Camp Weld

A MAP DEPICTING THE

MILITARY POSTS OF THE SOUTHWEST

IN THE 19TH CENTURY

BY HERBERT M. HART

SHOWING APPROXIMATE LOCATIONS AND DATES OF
MILITARY POSTS (INCLUDING SOME MILITIA,
CIVILIAN, AND NON-U.S. FORTS). ARMY USE
NOT NECESSARILY CONTINUOUS BETWEEN DATES
SHOWN. PREPOSITIONS HAVE BEEN DROPPED FROM
NAMES IN MOST CASES.

MODERN STATES · ARMY DIVISIONS, 1874

| | |
|---|---|
| CP CAMP | PP PICKET POST |
| FT FORT | PT POST |
| DET DETACHMENT | GN GARRISON |
| STN STATION | RT REDOUBT |
| CT CANTONMENT | C "CIRCA" |

SCALE APPROXIMATE

50    0    50    100

ILLUSTRATIONS FROM CONTEMPORARY SOURCES.

Fort Point, California

Fort Arbuckle

Fort Bliss, Texas

Fort Union

# OLD FORTS
## of the Southwest

# OLD FORTS
## OF THE SOUTHWEST

by Herbert M. Hart

Drawings by Paul J. Hartle

(Opposite Page) RUINS AT Fort Union, New Mexico.

SUPERIOR PUBLISHING COMPANY-SEATTLE

Sketch of the Alamo, 1836, is by Paul Laune from *A Time to Stand* by Walter Lord, copyright 1961 by Walter Lord, reprinted by permission of Harper & Row, Publishers, Incorporated.

Sketches of certain Oklahoma forts are by Vinson Lackey from the Thomas H. Gilcrease Institute of American History and Art, Tulsa, Oklahoma, used with permission.

FIRST EDITION

PRINTED IN THE UNITED STATES OF AMERICA

## DEDICATION

To the Troopers and Their Families
  Who Created History at the Forts
  Of the West

And to My Mother and Father
  Who First Taught Me that Yesterday's
  History Is Tomorrow's Future

# PREFACE

*"His summers are spent in campaigning; his winters in getting his horse in condition for the next campaign. He has scarcely any mounted drill for in summer he must save his horse for active work, and in winter his horse is unfit for it. He is building posts, stables, cantonments, driving a team or cutting firewood. He is a 'hewer of wood and a drawer of water.' That he can still contend with the Indian on anything like equal terms is his highest commendation, for the Indian is his superior in every soldierlike quality, except subordination to discipline and indomitable courage."*

—Colonel Richard I. Dodge writing in 1882 of the western cavalryman.

The story of the frontier trooper has been told many times and in many ways. The conclusions drawn have ranged from condemnation to commendation, usually depending on the writer's point of view.

What follows is this story told from the aspect of its officers and men who fought and frolicked, built and bled at the half a thousand forts in the southwestern United States. The writer has a point of view: the opinion that the Army deserves primary credit for the end of the frontier.

Because of Army protection the wagon trains moved westward on routes explored by Army expeditions into areas claimed for the United States by Army might. The towns sprang up in the shadow of Army forts, and sometimes earned their earliest livelihood from selling to the Army. The railroads that spelled the final close to the frontier moved across prairie and mountain with Army escorts. And the Indians, once gathered together into reservations, were kept there and protected by the Army.

Mistakes were made and the armchair diagnosticians have come forth with many ways that might have worked better. It should not be forgotten, however, that the Army was not the maker of policy, but merely the instrument of its execution. Just as in years previous, and in years later, the military and lawmakers occasionally disagree on policy, the fact remains that the government, and not the military, determines the national policy.

A century ago the policy dictated that the United States Army would clear the way westward. Between 1850 and 1890 this was what the Army did, undermanned, underpaid, and under-recognized.

This book does not attempt to explore any of the thinking and policies that sent the Army west. Instead, it hopes to take the reader on a tour of the west, stopping along the way at some of the many forts that the Army called home.

In preparing this second volume of the "Forts of the Old West" series, we had to draw an arbitrary line between the Southwest and the Far West. This could not be one of geography, because some matters of concern to one area overlapped into the other. Rather, an attempt has been made to place in this volume those forts that fit into events of primary concern to the Southwest—roughly defined east of the Rio Grande.

Volume III of the series, *Old Forts of the Far West*, also will overlap this geographical boundary, but its emphasis will be on forts and events of concern between the Rio Grande and the Pacific Ocean. If the delineation is annoying, an apology is submitted, but this was the only way that we could visit 130-some forts and still present something about each fort that set it off from its contemporaries.

The photographs in this book were taken during a 15,000-mile trip in 1963.

Every fort was visited with the exception of Brown, Ringgold, and Elliott, all in Texas. Their sites could not be squeezed into a rushed trip and National Park Service photographers had to be called upon for help. Park Service and other sources also assisted when our photographs were less than satisfactory. The trips were rushed and the author had little control over rainstorms, clouds, and the lateness of the day when he arrived at some sites.

The gathering of data on the posts was equally challenging. The bibliography and acknowledgments sections hint at the difficulty in finding out about what forts once existed and what went on at them. Only because of the wholehearted cooperation of many kind folks throughout the country was it possible to obtain what data were gathered.

If the reader is tempted to visit any of these sites, a few words of caution may be in order. Many are privately owned. Permission should be requested from the owner before investigating, and the courtesies of the west always should be observed. This means, leave things as they are found, close all gates, do not frighten the livestock, and do not carry off any souvenirs.

In rattlesnake country, take appropriate precautions. Many of these sites are so noted. In desert country, take along a shovel, some boards, some gunnysacks, and chains. And do not try to navigate the back roads in the family car; a jeep, pickup truck, or foot travel is recommended.

The routes given are the ones that worked for the author. They may not agree with road maps, which have a tendency to place forts on the wrong side of streams and mountains or at the end of non-existent roads. If we were going to return to a site, the directions given would be used and that is the spirit in which they are presented.

There were more than a thousand forts in the West of the nineteenth century. This treatment cannot help but touch lightly on the subject. It is hoped that the selection, based mainly on what happened there and what is left today, will give the reader an idea of the challenge faced by the Army, and how it solved it.

H.M.H.

New Haven, Connecticut
Saint Patrick's Day, 1964

# CONTENTS

Bibliography

(Because of duplication of sources and space limitations, the bibliography for this volume will appear in consolidation with that of Volume III of the OLD FORTS OF THE WEST Series.)

(Opposite Page) BARRACKS' INTERIOR, Fort Davis, Texas.

**SOUTHWESTERN FORTS** and their battles saw many officers, some of whom are pictured here. Left, Randolph B. Marcy (1812-87) led pre-Civil War expeditions and was Army inspector-general after war. Christopher (Kit) Carson (1809-68) was militia general who fought Navajos during Civil War. John M. Chivington (1821-94) defeated Confederates at Glorieta, then lost his own reputation at Sand Creek Massacre in 1864. Philip H. Sheridan (1831-88) was top departmental commander in post-Civil War Indian expeditions, later succeeded Sherman in command of Army. Egotistic George A. Custer (1839-76) led troops under Sheridan, especially as commander of Battle of Washita, but died at near-legendary Battle of Little Big Horn subsequently.

# WAR ON THE PLAINS

*"You will observe that whilst the country generally has been at peace, the people on the plains and the troopers in my command have been continually at war, enduring all its dangers and hardships, with none of its honors or rewards."*

—General Sherman in his 1868 Report to the Secretary of War.

ARMY RECORDS in the Southwest generally go back to Captain Zebulon M. Pike's 1806 expedition when he arrived at the headwaters of the Rio Grande in Colorado, built a stockade, and hoisted the American flag. The Spaniards did not appreciate this intrusion on their lands and Pike found himself a prisoner for a few months.

But when he returned, he published reports that broke through the "caballero curtain." The American commercial spirit quickly grasped the trade opportunities available in Spanish America. The 1821 Mexican revolution made it possible to exploit these opportunities. With much of this territory coming to the United States by the end of the War with Mexico in 1849, the barriers of foreign borders were down and the western rush began.

Explorers, trail blazers, gold seekers, settlers, soldiers all seemed to vie with each other in their enthusiasm to cut new ways across the plains. But the opponents of Mexican and Spanish domination were equally hostile to Yankee advances: the traditional wanderers of the Plains, the Apache, Navajo, Kiowa, Comanche, Cheyenne, and the rest. For 250 years these nomads had fought every incursion into their traditional hunting grounds, and they saw nothing new in these buckskin-clad bands of bead traders and buffalo hunters.

The United States found it had assumed an almost unwelcome burden when it took over the Southwest. It promised protection and peace to the settlers—and to Mexico—and it had not the wherewithal to do the job.

In 1851, more than 1,300 troopers were scattered at 11 tiny outposts in the Territory of New Mexico. In Texas in 1853 a chain of forts followed the westernmost line of settlements, and within three years a second line had to be established even farther west. Across Kansas, the Army spotted small sod affairs along the trails, garrisoned them with small detachments, and dignified them by calling them "forts." Oklahoma was known as "Indian Territory," and forts were built to insure that both whites and redmen recognized this.

The line of forts stretched between 1,300 and 2,500 miles and were from 30 to 300 miles apart. Some thought they should be closer; others felt fewer posts with bigger garrisons would be better.

While debates over the proper strategy were argued, the more earthy disputes of shot and arrow swept across the plains. In 1854, northern New Mexico saw an Apache War. Ute Indians chased and were chased by soldiers in 1855. In Kansas, Texas, and Oklahoma, the Kiowas and Comanches combined to ravage and rape and in 1860 the Army mounted a three-pronged expedition against them.

Then came the period of great confusion to the Indian. White turned against white and a

**HE TOOK MANILA** with Dewey, but during Indian Wars Wesley Merritt (1834-1910) served first as a Dragoon, then commanded campaigns and forts in Southwest. Eugene A. Carr (1820-1910) was aggressive young officer during his early Indian fights and carried enthusiasm into mature years, earning grudging admiration of Indians and nickname, "War Eagle." George A. Forsyth was hero of Beecher's Island fight when he led 50 men in holding off besieging Indians. William R. Shafter (1835-1906) patrolled intensively through West Texas, exploring many areas previously thought inaccessible; during Cuban War he led Army forces. Benjamin H. Grierson (1826-1911) was an ex-music teacher who led famed "Grierson's Raid" 600 miles deep into Confederate territory in Civil War, later commanded forces in Oklahoma and Texas, especially during Victorio War. (Carson photo courtesy Veterans' Hospital, Ft. Lyon, Colo. Chivington photo courtesy Colorado State Historical Society. All others from National Archives.)

new flag, with stars and bars, was seen in the land. By and large, the Indians watched on the sidelines of the Civil War, grasping the advantage whenever the soldiers moved to Eastern battlefields.

The historically ignored California Volunteers headed East and stopped in New Mexico. They reestablished United States supremacy over most of the Southwest, employing vigorous and sometimes drastic measures to control the raiders of the plains. Kansas saw midwestern Volunteers take equally stringent steps. Oklahoma was split by the Yankee and Rebel seesaw, and Texas was almost unprotected. There the Federals knew they were unwelcome, and the Confederates drained most able-bodied men into their front on the other side of the Mississippi. Only rangers and state militia were available to keep order, and they were so undermanned that most of West Texas had to be abandoned for lack of men and money to protect it.

"With the expiration of the rebellion," General of the Army U. S. Grant reported hopefully in 1866, "Indian hostilities have diminished. With a frontier extending and encroaching upon the hunting-grounds of the Indian, hostilities, opposition at least, frequently occurs.

"To meet this, and to protect the emigrant on his way to the mountain territories, troops have distributed to give the best protection with the means at hand . . . These troops are badly sheltered and supplied at great cost . . . The labor of putting up temporary quarters is performed by the troops intending to occupy them."

The Army of 1866 was set at 54,302 men, but it was able to muster only 38,000. Of this, only 5,000 were available for the Army of the frontier. From every corner of the Southwest the call came for protection, sometimes from legitimate settlers and politicians, but just as often from those who wanted to profit from having a fort nearby.

When a fort was built in tillable terrain, its neighbors came to ranch and settle down. But when it was in the desert or in the wilds, the so-called settlers seemed more concerned with illicit trading with the troops than with farming and cattle grazing. And when a fort's abandonment was rumored, usually the latter generated the loudest howls.

The future was written along the ruts of the trails and in the steel of the plodding railroad construction crews. Indian depredations were conducted with the naiveté of tribes that did not seem to know their way of life was ending. In his campaigns of 1868-69, General Sheridan revealed this to them. The Comanches lost their food supplies in the Battle of Soldier Spring on Christmas day, 1868; a month earlier, the Cheyennes had been routed at the Battle of the Washita.

In 1874, Sheridan again drove across Oklahoma and Texas' Panhandle and in 25 skirmishes broke the resistance of the Plains Indians. Periodic uprisings, including Victorio's War in West Texas in 1879-80, occurred, but resistance grew weaker and weaker.

Finally in 1900, the Army could close its records on the Indian Wars. From 1789, it had met the Indians a total of 1,240 times, had 1,105 officers and men killed, 1,391 wounded. But its record was more than mere statistics, for in shepherding the settler and stage across the plains, it had tamed the frontier.

# THE FORTS

The Army fort in the Southwest had no common denominator. It could be the rude stockade of Camp Supply, Oklahoma; the adobe shacks of Fort Fillmore, New Mexico; the stone bastillion of Benicia, California; the pole shanties of Camp Cooper, Texas; the mud soddies of Fort Aubrey, Kansas.

Its appearance reflected the times. In its earliest days, it was far from civilization and any sort of shelter seemed near luxury. Sometimes this shelter included a stockade in the modern tradition of romanticized Western tales. More often, the "fort" was a fortress in name only. It was a cluster of buildings built by the soldiers themselves.

The idea of holing up behind a barricade was unpopular with both officer and man. Psychologically, this seemed to foster a defensive, "let 'em come" spirit. Without a wall behind which to hide, the troopers had to keep on the alert. They were not in the West to watch for Indians, but to keep order and this gave them the offensive, "go get 'em" spirit.

Forts of all of these varieties are visited in this book. The open fort predominates because it was more common. Because of its arrangement that approximated a tiny village of houses and stores, usually it lasted longer. When the Army left, the buildings were auctioned off, or carried off, as the case may be. Many of these structures are left today because they are still being used today.

Every effort has been made to present a true picture of each fort. The old photographs and sketches came from a variety of sources. Only when the most conscientious efforts could not locate one does a fort appear without a representation of its early appearance.

This holds true as to ground plans, too. Many fort plats were located in official War Department reports, others in the files of the National Archives, some in state historical society collections, a few in the hands—or memories—of local residents. A few were drawn after a careful search of available descriptions and actual walks over the ruins and foundation holes that are left today.

At one time, it was thought that the actual plats could be reproduced here. It was found that usually they were such a maze of rough sketches, jumbled buildings, and other things it would be impossible to reproduce them in the space available. To provide legibility and consistency, these plats have been simplified and minor buildings have been left out. It was hoped that a scale could be included with each plat, but many original plans lacked this. An attempt to reconstruct scales would provide more errors than it would prevent. Whenever possible, the dimensions of buildings or parade grounds have been given to suggest approximate scales of the plats.

Comparison of ground plans with surface remains or old pictures may reveal discrepancies. It is for this reason that a date is included with each plat. Buildings went up or were moved or torn down with such regularity that a ground plan of one year should be considered accurate for that year only.

For ease in identification, here are the abbreviations used most frequently for the buildings:

HQ, OFF, or ADJ-Headquarters
　　　　or Adjutant's office
S or ST- Stables
B - Barracks
BK- Bakery
SH- Storehouse or warehouse
H- Hospital
GH- Guardhouse
C or CHAP- Chapel
EM or NCO- Married enlisted quarters
T- Tower or blockhouse
Mess or MH- Messhall
PO- Post Office
SURG- Surgeon
GRAN- Granary

LAUN- Laundry or laundresses' quarters
OQ- Officers' quarters
CO or COQ- Commanding officer's quarters
BLK - Blacksmith
TR, SUT, or TRAD- Sutler or Post Trader
K or KIT- Kitchen
MAG - Magazine
CEM - Cemetery
COM or COMM - Commissary
CARP - Carpenter
CAV - Cavalry
INF - Infantry
ART - Artillery
SHOP or WORK - Workshops
LIB - Library

"AN ARMY CAMP beyond the border" was the original caption on this old engraving that was representative of the pre-Civil War Western Army.

From Glisan *Journal of Army Life*, 1874.

# THE EARLY DAYS

*"Our national flag is waving in mute mockery on our frontier without sufficient force to prevent its being torn down and trampled in the dust . . . The garrisons . . . are scarcely large enough to protect themselves."*

—Corpus Christi *Star*, May 26, 1849.

WHEN THE Mexican border was pushed southward to the Rio Grande, the American Army found itself caught in the middle. On one hand there were the Indians and the lawless. On the other, the settlers and politicians who wanted protection from the Indians and the lawless.

Fifty-some forts provided a semblance of this protection before the Civil War. "Forts" dignifies many of them because "tent camp" probably would be more appropriate. The Army was feeling its way, sometimes hardly ahead of the settler.

Before the Mexican War the U.S. Army had 6,500 men spread over the 100 posts and stations throughout the country. The strength jumped to 47,000 by 1848, but most of these men—and that includes many of the western fort garrisons—fought in Mexico.

After the war, the Army totaled 10,000 men in 166 companies. The bulk of them, 126 companies, were in the West. In 1855, the strength went to 15,000 and by the start of the Civil War 181 of the 198 companies were outposting the 79 forts of the western frontier.

But even with 90 per cent of its troops in the West, the Army was hard-pressed to keep the peace. Some order resulted, and many men received experience of value in the Civil War.

Most of all, the early days in the West convinced the Army and the nation here was the future. Raw, untamed, and hostile, but still the future.

# FORT WASHITA, OKLAHOMA

American forts usually were expected to defend beleaguered settlers and emigrants from wild and ferocious Indians.

This was not always so. Sometimes the main idea was to defend beleaguered Indians from wild and ferocious members of the "other tribes"—the latter being the ones not being defended.

That was the case with one of the first forts of the Southwest, Fort Washita. It came on the tail end of one of those black chapters in American history, when all Indians east of the Mississippi were ordered by the Indian Removal Bill of 1830 to be evicted.

Cherokees, Choctaws and Creeks were uprooted, some voluntarily, others by force, from homes in the southern states and located in what was then known as "Indian Territory." We call it Oklahoma today.

The eviction did not set well either with those being evicted, or those crowded aside to make room for them. That is why the Army was called in, and why Fort Washita was built.

A general named Zachary Taylor selected its site and also its name. That was seven years before he became the twelfth president of the United States. At this time, however, he was the commander of the Second Military District, which included today's Oklahoma.

The site was selected in 1842 on a spot that commanded the fertile valley of the Washita river. The river was one of the reasons for its selection, apparently, because in 1841 Taylor reported, "Whenever boats can ascend Red River as high as the mouth of Washita it will be navigable or can easily be rendered so as high as the point selected for a military post."

The river proved helpful to the post but it almost backfired. Some of the steamboats that used it to Fort Washita brought in grain and other materials. This undercut the Indians at the nearby agency who had hoped to trade their harvests to the post. This must have been settled some way, though, because the records report frequent trips. Some boats had to unload a mile or so below the fort, and others had to hold over until the rainy season to make a return trip, but the turgid Washita usually could float boats drawing less than three feet.

Taylor's fort was a slow starter after troops arrived in 1842. It was not until the following summer that any progress was made in its construction. Part of the delay was an early hint that the Army was to abandon the site.

Taylor defended his selection, pointing out, "It bears immediately upon the numerous predatory bands who live by the chase, who here approach nearest to the Chickasaws, and against whom the latter nation, by every consideration of humanity and policy, is to our protection.

"The establishment of the post has invited many Chickasaws to move into the desirable position of their country, commanded by it, who were before deterred by the plundering expeditions of the wild bands referred to."

After the months of indecision, Fort Washita was determined to be a permanent selection and construction got underway with a will.

Solid buildings of walnut shingles were placed on limestone foundations, ash and walnut logs were hauled ten miles to the site, and the fort took on a sudden but permanent appearance. The officers' quarters prompted the post adjutant to report by fall, 1844, "The frame is the best and most substantial that I have ever seen erected."

At the same time, the alter ego of most western forts came into being, the "hog ranch." This venerable but not necessarily reputable institution for Fort Washita was described by an Army surgeon in 1850. "A little village has sprung up near the post called Rucklesville, but can never grow into that importance that such nuclei of larger towns near military stations sometimes assume," he wrote.

After awhile it did assume an air of respectability, however, and married soldiers and their families had their homes there. So many lived there that the morn-

FORT WASHITA
OKLA – 1854

**BARRACKS** of Fort Washita was 110 feet long, 40 feet wide. Balcony extended around its second story. Cemetery still stands down hill to west with gravestone of General William Belknap although his body now is in Arlington National Cemetery. One grave is of an "Aunt Jane," supposedly killed by robbers. She now haunts ruins. Or so the legend says. (Redrawn from National Archives.)

**FORT WASHITA** in 1854 was dominated by the two-storied barracks just as it is dominated today by the barracks' ruins. Officers' quarters were to left of flagpole. Low building behind pole was hospital. Locations of most of these buildings can be traced today. They are carefully marked by State Historical Society after civic-minded citizens bought the site and donated it to the state. They even paid for it to be cleared of years of brush and evidences of farm use.

**BARRACKS RUINS** are unusual for a frontier fort. Building was used as private residence until fire in the 1930's.

**INSIDE OF BARRACKS** shows thickness of walls that have withstood more than 100 years of use, two fires, and farmhouse builders who made off with most of the stones of Fort Washita including wall that once surrounded it.

ing bugler at the fort usually posted himself on an elevated position so his calls would summon the troopers to the reveille formations. This town has also been known variously as Hatsboro and Rugglesville.

In 1854, Fort Washita was almost abandoned. It was reported to be in a dilapidated condition, the equipment all but useless, and the stables so inadequate for the 104 artillery horses that they and the cannon had to be sheltered under porches and trees.

Fort Washita assumed fairly magnificent proportions by the time it was completed. Its double-storied brick barracks and the rock wall that surrounded the entire post almost brought an air of the East to what was then the wilderness. Gradually this isolation lessened as the gold lure of California beckoned. Washita became a stopping place where travelers laid over for several days to elect wagon train officers and get things in order before venturing farther.

They saw evidences of the fact that almost a quarter of a million bricks had been brought in to build the fort. An official report termed it as good as any other military post in the United States.

Washita's claim on history was not destined to

be etched in tradition and glory. It performed its mission in a businesslike manner until a consolidation of troops at the start of the Civil War caused its abandonment.

Confederates used it alternately as their territorial headquarters or supply depot until the end of the war. When they left it, local settlers apparently burned it down to prevent bandit bands from using its buildings.

The desolate remnants stood idle for several years until the government was asked by the Chickasaw Nation if it had been abandoned. They suggested, "The old fort having been burnt down is of course no use to the government."

Fort Washita's end was signalled when an Indian agent, acting for the government, inspected the site in 1869 and reported: "There are no buildings at old Fort Washita that are habitable or can be made so."

TO GET THERE: From Durant, go north on U.S. 69-75 three miles to State 78. Go a mile west to State 199. Follow this north and then west a couple of miles to where the road takes a sharp turn to the southwest. The Fort is north of the road and within view.

16

# FORT ARBUCKLE, OKLAHOMA

As far as Oklahoma is concerned, Arbuckle seems to have been just about the most popular name around when it came to naming forts.

There were four of them, not counting miscellaneous overnight types in the Fort Gibson vicinity. Apparently the fact that Colonel Matthew Arbuckle was top Army commander in the area had a bearing on the popularity of the name.

Camp Arbuckle, the first that is, was a winter cantonment near Fort Gibson in 1832-33. "Old" Fort Arbuckle was a five-month post in 1834 about 20 miles west of present-day Tulsa.

The second "Camp" Arbuckle, actually the parent of the fourth post, was not too far from today's Purcell. It lasted from fall, 1850, had a 200-foot-long barracks and four officers' "huts," but also a brand of malaria that hit almost unanimously.

In April, 1851, Captain Randolph Marcy supervised movements of the post 40 miles to the south, near modern Davis. The post was believed to be clear of the malaria threat—it was 500 feet above the Washita River— and had a spring that gushed forth ice water in near-millrace velocity.

"It would be a great blessing if the men were content with this wholesome beverage of nature, but such is not the case," reads the diary of the post surgeon of the time. He said that the troops usually were able to obtain something stronger than water and "however faithful soldiers may be in all other respects, there is no dependence to be placed in many of them in regard to the indulgence in strong drink."

The good doctor, a teetotaler, had one consolation. "Fortunately the price of intoxicating spirits is, in this isolated place, so high that even the most inveterate tiplers cannot afford the indulgence of a big spree very frequently."

This final Fort Arbuckle, called by Oklahoma "New Fort Arbuckle," was destined to live an up-and-down existence. Garrisoned and then abandoned almost with regularity before the Civil War, it also saw Indian Militia and Confederate troops. After the war it was destined for big things in General Phil Sheridan's scheme to flush out the winter Indian camps. In the long run it was a glorified stables for the mounts, and little else.

Active as it was with trying to protect the Chickasaws from the Choctaws and both from the Comanches, and the California emigrants from all of them, still its biggest action was during a lull in its official life.

In 1858, most of Arbuckle's troopers had been sent to Salt Lake City and the so-called non-shooting "Mormon War." The single company left at the fort had its full share of troubles just keeping the Comanches from border jumping into Texas and raiding the ranches.

Finally things got so out of hand that a company of Texas Rangers chased them back to the reservation. The Rangers were persuaded that "it will never happen again." The Indian Agent, former Colonel Douglas Cooper, reactivated his title and mustered a 100-man force of Chickasaw and white settlers and tried to carry out the promise.

But the Comanches disappeared every time the militia took after them. Finally help from the regular Army was requested and a company of infantry marched up from Fort Belknap, Texas.

Foot soldiers being somewhat less than invincible against mounted Indians, "Colonel" Cooper kept his mounted militia on active duty and added another

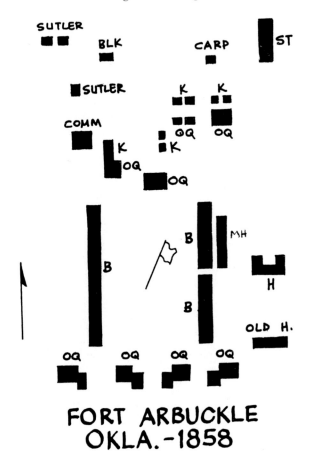

FORT ARBUCKLE
OKLA.-1858

STABLES IN northeast corner were longest lived buildings of post. Only in recent years did present owner try to dismantle mammoth barn, dragged it 100 feet with a bulldozer but to no avail. He found dowel-pinned log construction almost impossible to dismember, but now only two chimneys from the officers' quarters remain of elaborate Fort Arbuckle. (Redrawn from National Archives.)

hundred. The fact that he used them to roam the western country looking for "a site for a new agency" did not set well with higher powers. His efforts paid him off with a severe reprimand and an order to dissolve his personal army posthaste.

With the militia out of the way, the regulars were able to gather together the Comanche elders and get them to promise they would war no more. And to clinch the bargain, they would return all of the horses they had stolen and would keep the young braves in line.

Word of this agreement was slow in getting around. A mixed Texas Ranger-Indian detachment intercepted the herd of horses, assumed they were being stolen rather than returned, and stampeded them. They passed the word to a Fort Belknap 400-man cavalry detail in the area and, after a forced march, the soldiers attacked the Indian camp. The pre-dawn fight killed 60 Comanches and four Wichitas.

The Comanches assumed that they had been betrayed by the Wichita tribe. Rather than debate the question, the latter quickly folded their tepees and rushed to Fort Arbuckle for protection.

Only fast talking and prolonged period of government handouts from the Arbuckle commissary kept the situation from getting further out of hand.

TO GET THERE: From Davis, Oklahoma, take State 7 west for seven miles, then north one-half mile on a gravel road. The site is on the west side of the road on the privately owned Grant ranch.

TALES THIS FIREPLACE could tell from Fort Arbuckle would fill many books, but it stands mute. Background buildings are modern ranch sheds.

**FORT ARBUCKLE** was a staunchly built post of 30 buildings of hewn logs, chinked with wood and clay. This view is from southeastern corner, shows officers' row on left, and looking across parade ground past barracks to another row of barracks. Officers' quarters were to right of flagpole, too. Despite snug appearance, Army inspectors in 1857 found it had a hospital with a roof that leaked "from one end of the building to the other," and had troops "almost destitute of clothing and working at daily labor for the protection of their horses for the winter." Inspectors also noted ammunition storage was so poor that "nearly all of the powder of the post is buried underground for safety."

**PARADE GROUND** of Fort Arbuckle still shows traces of trees probably planted during Army's occupancy. In 1868 General Sheridan planned to make Arbuckle center of his winter campaign, shipped supplies to Fort Gibson by water and then overland to Arbuckle by wagon. Hay and feed piled up but wagons had trouble getting to fort, so Sheridan sent his horses and mules to be fed but decided against using it as supply center. With 21-year-old lieutenant as probably youngest post commander in Army, Arbuckle was retained until the feed was exhausted in spring, 1870, and it was abandoned.

# FORT BELKNAP, TEXAS

The old adage about "possession being nine points of the law" seems to have had a reverse effect when it came to Army forts in nineteenth century Texas.

When Texas joined the Union, it was agreed that property taken by the Army for its posts would continue to belong to Texas. And that is why the Army at Fort Belknap found itself literally an outsider on its own reservation. Once it had built a relatively elaborate stone fort overlooking the Brazos River, it found that an enterprising citizen had surveyed the land, used fort buildings for his bearings, and obtained legal title to the land from the state of Texas.

Although the Army stayed, there was little it could do about the new landlord. It never owned the ground it stood on.

This did not prevent the Army from using Fort Belknap as an active post between 1851 and 1861 to maintain a shaky peace between the Indians and settlers. Two Indian reservations were near the fort and friction was inevitable, especially with hotheaded and sometimes self-styled "rangers" roaming the countryside, keeping their brand of peace.

On one occasion a hunting camp of 18 friendly Indians were attacked at night. Eight Indians died before they could get out of their blankets. Five months later, a group of white men scalped an elderly Indian and then killed an old Indian woman whom they thought was a witness. They were bold enough to warn the Army that interfering troops would be treated as Indians.

When the post adjutant was asked by the "rangers" if the soldiers would fight for the Indians, he answered curtly, "I will fight for the Indians as long as I have a button on my coat!"

But after a time, the only solution seemed to be abandonment of the Fort Belknap reservations. The morning of July 30, 1859, the Army shepherded a caravan of Indians from their Texas homes to the Washita reserve in Oklahoma. More than a mile wide, the tearful procession walked for two weeks to their new reservation, one elderly Indian dying along the way and two babies being born.

The Indian eviction did not solve the problem, however. The former agent, Major Robert S. Neighbors, returned to Fort Belknap after the move, only to be shot in the back by a total stranger, an anti-Indian fanatic. Neighbors had ignored warnings that his life was in danger and he died at Fort Belknap where a monument today memorializes his humane treatment of the redman.

Belknap originally was located about two miles north of its present site. After two wells were dug without success, the post was moved to what looked like a well-watered spot. This, too, failed and was the prime reason Fort Belknap had only a checkered life. After the Civil War, plans to rebuild the post were started but abandoned because of the water situation.

Before the final abandonment decision came in 1867, work actually began on repairing Fort Belknap. During the war only three families had remained at the combination town and military post, but Texas Rangers, Confederate soldiers of the Texas Frontier Regiment, and other forces moved in and out of it.

The dilapidated fort that greeted the restoration troops caused one sergeant to write: "The quarters and hospital were roofless and most of the woodwork had been removed. The village adjacent to the fort had been a station of the Overland Mail Route, and when it was occupied by settlers and the fort filled with troops I have no doubt it was, as I was informed it had been, the prettiest frontier post in Texas.

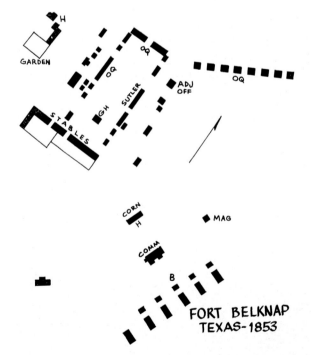

FORT BELKNAP TEXAS-1853

**SOME OF THESE** buildings remain today: commissary, two right-hand barracks, magazine, and corn house. Town of Fort Belknap occupied almost same site as fort; Belknap general store was immediately north of commissary, saloon was next to westernmost barracks and, next to saloon, once stood Lauderdale Hotel. (Redrawn from Fort Belknap Museum data.)

**BEFORE RESTORATION,** Fort Belknap ruins attracted outings from nearby towns. Stone construction minimized natural destruction of buildings; most loss was caused when settlers decided they could use materials. From attire of these visitors, it appears this was Fort Belknap circa 1900.

(BARBARA LEDBETTER COLLECTION.)

"But now desolation reigned supreme. Sand, sand everywhere; dead buffalo lying on the parade ground; a few ancient rats and bats looked on us with an evil eye for disturbing their repose, and my first night's rest in the old commissary was broken by visions of infantry sentinels stalking ghost-like on their beats, and the wind howling through the broken roof."

Soldiers turned builders worked throughout the summer of '67 in restoring the fort. The work was pressed with a sense of urgency. Guards and a rigid system of passes insured that every worker toiled his full share. But after five months, the verdict was reached and Fort Belknap was written off the Army books. Fort Griffin, to the south, was to be the mainstay in the area and Fort Belknap and its water problems went back to the Texas owners.

TO GET THERE: Take State 251 south from Newcastle, Texas, until it ends at Fort Belknap, two miles.

**COMMISSARY** was rebuilt and now is museum. Nearby was Niuehouse General Store and museum still has its ledger for 1856 to 1858 which records charge accounts to soldiers. Whiskey, beer and "seegars" accounted for bulk of purchases. Although kept only by man's last name and unit, rank could be guessed by $1 champagne and 75 cent wine purchases of officers and 25 cents a pint tabs for beer by privates.

**WELL AT FORT BELKNAP** serves for good luck wishes today. It is 65 feet deep, was dug by hand and walled by stone using candlelight. Two barracks have been restored. They were double-storied, 80 feet long. Today's use is as dining hall for family reunions, an auditorium, and archives of the Fort Belknap Society.

**MOST OF FORT BELKNAP** can be seen from edge of corn house in foreground. Commissary is to right behind corn house, two barracks with 30-foot kitchen in between, are to left of flagpole. All buildings were reconstructed on original foundations. One building now standing today was two-room guardhouse used jointly by fort and town. Each had its own jail, but usually one had to suffice while other was being repaired. Prisoners had little trouble kicking out rocks or tunnelling from under, but some nail-studded logs exist showing that at least prisoners could not saw their way out.

# CANTONMENT BURGWIN, NEW MEXICO

Christmas, 1852, was the first time that holiday was celebrated at brand new Cantonment Burgwin, and it was an occasion long remembered.

"A Christmas dinner that would do honor to the Astor House," recorded Sergeant James A. Bennett in his diary. "Many got jolly. A few good toasts were given. I had to give a short address. Ended by a dance at night in our quarters."

Bennett reinforces the suggestion that it was a memorable event: "The dance broke up at the sound of the drum, announcing the morning of the 26th."

For the men of the 1st Dragoons at Cantonment Burgwin, anything was welcome to break the monotony. They had been at the post 11 miles south of Taos, New Mexico, since August 7. They found it only a site, and the fort was to be the result of their labors.

"Surrounded by mountains, it looks as though we were shut out from the world," Bennett wrote, but two months later and the command was in its new buildings. They were of adobe in a hollow square enclosing a parade ground. When he visited in 1853, the Army inspector declared the post "for its size, being calculated for a company of dragoons, deserves commendation as well adapted to the service."

"For its size" frequently was almost the undoing of the fort, however. With several thousand Indians in the area, Cantonment Burgwin was hard pressed to keep things in check. In March, 1854, it faced its worst test and was found able.

That was the so-called Battle of Cieneguilla. Led by Second Lieutenant John W. Davidson, 60 Dragoons had left the cantonment to meet with 150 Apaches. The Indians agreed to proceed to the post and discuss a possible treaty, but instead joined another tribe and headed toward Taos Rancho, not far from the town of Taos. The soldiers followed.

Ten Indians were surrounded in the Rancho and were taken as prisoners to Burgwin. Here three chiefs agreed to go to Fort Union to conclude a treaty, but later ran from their escort.

By now the Army was getting the hint that perhaps treaty-making was not on the Indians' minds.

"We were, 60 of us, to saddle up immediately and pursue the band to prevent them from crossing

the Rio Grande and joining the Chachon band of Apaches," wrote Sergeant Bennett. "We mounted and left at 11 o'clock that night."

The next day, March 30, "at sunrise this morning we started, found the body of a white man who was killed by the Indians. Followed their trail; found ourselves at 8 o'clock a.m. in ambush, surrounded by 400 Indians; fought hard until 12 noon when we started to retreat."

Bennett records the desperate battle calmly, and with equal aplomb adds: "I was wounded shortly after by a rifle ball through both thighs. I then ran about a mile; found I was not able to walk alone any farther; got between two horses, seized their stirrups. The horses dragged me one-half mile when I managed to mount my horse."

He was one of the lucky ones. More than 40 of his fellow soldiers died in the battle and most of the survivors were badly wounded. Their opposition had been a war party of 250 Utes and Jicarilla Apaches. Six weeks later, the Army overtook the tribes and exacted a measure of revenge by confiscating their horses, provisions and equipment.

Bennett was eye-witness to the situation back at the cantonment while the Cieneguilla pursuit was underway. "Few soldiers are here now," he recorded. "What a pleasant situation: to lie in bed, helpless, and

"THE BUILDINGS are built of mud brick in a hollow square, leaving in the center what is called a 'parade ground' where the military parades are held every morning," wrote sergeant in 1852. "One side of the square is used as officers' quarters; the opposite side is a guardhouse, commissary department, offices, etc. The other two sides are soldiers' barracks. There is a flag staff in the center from which the Stars and Stripes flash and wave in the breeze." Apparently some additions were made by the time this plat was drawn. (Redrawn from Mansfield Inspection Report, 1853.)

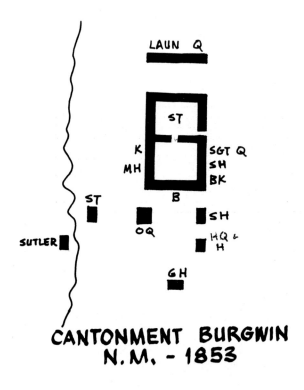

CANTONMENT BURGWIN
N.M. - 1853

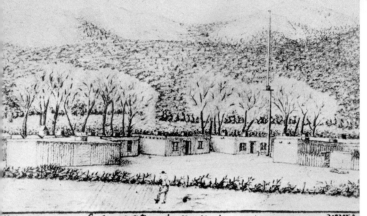

1857.  Cantonment Burgwin New Mexico  W.W.A.

**CANTONMENT BURGWIN** in 1857, three years before it was abandoned in 1860, presented compact appearance. It was centrally located to reinforce garrisons at Fort Union, Santa Fe, and others in area, and commanded only wagon road between Taos and Santa Fe. In early sketch, it appears buildings have been added to those shown in the earlier plat. As described by a former sergeant, "Buildings are all of one story with flat roofs, having a parapet on the top of the outer walls. There are no windows on the outside of the square and only port holes in the parapet through which one may look or shoot."

**GARDENER** coincidentally was matching old sketch when this photograph was taken, although duplicate view was not. Building is at site of guardhouse noted on plat, and main portion of fort is in background. Buildings have been restored on former sites following careful archaeological research. Despite absence of foundations and other ground clues, experts were able to locate site after several false starts, and located fireplace and wall traces under surface.

expect to be massacred at any moment. The Indians came quite near to the fort just now. We momentarily expect an attack."

This was in May. In June, 15 sick and lame manned the fort while the command tracked Indians. On July 1, Bennett wrote, "Company away again. Twenty-one of us here in the fort are surrounded by Indians."

On the 4th of July, Bennett decided that enough was enough.

"Today I walked out upon my crutches about 300 yards from the fort into the bushes," his diary tells. "I heard a noise. Supposing it was a deer, I secreted myself.

"In a few moments I discovered it was an Indian spy who was crawling through the bushes. When the Indian got within eight or ten paces from me, I fired my pistol and struck his neck.

"He fell but still exhibited signs of life. I fired again and the ball passed directly through his head."

Cantonment Burgwin's troubles apparently had tainted its occupants by a touch of the savagery they were fighting. Bennett adds, "I then approached him, cut off his scalp or 'took his hair' as some say here, and hobbled to my quarters, bearing my trophy of war.

"We had a regular war dance around it. The captain congratulated me on my success as a 'lame warrior.' Thus I celebrated the anniversary of independence."

**CANTONMENT BURGWIN** as it appears today. Southern portion of square has been restored, while one wing of stable square is only portion of that segment completed. Traces of remaining portion of square have been located. Objective is to restore it to earlier appearance when Army inspector declared, "This post is in good discipline and police, and the comforts of the troops, both sick and well, cared for . . . The troops are well instructed in the drill and the arms and equipment in good serviceable condition although much worn." His only complaint was that "of ten recruits recently joined this company, one is nearsighted and one left handed . . . and a left handed man is quite awkward in ranks."

TO GET THERE: From Taos, N.M., take U.S. 64 south four miles and turn left on State 3. Seven miles south is Fort Burgwin Research Center on the right side of the road, directly across from Pot Creek Lumber camp. Fort site is now being restored as part of research foundation founded by Wichita lumberman Ralph M. Rounds. It specializes in fields including history, archaeology and pollen research. Due to scholarly nature of center, visitors would do well to make arrangements beforehand by writing, care of Taos.

**HOSPITAL STOOD** at this point, as evidenced by slight mound and rock traces, results of archaeological work.

# THE ALAMO & FORT SAM HOUSTON, TEXAS

San Antonio's military story has at least three chapters, and in each of them it played a key role in the development of the United States. It may seem unlikely that activities at this relatively distant spot would have national and even international repercussions, but that was the case.

It might be said that San Antonio's first military era was that of the Spaniards, the Mexicans and the Texans. It began on June 13, 1691, when 50 soldiers escorted Spanish missionaries to this point near headwaters of what was later called the San Antonio River. And it ended on March 6, 1836, when Santa Anna's 5,000-man Mexican Army captured the Fort, or ex-mission, of the Alamo in the center of the town after it had been defended to the last man.

Previously, Texas revolutionaries had stormed San Antonio and forced the surrender of its Mexican commander. Knowing that Mexico would not permit this rebellion to go unchecked, they attempted to restore the 91-year-old mission-turned-fortress. The Mexicans had left 12 cannon but these were nearly useless at the hands of the amateur artillerymen.

When Santa Anna's advance force arrived on February 22, 1836, it was faced by 156 men. These were led by Lieutenant Colonel William B. Travis, by appointment of Texas President Sam Houston, and Colonel Jim Bowie, by popular election of the men. David Crockett, famed in modern folk song, was one of the defenders.

Tradition says that Travis, realizing the desperate predicament that could spell only death to the defenders, drew a line upon the ground. He asked that all men volunteering to stay and fight cross the line. Every man crossed, even Bowie who was sick and had his stretcher carried across.

The Mexican answer to the Texans' stubbornness was siege of the Alamo from February 24 until March 6. Other than 32 volunteers from Goliad who crawled through the lines, the Alamo received no outside help. When the waves of Mexican troops charged on the morning of the sixth, the outnumbered Texans' resistance was to little avail. The outer walls were conquered and the fight became a running affair from room to room.

Travis was felled with a single bullet. Bowie was killed on his sickbed, but not before he shot several of his attackers. The chapel, today's main reminder of the Alamo, fell last. The Texans fired from its upper floor as the Mexicans forced their way into the main room. Legend says that one officer tried to leap from the east embrasure with his child strapped to his back. Both were shot.

All 188 Alamo defenders died, and the Mexican dead has been placed in the area of 500. Right after the battle, the Texans' bodies were placed in three piles and burned. A year later Sam Houston had the bones and other evidences buried a few hundred yards away, although some San Antonions think they may have been buried beneath the floor of San Fernando Cathedral. Still standing on the Main Plaza, from its tower Santa Anna had watched the Alamo siege, flying from it the red flag that signified "no quarter."

The Alamo was never intended to be a fort, but by the fate of destiny it played a military role. When Texas joined the Union and, in 1845 the Army came to San Antonio, it was only natural that this crumbling building should be part of the new Army establishment. Company G, 2nd Cavalry, reported on October 28, 1845, that it had arrived at "Camp Almus," the closest phonetic spelling the Army clerk of the day could record.

While the San Antonio City Council tried for 30 years to give land to the Army for a permanent post, the Army seemed content to erect a camp at the Alamo plaza, using rented buildings and the old chapel.

Into this situation came troops gathered for the Mexican War in 1846. The Post of San Antonio was a

FAR CRY from the Alamo was this ground plan of Fort Sam Houston. This shows only one part of post, including the walled Quadrangle; bulk of training and infantry barracks area was east of here. Quadrangle had all of its windows facing inward and presented solid rock face to outside in event of Indian attack. Modern use by Fourth Army shows fear of Indian attack has abated. Exterior walls now have windows. (Redrawn from National Archives data.)

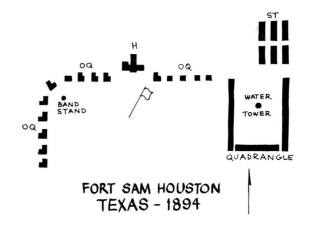

FORT SAM HOUSTON
TEXAS - 1894

# THE ALAMO—1836

Gonzales
(70 miles)

Goliad
(95 miles)

Where Col. Travis fell

Artillerymen's quarters

Hospital

Northern Postern

Infantry barracks

Powder magazine

Officers' quarters

Headquarters of the Alamo

Palisade defended by David Crockett

Pecan tree

Guardhouse

Jim Bowie's room

San Antonio (San Fernando Church, 800 yds)

The 18-pounder

Artillery command post

**THIS WAS THE ALAMO** in 1836 as depicted by Paul Laune for Walter Lord's 1961 book, *A Time to Stand*. Five different ground plans were studied to produce this representation of how the Alamo looked before Santa Anna's siege began. Today only the chapel, considerably restored, and some walls of hospital and nearby stables remain. Downtown San Antonio and Alamo Plaza cover "parade ground" area.

(HARPER & ROW, PUBLISHERS, INC., USED WITH PERMISSION.)

quartermaster depot at this time and it was charged with obtaining 1,112 wagons for the invasion of Mexico. Every available set of wheels was commandeered and many travelers were left high and dry on the back roads of Texas.

Robert E. Lee was here as a lieutenant and while here gathered the tools, pontoons, and other equipment he needed to prepare a road for the Army that was forming to invade Mexico.

The Army officially took over the Alamo in 1849. Some $5,000 was spent in restoring the buildings, including the almost destroyed chapel. The Alamo was used as a quartermaster storehouse for forage and equipment and also for some workshops. The Army post grew around it, but in leased buildings.

Four blocks away, at St. Mary's and Houston streets, the Army persuaded local businessmen to erect a two-story building. Leased to the Army, it was post headquarters until the Civil War. The Confederates gave it similar duties, but after the war it became a hotel. The modern Gunter Hotel now stands on the site.

San Antonio served two functions in the 1850's. It was the Quartermaster Depot for more than 20 Texas forts, and the headquarters of the Eighth Military District. It lost this latter assignment for a short time

**CHAPEL OF THE ALAMO** is silent reminder in bustling San Antonio of heroes whose sacrifice made Texas part of United States. Battle cry "Remember the Alamo" rallied Texan Army at Battle of San Jacinto 46 days after Alamo defeat, and capture of Santa Anna signalled freedom for Texas. Chapel has been restored and upper story does not match former appearance; two towers chapel had also are missing. Added, though, is the epitaph of the Alamo: "Thermopolae had its messenger of defeat; The Alamo had none."

ALMOST SIXTY YEARS later, this was Alamo's descendant, Fort Sam Houston as it appeared in 1890. Appropriations for post had to be made twice by Congress when Army failed to act in time when money was first given. San Antonions share credit for location of fort; fearing it would be moved to Austin, they sent delegations to White House and Congress in 1873 to argue for it despite opposition of Army.

(NATIONAL ARCHIVES.)

in 1853 when district headquarters was moved to Corpus Christi. The district commander, General Persifer Smith, was ailing and doctors thought a sea atmosphere would help him.

Robert E. Lee returned to San Antonio as a lieutenant colonel and acting district commander in 1857 again in 1860. During this last tour, the war clouds were gathering and he was going through an agonizing self-examination as to his future course.

He rented a small house on the river near N. St. Mary's Street and worked in a one-room office in the Army's leased headquarters. Much of his time was spent with fellow West Pointer Lieutenant Thomas G. Williams and his wife, a daughter of President Tyler. Their daughter later recorded that Lee and her father "often talked of the coming events that were casting their shadows before them.

"They discussed what they would do in the event that Virginia, the native state of both of them, should secede. They both decided they could not remain in the service if that happened."

Lee returned once again to San Antonio after his temporary district assignment was over. This was when he was summoned to Washington in 1861 to be offered command of the Federal Army. He found drastic changes.

LOOKOUT POST for Indians was original intention of this tower in center of Fourth Army Quadrangle. Tower was built in 1876, is 87 feet high, once had 30,000-gallon water reservoir on top, along with an open lookout perch. Bell in tower came from gunboat that sank in Galveston Harbor, then was used in mule compound at the Alamo. When Alamo was gutted by fire in 1861, bell was undamaged and ultimately found its way to Quadrangle tower.

**SALLY PORT** of Quadrangle is only entrance into interior where deer and ducks roamed uncaged under tower's protection. Tower originally was located so that sentry atop it could see all doors in Quadrangle, and all entrances to warehouses outside of square. Quadrangle is 499 feet long and 33 feet high along its south side, and 624 feet long and a single story high along the north. Originally only loopholes near the top pierced the walls. Quadrangle had 36 storerooms, 20 offices, many shops and a cellar.

A contemporary newspaper described the scene: "Eight o'clock Saturday morning our usually quiet city is full of soldiers. All the important streets are guarded, and the main plaza looks like a vast military camp."

In answer to Lee's inquiries, he was told that the soldiers were rebels under Colonel Ben McCulloch and that the district commander, "General Twiggs surrendered everything to the state this morning, and we are all prisoners of war."

Lee noted the Lone Star flag flying over the Alamo and he was asked to declare whether he would support the South. Angrily he pointed out that he was a sworn federal officer and he would not be pressured. He was permitted to leave Texas, but was required to leave his baggage behind. He never got the baggage back.

Lee's old regiment, the 2nd Cavalry, next moved through San Antonio. They were enroute to the Gulf Coast and a voyage to the East. According to a regimental history, when "they arrived at San Antonio the state troops were flying the 'Lone Star Flag' over the Alamo. The next morning the command marched through the principal streets with the regimental standard and company guidons displayed and the band playing 'Yankee Doodle' and 'Hail, Columbia.' A large number of citizens followed the troops beyond the city limits and presented them with a United States flag."

They found the same situation at Goliad, but this time pulled down the secession flag during the night. "The next morning it was used to make head-streamers for the train mules, and was thus displayed as the troops marched through the town."

San Antonio's role in the Civil War was minor. It was a Confederate headquarters but was far from the center of the stage. Apparently the liveliest event was Christmas Eve, 1862, when some Confederates clashed with a company of local Mexican volunteers in a riot that broke more windows and smashed more chili stands than any event since.

The United States Army returned to San Antonio in 1865. Soon the city became a bustling trade center. The cattle drives and the stages to the west brought in money and business and all that went with it. The saloons and other dens became so bad that an 1870 surgeon's report suggested by moving farther from town "the government would certainly gain much in point of economy in the health and discipline of the garrison."

This came about finally in 1879 when the "Infantry Barracks, San Antonio" was established two miles to the northwest. On a 3,300-acre plot, the Army built what is today one of its largest installations. It is also one of the most historic. Here Teddy Roosevelt organized his Rough Riders for the Spanish-American War. Here, too, military aviation was born when Lieutenant Benjamin D. Foulois rebuilt a Wright Brothers airplane and made the Army's first flight on March 2, 1910.

The Mexican Border troubles before World War I found San Antonio again a troop center. Today it is the headquarters for the Fourth Army and the site of Brooke Army Hospital, one of the country's largest.

With the number of soldiers who have been stationed and married locally in San Antonio since the days of the Alamo, it is almost with pride that the city lays claim to being "The Mother-in-law of the Army."

TO GET THERE: The Alamo is in downtown San Antonio on Alamo Plaza at East Houston and Alamo Streets. Fort Sam Houston, for that was the name the post at San Antonio was given in 1890, is at the north end of New Braunfels Street (take East Houston from Alamo and turn right on New Braunfels, about 20 blocks to the east).

BANDSTAND at Fort Sam Houston appeared on original plan of post. It is at end of parade ground along officers' row. Watch tower and Quadrangle can be seen through bandstand.

HOSPITAL AREA of the Alamo is shown by three reconstructed walls to northwest of chapel.

# FORT LANCASTER, TEXAS

Things might have been primitive back in pre-Civil War Fort Lancaster's frame and shanties, but that did not seem to affect the troops' tactical skill.

When it came to Indian fighting, the soldiers had a few tricks of their own. A case in point occurred in 1857 when 14 men and two wagons were ambushed 25 miles away. The Indians first approached under a white flag. When it was obvious the soldiers were not to be fooled, the Indians opened fire, killing one of the sergeants.

The remaining sergeants ordered a retreat. While the Indians tarried to loot the wagons, both military and civilians got away, although the dead sergeant's body had to be left. It was found later scalped.

Eighty men at Lancaster, including 40 camped there from a Fort Davis unit, pursued the hostiles on the "trojan horse" principle. The troopers were hidden in wagons, the canvas covers closed, and the "supply train" headed west.

Forty-five miles from the post, the Indians jumped the apparently civilian wagon train. The covers came down and the soldiers blasted back. Half of them advanced as the shocked braves pulled back.

The Indians set the prairie on fire, hoping to sneak up under a smoke screen. This did not work when the troops moved to a bare depression and waited out the flames, then advanced again. Bested at their own game, the redmen disappeared.

It was not always this clever around Lancaster,

though. Established in 1855, the post was not a year old when the Army Inspector found the troops so untrained he feared to let them demonstrate rifle firing.

At least half of the two companies of the 1st Infantry were recruits, and the inspector complained, "They could not drill as skirmishers . . . nor could they drill at the bayonet. I dispensed with target firing for the same reason."

He blamed the absence of qualified instructors for most of the difficulty. Apparently a captain was trying to do all of the training because his company had not had any lieutenants for nine years, and this was too much for one man. "The labor of instructing inferior recruits . . . at the squad drill is great," it was commented, "and most of it should fall on subalterns. The noncommissioned officers, in most instances, are not properly qualified. Add to this the labor of building a post in such a locality."

This last remark probably was the crux of the situation. The garrison was living in what were termed "hackadales," portable frames covered with canvas. Some officers lived in adobes and the stores were in a stone building that had a canvas roof.

Improvement in the housing situation is evident from the elaborate ruins remaining today. Heavy stone walls with crumbling but impressive fireplaces indicate that the hackadales were replaced by sturdy buildings before the post was finally abandoned in 1867.

It was surrendered to Texans in 1861 and they maintained it with companies of so-called "Minute Men" sporadically. General Sibley inspected the post in November 28, 1861, but was not pleased by what he saw.

At 7 a.m., the uniformed company gave Sibley a review on the parade ground. As they trotted by him in a column of twos, the Confederate general commanded, "File left!" Apparently the order was unheard. The volunteers cantered across the parade

## FORT LANCASTER
## TEXAS — 1856

HACKADALES made up most of post in this early ground plan, apparently pre-dating stone construction. At this time 150 men and three officers were stationed there. Army Inspector reported that there were 76 prisoners in guardhouse, 15 of them for drunkenness "by liquor given them by travelers." Although post sutler was not permitted to sell whiskey except by special permit, inspector complained, "I presume the error is in enlisting confirmed drunkards who desire nothing better than to get drunk and lay in the guardhouse." (Redrawn from plat at College of William and Mary.)

**FORT LANCASTER** in 1861 flew Stars and Bars over buildings that were obvious improvements to temporary structures of early post. Fort was reactivated as sub-post during Kiowa-Comanche troubles of 1871 and a lieutenant and six Indians were killed in skirmish here a year later. Two years after Civil War fort was site of two-day battle between Indians and 9th Cavalry troops, resulting in deaths of three soldiers.

(MRS. M. C. ROBERTSON, OZONA, TEXAS.)

ground, through the outbuildings, then across the mountains and out of sight. Sibley had but one comment. "Gone to hell!" he snorted and stamped away.

The troops finally realized their situation and returned to the post in the evening. They were relieved to find Silbey had left for New Mexico.

TO GET THERE: From Sheffield, Texas, take U.S. 290 ten miles north to where marker is on right of road after crossing Live Oak Creek. Fort Lancaster chimneys can be seen to left of highway. Watch for rattlesnakes.

**SUBSTANTIAL BUILDINGS** at this point probably served as barracks row. Fireplace and wall in foreground belonged to one building, wall in background was for one next to it. Entire area is dotted with ruins half covered by sagebrush and mesquite and protected by rattlesnakes.

# FORT TERRETT, TEXAS

If local legends in West Texas are any indication, Fort Terrett was closed down because of a bad reputation. Supposedly the whiskey traders from Fredericksburg set up shop nearby, and the soldiers became too frequent clients of their emporiums.

The tale is told that conditions at this post were so bad that the scandal reached Departmental Headquarters. Despairing of improving the morale and morals, and noting the high incidence of sickness, it was decided to abandon the place when it was a month and a half shy of three years old.

No official records seem to exist to corroborate this story, although an 1853 inspection mentions "an unfavorable opinion would be formed of the healthfulness of the climate" from the fact that there were 22 men on the sick report the day of the inspection. "In the year ending June 30, 1853," it continued, "there were 1,577 cases of disease for a mean strength of 194 men, or about 800 per cent — the prevailing diseases being intermittent fevers, diarrheas, and dysentery."

The post commander apparently felt he was doing a good job with his men, but reported that Army policies hampered him.

"Teamsters detached from the command and engaged in supplying the post," the Army Inspector complained, "were taken from under the control of the commanding officer and placed under the exclusive control of the Quartermaster at San Antonio, who can, at pleasure, relieve any of the men and is authorized to call for others to supply their places.

"Men thus taken away from the restraints of discipline soon contact bad habits, become drunkards, and are soon relieved by other good men, and sent back to their companies to be remodeled by their Company officers.

"The effect of this is readily seen," he pointed out. "It destroys discipline, not only in a few, but in course of time an entire company may have to undergo the same thing."

To complicate the military situation, apparently from the day the post was started most of the troops stopped soldiering to become builders. Almost 75 per cent of them were thus occupied, but when the Army Inspector observed their drilling he said, "The display was creditable to them."

A higher commendation might be earned from his comment on the post buildings: "The quarters were in as good order as buildings of their character are capable of being rendered."

Most of the fort was of stone, though at the time of inspection the barracks were a long way from complete. "The quarters as far as completed are merely shelters for the men, without doors, floors, or windows," the report commented, adding, "No timber suitable for flooring can be cut in the vicinity."

Records of Fort Terrett's military endeavors are sketchy, usually tacked on the end of a report for another fort. Generally, the post is mentioned as filling a gap between Fort Clark, along the lower line of forts on the Rio Grande, and Fort McKavett, on the upper line.

It was the headquarters for the 1st Infantry Regiment. At the time of its founding, the post had almost 250 personnel on its rolls, plus almost 200 more on duties elsewhere. The regimental commander was tied up on court-martial duties in Florida, and the duties of post commander were left to the senior captain.

This situation did not last long, however. By the end of 1853 there were only 100 men at the post. Two months later it was abandoned. Regardless of what factual seeds might exist in the local legends, an obvious fact is that Fort McKavett was only 30 miles to the north. It was on a direct road between forts; Terrett was on a tangent.

Perhaps the facts of geography had more to do with the closing of Fort Terrett than the excesses of a not-so-temperate garrison.

FORT TERRETT
TEXAS - 1852

**MANY OF THESE** buildings still remain, and foundation traces are left of those now in ruins. Officers' quarters were stone, barracks were wooden but plans were to replace them with stone. Band barracks, right end of barracks row, was occupied by what inspectors termed "though small, the band is quite good, and does much to relieve the montony of a garrison at an isolated, frontier station." (Redrawn from National Archives.)

COMMANDING OFFICER'S quarters and parade ground probably have changed little in 100 years. Original ground plans showed considerable brush and trees dotting parade ground, a condition still existing in this view from officers' row toward CO's house.

TO GET THERE: From Junction, Texas (96 miles southeast of San Angelo), take U.S. 290 west 26 miles to intersection with dirt road beyond Roosevelt. This is River Road and also has a sign to Fort Terrett. Go north one mile to Fred Rowsey Ranch, the site of fort which uses remodeled fort buildings.

BARRACKS at Terrett were replaced at least in part by stone. This building now is used as garage, but its early appearance is virtually intact. Note entrances in doors, especially far doorway.

# FORT MARTIN SCOTT, TEXAS

When the wonders of modern ingenuity came to the Western frontier, often they came via the Army and the Indian was the mystified observer.

So it was at Fort Martin Scott, a tiny outpost of the Army amidst the German emigrant area of West Texas. As described by Colonel Richard I. Dodge in later years, once while talking to an Indian a Fort Martin Scott officer "took from his pocket a box of what, to the Indian, were merely little sticks, and, scratching one on a stone lit a pipe."

The Indian's amazement was increased by the lighting of several more matches. "Going to his camp nearby, he soon came back, bringing half a dozen beautifully dressed wildcat skins, which he offered for the wonderful box. The exchange was accepted . . .

"Some time after he was found sitting by a large stone, on which he was gravely striking match after match, holding each in his fingers until forced to drop it, and then carefully inspected the scorched finger, as if to assure himself that it was real fire. This he continued to do until every match was burned."

Perhaps all of the Indians in Martin Scott's vicinity were equally gullible for there is no record of hostile activity during its five years of activity, 1848-53.

One of the lone incidents involved soldiers rather than savages upsetting the settlers. As the story is told in Fredericksburg today, on one occasion an imbibing soldier was refused further service by a town barkeep. The result was a fight in which the trooper was killed.

The next day, his comrades came to town and burned the saloon. All of the legal and court records for the three-year-old town were stored in the building and were lost.

In 1853, the Army Inspector visited the post and was less than pleased with what he saw. By this time the fort was only a 19-man forage depot for trains that serviced the northern posts.

He found the men had various weapons, one had none at all, and "almost all had a very limited supply of clothing." Their training seemed to be neglected and they "made but an indifferent appearance on parade."

He had a good comment on the buildings. "They are of a better description than at most of the posts in Texas," he reported, but with a reservation. "It is believed no rent is paid for the land, but the owner has received a considerable sum for fuel and timber cut, and the improvements will belong to him when the troops are withdrawn."

Summed up, he said, "There seems to me little advantage in continuing to occupy Fort Martin Scott, and I think the discipline of the service would be promoted by sending the detachment to its regiment."

Four months after this visit, the Army took action and Fort Martin Scott was abandoned. It was used periodically by Confederates and Texas Rangers but in later years the only remaining trace was the limestone officers' quarters used as a private residence.

TO GET THERE: From courthouse in Fredericksburg, go east on East Main (U.S. 290) in direction of President Johnson's "Little White House" 2.4 miles to marker on left side of highway.

ARMY INSPECTOR considered Martin Scott one of best in Texas, even if it had little combat action. (Redrawn from Mansfield Inspection Report, 1853.)

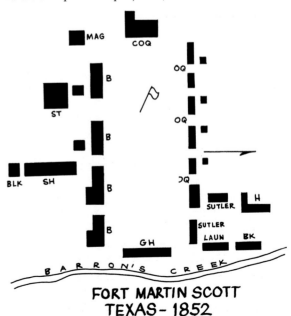

**OFFICERS' QUARTERS** from Fort Martin Scott do not show age; only local stories support idea that this building once was part of fort. Supposedly it was used as residence by settler and post-Army use accounts for its good condition.
(KILMAN STUDIO, FREDERICKSBURG, TEXAS.)

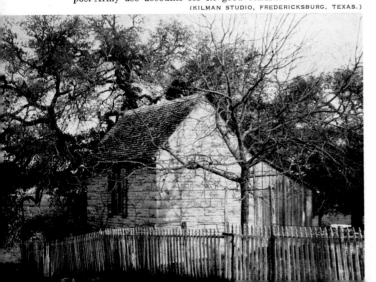

# ROBERT E. LEE WAS HERE

*"As an American citizen I take great pride in my country, her prosperity and institutions . . . I can anticipate no greater calamity for the country than a dissolution of the Union . . . Secession is nothing but revolution."*

—Lee writing from Fort Mason, Texas, January, 1861.

ROBERT E. LEE went to Texas three times, once to fight Mexicans, twice to fight Indians and bandits. The lessons learned prepared him for leadership of the Confederate Army in the Civil War.

He first came to Texas in 1846 for the Mexican War. He was at San Antonio, Eagle Pass, Brazos Santiago, and Rio Grande City for a short time, but most of the tour was spent in Mexico. From Vera Cruz to Chapultapec he fought, received three brevets, one wound, and a firsthand knowledge of other officers that would serve him well when he faced them on Virginia battlefields.

When the 2nd Cavalry was organized in 1885, Lee was designated its second-in-command. From 1855 to 1857 he was back in Texas, serving mainly at San Antonio, Fort Mason, and Camp Cooper, but his patrols and six court-martial tours took him to many forts on the Texas line. Even Leavenworth and Riley in Kansas saw him as a court member.

He was called East in 1857 on family matters. While there, he commanded the Marine and militia units that captured John Brown at Harpers Ferry in 1859.

His last tour in Texas was short. He arrived on February 19, 1860, and assumed temporary command of the department at headquarters in San Antonio. He chased bandits and experimented with camels until December when he resumed his command at Fort Mason.

He was at Fort Mason when he received orders to proceed immediately to Washington. Secession was on the land and Lee was to be offered command of the Federal Army. On April 22 he doffed the Union uniform he had worn for 32 years and went to Richmond. Loyalty to his home state was stronger in him than his dislike of secession.

# FORT BROWN, TEXAS

The last battle of the Civil War was fought near Fort Brown, Texas, but that is getting ahead of the story.

Nineteen years ahead, in fact. For Fort Brown, these were years of action that began in a state of siege during the Mexican War.

It was in April, 1846, that General Zachary Taylor took possession of Southern Texas, claiming it from Mexico in the name of the United States. Expecting less than a hospitable reception, Taylor built an earth fort and left a 50-man garrison for its defense. The post was in the direct line with Matamoros, across the Rio Grande, and Taylor included a battery of four 18-pounders—all aimed at Matamoros.

No sooner had the bulk of his Army left than the Mexican Army splashed across the river and bottled up what had been named Fort Taylor. In the ensuing fight, Major Jacob Brown, its commander, was killed.

The sound of the bombardment alerted Taylor and he rushed back to its relief. Fighting and winning the Battles of Palo Alto and Resaca de la Palma enroute, Taylor caused the Mexicans to turn tail across the river. Fort Taylor was strengthened, its name changed to honor the late commander, and it became a key to the Texas defense line until the Civil War.

Lieutenant Colonel Robert E. Lee made at least two trips to Fort Brown in the between wars period, once for a court-martial and once to chase Mexican bandit Juan Nepemuchene Cortinas back and forth across the border into Mexico. Even earlier Lee had passed through Fort Brown during his Mexican War service.

When Lee arrived at Fort Brown in November, 1856, he was not impressed. The countryside bore the scars of bandit raids and the town of Brownsville, next to the fort, was a typical border town. Lee saw the plight of Army families stationed at the post and wrote his wife back in Virginia, "The more I see of Texas Army life, the less probability do I see of your ever being able to join me here."

His summary comment on Matamoros, and probably equally applicable to Brownsville, was that it was neat "though much out at the elbow."

Lee returned to Fort Brown in 1859 while he was acting as commander of the Department of Texas. The aforementioned Cortinas had invaded Brownsville at the head of somewhere between 40 and 80 mounted bandits. After shooting up the town and opening the jail cells, his crew took over Fort Brown which had been abandoned by the Army eight months before. Without success, they tried to break down the door of the powder magazine.

Summoned by the frightened citizens, Mexican troops rushed across the river to enforce a truce until relatives of Cortinas could quiet him down. Several days later he again came to Brownsville, but found the citizens armed and ready. An impromptu militia had been organized under the name "Brownsville Tigers" and they joined with Mexican militia into a joint 60-man, 2-cannon chase of the bandits.

When Cortinas stopped running and faced his chasers, he sent them rushing in disorder back to Brownsville, their cannon left behind.

Into this situation came Lee. Cortinas was robbing and plundering, even capturing and reading the mail between Brownsville and Point Isabel because, as Lee later wrote, "it was a matter of necessity for him to know what steps were taken against him."

The Army sent 117 men to re-garrison Fort Brown. With rangers more than doubling this force, the troopers met and defeated Cortinas in several engagements. Then Lee led a cavalry force through a snowstorm to find the 120-mile-long Rio Grande valley had been desolated. Citizen claims against the government exceeded $300,000 and 95 Americans and friendly Mexicans had been killed.

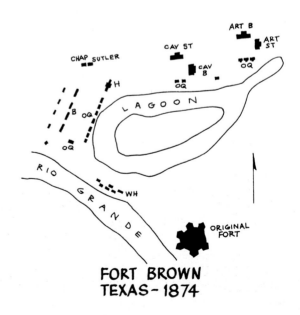

**FORT BROWN
TEXAS - 1874**

**A NEW FORT BROWN** was built in 1868 north of the maligned and battered earthen fortification. After Civil War, post was rendezvous for 25,000 men mustered by General W. T. Sherman as a "show of force" to prevent Mexican intervention in postwar reconstruction. Troops were quartered in temporary huts in town for two years until 1867 hurricane demolished most buildings. New fort was built in 1868-69 while troopers lived in town houses. (Redrawn from NPS data.)

**ACTIVITY** at Fort Brown ranged from minor role in Indian Wars to a major one in controlling border disturbances of 1914-16. National interest focused on it in 1905 when President Theodore Roosevelt mustered out of service an entire battalion because a dozen troopers involved in a bar killing could not be discovered. When abandoned in 1946, it was southernmost military post in United States. Above, Fort Brown in 1876.

But Lee spent five months at Fort Brown in chasing what he termed the "Cortinas Myth" without luck. On one occasion, he determined to surprise Cortinas in Mexico and mounted two columns of troopers in a sudden attack across the Rio Grande. Again, no luck.

Lee occupied much of his energy in trying to get Mexican officials to arrest Cortinas. Finally, reports of depredations dropped off and, with the feeling that Cortinas had appeared in Mexico, Lee gave up the chase.

The Army was left at Fort Brown, though, but its condition two years later did not speak well for any care and maintenance rendered. After it was taken over by Confederates in 1861, survey of its seven officers found them unanimous in their disgust with it.

One officer estimated that it would take 500 laborers three months to make it defensible. Its commander did not think its defense advisable at all. Another thought it could hold for 15 to 20 days "against five times the garrison, provided five days labor of said garrison is bestowed upon it." Four other officers had only one opinion: "untenable."

The fort they found was a field work of six bastion fronts with a 950-yard defense line which the Confederate commander said would require 2,000 men.

It had a miscellaneous collection of 25 howitzers, cannon and mortars. The garrison consisted chiefly of Mexicans, "old soldiers and deserters from the Federal Army, with few exceptions a class of men in whom no dependence can be placed," according to their commander. "A few dollars and a little whiskey is quite sufficient to corrupt and entice them away."

Brown was burned in 1863 by the Confederates when 6,000 Union troops approached, but eight months later the Federals were driven out and the fort again saw the "Stars and Bars." Brownsville was too important a shipping port to Europe for the Confederacy to permit its loss.

The Confederacy held on for a month after Appomattox at Fort Brown, finally surrendering after the Battle of Palmetto Hill on May 14, 1865. Ironically, according to its regimental commander, "The last volley of the war, it is believed, was fired by the Sixty-second U. S. Colored Infantry about sunset of the 13th of May, 1865."

TO GET THERE: Thriving Brownsville is a far cry from Lee's border town of 100 years ago. Fort Brown is next to the city at the south end of S.E. Elizabeth Street. So-called "Quartermaster's Fence" built in 1850 separating the city and the post was torn down in 1950 to widen International Boulevard, but its location is marked in the cement of the boulevard.

**CHAPEL** at Fort Brown now houses Brownsville Historical Society. Early appearance is evident. Earliest American military battle in area was Thornton skirmish on April 25, 1846, 20 miles west between U.S. and Mexican soldiers. President Polk said of it to Congress, "American blood has been shed on American soil and war exists by act of Mexico."

**ORIGINAL FORT BROWN** can still be seen on Brownsville golf course. Marker and upright cannon are where earthworks once were. (Modern photos courtesy Robert Utley, National Park Service, Santa Fe.)

YELLOW FEVER'S opponent, Dr. William C. Gorgas, began his experiments when he was a surgeon at Fort Brown's hospital in 1882. Building is now administration building of Texas Southernmost College. Building was finished in 1868, first used temporarily for officers' quarters. It is 136 feet long, 40 feet wide, was considered excellent for hospital. Its sandstone and wood construction of 1868 have been remodeled but building still resembles early years.

HEADQUARTERS for fort was this building, now used as police headquarters by Brownsville. It dates from 1869 era but remodeling gives it appearance of turn-of-century Army building.

# FORT RINGGOLD, TEXAS

"This was a brilliant affair and reflects huge credit upon the soldiers," so said Army General Order Number 11 of November 23, 1860 speaking in general of the major action in the annals of Fort Ringgold, Texas.

Major Samuel P. Heintzelman was more specific about the actions of his men: "The enemy were driven from every position taken for ten miles, when they dispersed. Captain Stoneman dismounted his company and drove a party across the Rio Grande. About 60 of the enemy were killed."

Both reports referred to the defeat of bandit Juan Cortinas—he of the "myth" that plagued General Lee during the activity around Fort Brown.

Actually the business at Fort Ringgold—or Ringgold Barracks as it was then known in 1859—came before Lee got into the bandit-chasing duty. And, to be frank, what happened at Ringgold just about closed the chapter on Cortinas, but no one could say that at the time.

Cortinas had pillaged the Rio Grande area of Texas almost at will, but finally had to take the defensive when both Army and militia ganged up on him. Major Heintzelman's troops attacked a Cortinas blockade near Fort Brown on December 14, 1859, forcing them to flee from their main body. At Rio Grande City on December 27, the full Cortinas force faced a combined Army-Texas Ranger outfit of 380 men.

As Captain G. Price writes in his *Across the Continent with the Fifth Cavalry*, "A severe engagement followed, and the troops gained a brilliant and decisive victory.

"The enemy, 550 strong, were driven for ten miles, when they abandoned their arms, ammunition and supplies, and sought safety in a hasty retreat across the Rio Grande into Mexico. They suffered a known loss in the engagements of 66 killed and many wounded. The troops had 17 men killed and wounded."

More colorful, and definitely to the point, was the reported battle cry used by Texas Ranger Major John S. Ford as he led his men against Cortinas: "You damned sons of bitches, we have got you!"

Lee arrived at Ringgold after the fighting had ended, but he found talk of new Cortinas raids on every lip. Most of this was based on fiction. Only a few days before, the Heintzelman-Ford combination again had whipped Cortinas to the tune of 59 casualties when he tried to capture the steamer *Ranchero*.

Noting that Cortinas took refuge into Mexico after his defeats, Lee addressed a message to the governor of Tamaulipas. He warned him that the Mexican government "must break up and disperse the bands of banditti which have been concerned in these depredations, and have sought protection within Mexican territory."

Then he left Fort Ringgold to observe the effects of his ultimatum from Brownsville. His statesmanship, coupled with the vigorous military actions caused the Cortinas threat to die a natural death and the border returned to its normal confused quiet.

This was not the first time Lee came to Ringgold. He had been here three years earlier while on court-martial duty, but found the post so crowded that he had to live in a tent outside the post. His memories of that five-week court-martial visit were of hours of listening to the court testimony and of watching the problems of the families some of his fellow court members had brought to Ringgold.

With tongue in cheek after watching one wife shepherding her children, chickens, goats and pigeon around a tent, he wrote his own wife back in Virginia: "If officers of the Army will get married, I think they should insist that their wives have no children. This will help the matter much."

RINGGOLD BARRACKS
TEXAS - 1875

TO GET THERE: Fort Ringgold is immediately next to Rio Grande City, and is now used for school purposes by the school district.

AFTER CIVIL WAR and Confederates no longer occupied Fort Ringgold, it underwent complete renovation. Although post surgeon reported in 1870, "The buildings . . . are constructed of wood, ill adapted to the purpose, and liable to be blown over by the first heavy gale," this soon was remedied. Post took on this appearance, retaining it basically throughout border bandit troubles in 1875 and until Army abandoned it in 1944. It was known as Ringgold Barracks until 1878. (Redrawn from Division of the Missouri Report, 1876.)

(NATIONAL ARCHIVES.)

**FORT RINGGOLD** in 1878 was an impressive version of permanent Army post era. This view of parade ground apparently was taken from hospital and shows officers' quarters in background.

**BARRACKS PICTURE** today fits 1870 description: "Two stories high, 130 feet long and 43 feet wide, inclusive of a porch, 9 feet wide, upon Moorish arches, in front and rear. It contains on the first floor a reading room, storeroom, and a room for the first sergeant. The second story is to be occupied as a dormitory." (Modern photographs courtesy Robert Utley, NPS Santa Fe.)

**OFFICERS' ROW** from across former parade ground was intended for three families each, two lieutenants and a captain. As late as 1935, an old three-room cottage was pointed out as General Lee's headquarters while he was at Ringgold; visitors also were told that both Lee and U. S. Grant were brother officers at Ringgold, a statement supported more by tradition than history. General Pershing served there as a lieutenant.

# CAMP COOPER, TEXAS

When Robert E. Lee and Camp Cooper first met, each was somewhat of a sight.

It was April 9, 1856, when Lee arrived at Cooper, fresh from two years as superintendent of the Military Academy at West Point. He was prepared for the tour, at least in one respect. Before leaving his last stop, Fort Mason, he had nailed to his wagon a coop with seven chickens. With the cackling and flying feathers behind him, Lee crossed the Clear Fork of the Brazos, worked his way up the steep bank, and came onto the parade ground of Camp Cooper.

"Parade ground" might be too dignified a term to use, however. The post had only been occupied by troops for three months. In *Across the Continent with the Fifth Cavalry*, the appearance of Camp Cooper when Lee arrived is described:

"The companies lived in tents during the winter, which was one of the most severe ever experienced in that section. Northers followed each other in rapid succession, and as there were no stables the horses suffered severely and were frequently covered with frozen sleet.

"An attempt was made to erect shelter for them, but failed because of the poor material at hand; and the picket-lines of two of the companies were located under the shelter of the high banks of the creek, while the others located their picket-lines on two benches on the mountain-side."

During Lee's time at Cooper, many of the tents were replaced by rough buildings. Barracks were built of "mud walls," a close cousin to adobe, and shingle roofs. Stone and boards, some simply placed upright in the ground, served many of the buildings, while storehouses were tarpaulins stretched over wooden frames. Tents continued to be used because throughout its five-year existence Cooper was considered only temporary. Lee was under standing orders to locate a better site, negotiate a lease from the owner, and prepare plans for buildings. He made frequent trips for this purpose, but nothing came of them.

Activity at Cooper was centered around the Brazos Indian Reservation, a mile to the north. About 500 Comanches, under Chief Katumse, were here, trying with a minimum of success to plant crops and run cattle.

The elements conspired against these domestic arts. Both the Indian and Army planting attempts were defeated by a combination of drought and grasshoppers. The Indians had to sell their livestock to live, and all of this contributed to a continual feeling of uneasiness.

As the second ranking officer in the Second Cavalry, at first it seemed that Lee was being exiled at this out-of-the-way fort. He soon realized that it was of an importance far exceeding its rude appearance. The Comanche reservation was an experiment and it fell to Lee to help it succeed. With success in domesticating the Indian, a peaceful solution to the Indian question might have been found. In addition, centering two squadrons of cavalry at this point permitted the Army to range far and wide on reconnaissance and patrol duties.

Shortly after Lee arrived at Cooper, he took out its first major patrol. Intending to locate three hostile tribes, he took two Cooper companies while a company from Fort Chadbourne reinforced Cooper's remaining squadron in its defense.

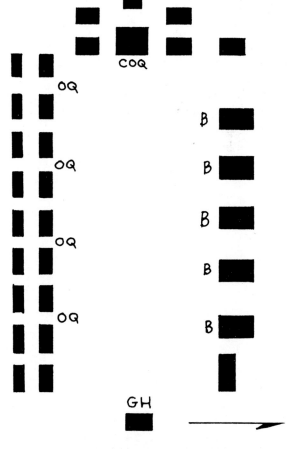

COQ

OQ

OQ

OQ

OQ

B

B

B

B

B

GH

## CAMP COOPER TEXAS - 1859

BOTH TENTS and makeshift mud-stone-wood buildings made up Camp Cooper, although this ground plan does not indicate this. More permanent-type construction was used along north and east side of parade ground, but it appears remainder of camp was tents or canvas covered frames. (Redrawn from data in National Archives.)

TRAGEDY IS RECORDED next to Camp Cooper site. Gravestone is of 24-year-old John M. Larn, county sheriff in 1878. He built house in background of stones and glass from Cooper, put cupola on roof in which lookouts were posted. Legend is that he supplied beef to Army at Fort Griffin, but neighbors did not consider his herds large enough for the quantity he was able to sell to the Army, suspected he was rustling their cattle. Jailed in Albany, he was never tried. Mob broke into jail and shot him. He and one child now are buried in this tiny plot next to his former home, ranch house now occupied by cattleman J. Carrol Putman.

The patrol lasted 40 days and went 1,100 miles. Bad water and heat plagued it all of the way and only one contact was made. This was with a small Indian looting party; three braves were killed and a squaw was taken prisoner and turned over to her parents on the Brazos reservation.

Lee was in and out of Cooper on his perennial courts-martial, and left it for the final time in 1857 when he became acting Department commander, headquartered in San Antonio.

Hardly had he left Major George F. Thomas in command when the post Lee described as a "desert of dullness" became just the opposite. Rumors of Comanche raids against the post proved usually to be false, but the troops were kept busy protecting the Indian reservation.

On one occasion an 11-man detail found itself between opposing groups of Indians. The soldiers hastily retired to the post when they realized they carried only enough ammunition for one round from each rifle.

On another occasion, 250 white settlers descended on the reservation and Thomas had to call out his troopers to drive them away. Comanche and whites engaged in a running fight before the Army stepped in. Later, groups of vigilantes camped along the reservation's borders, keeping Camp Cooper on continual alert.

Camp Cooper was the center of numerous expeditions against the Indians until the Civil War came along. Texas state troops surrounded it on February 21, 1861, and its commander surrendered, first burning many of the storehouses and permitting the soldiers and civilians to come and carry off anything they wanted. Generals who received training as junior officers here included Lee, William J. Hardee, Earl Van Dorn, E. Kirby Smith, John B. Hood, George H. Thomas, I. N. Palmer and George Stoneman.

DATING FROM early 1870's, this building is in vicinity of southern edge of Camp Cooper parade ground. Not contemporary with active years of fort, it was probably built with fragments of Army buildings and in their style. Post was used occasionally by state militia and Texas Rangers in post-Civil War activity. Graveyard nearby has two markers from this non-Army period.

TO GET THERE: From Albany, Texas, take U.S. 283 north about 13 miles to road intersection with farm road (2 miles south of Ft. Griffin State Park). Sign for Matthews Ranch is at this point; turn left. Follow signs for eight miles, turn right to Putman Ranch five miles. At Putman ranch house, it is a one-mile hike west, including wading the hip-deep Clear Fork of the Brazos. Permission should be asked. Beware of rattlesnakes.

# FORT PHANTOM HILL, TEXAS

Unquestionably Fort Phantom Hill has the most romantic name of any western fort, even if it was not its legal one. Officially the "Post on the Clear Fork of the Brazos," the most colorful title was the most commonly used, and the one which remains today.

As if in recognition of its near-legendary status, the site of Fort Phantom Hill probably is one of the most picturesque. When the soldiers left it in 1854, the buildings went up in flames. Only the stone chimneys were left. For more than 100 years, these stone chimneys have remained, sixty-some eerie and silent sentries of a frontier that is no more.

Mrs. Emma Johnson Elkins lived at the post in 1852 as a child and in 1908 wrote about the source of its unusual name.

"On a bright moonlight night," she recounted, "a group of officers and a party of men were encamped a short distance from the post when one of the party, seeing a tall white figure on the hill (probably an Indian with a white blanket around him), exclaimed: 'A ghost!'

"Another said: 'A phantom on the hill!'"

" 'This,' said one of the officers, 'suggests a name; we will call the fort Phantom Hill.' This name was unanimously adopted."

Regardless of the degree of truth to this version, it seems as logical as any. At least the name lent a certain air to an otherwise drab installation.

The Army Inspector visited in 1853 and suggested it "would be a real charity" to move the soldiers away from Phantom Hill. He noted that water had to be hauled four miles and fuel, five to eight miles.

"The buildings, which are of a very inferior character, were put up by the labor of the troops," he reported. "The aspect of the place is uninviting. . . .

"The officers and soldiers are living in pole huts built in the early part of last year. They are now in a dilapidated condition. The company quarters will, in all probability, fall down during the prevalence of the severe northers of the coming winter."

The inspector's disenchantment with the post probably was not eased when he checked the personnel and armament situation. When he visited, of nearly 200 men it was impossible for the garrison to have a parade because 123 of them were raw recruits and most of the seasoned troops were on patrol duties.

To compound the problem, 55 of the recruits "appeared on parade without arms," he reported, "there being none in the company stores for issue."

He said the post commander had several requisitions for arms, but no action from higher headquarters. Those who had weapons carried percussion muskets or musketoons. Two brass six-pound cannon completed the defenses.

Considering the Indian situation, the weapons inventory was not too promising. Mrs. Elkins wrote that Comanches, Kiowas, and Kickapoos camped around the post "and they become a nuisance; crowding into houses and prowling around until the commander would have to send a squad of men to drive them out of the garrison."

The fort was threatened at least once, she recorded, when the Northern Comanches proclaimed that no white man should settle west of the Red River.

"Preparations at once began for the reception of the Indians in case an attempt was made for the execution of their threats," Mrs. Elkins remembered. "A trench eight feet wide was cut around the garrison and the artillery was placed on a parapet in the center, ready to sweep the environs."

The Indians appeared in the distance one day and the troops turned out. Although Mrs. Elkins says

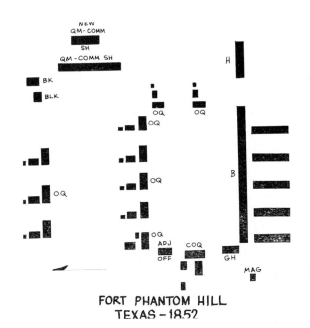

FORT PHANTOM HILL
TEXAS – 1852

**EXCEPT FOR MAGAZINE,** all buildings had thatched roofs and most were of logs or jackel (upright timber stuck in the ground). Officers' area was the north, enlisted to south, with commanding officer's log quarters almost in between. Quarries were within a mile or so of post and plans were to rebuild it of stone. Its abandonment in 1854 stopped this. "It is said," a contemporary diary records, "that the officers and men were heartily disgusted with the station and wished to make certain of never going back; that, as they were leaving the fort, one of the principal officers was heard to say that he wished the place would burn down, and that the soldiers taking him at his word, stayed behind and fired the buildings." (Redrawn from NA data.)

**MAGAZINE** was one of few stone buildings, and is most intact today. Fort was used by Overland Mail line after abandonment and, despite fire ravages, 1858 traveler stated, "Phantom Hill is the cheapest and best new station on the route." Magazine became storehouse and the stone storehouse indicated in plat also was used. Traveler said, "There are the ruins of from 40 to 50 buildings, including an observatory."

that there were about 2,500 Indians in all, "Seeing the preparations for their reception, it was too much for the noble redmen and they passed on with scowls and angry looks, going in a westerly direction."

Robert E. Lee was commander of Fort Phantom Hill, according to local tradition upheld even in a current Chamber of Commerce news release. Mrs. Elkins is positive in denying this point and the historical facts bear her out: "Colonel Lee never commanded at that fort; of this I am quite certain."

Lee was at Phantom Hill during his first major

patrol from Camp Cooper. This was in 1856, however, and all he saw of it were the smut-scarred chimneys. His troops camped under tents nearby and after an overnight stop, moved out on the 1,100-mile expedition that taught Lee much about Texas and troops, little about Indian fighting.

TO GET THERE: From Anson, Texas (24 miles north of Abilene), take U.S. 180 to intersection with Farm Road 600, about 10 miles. Turn right to Nugent, about five miles, and go three miles farther south. Sentinel-like chimneys are scattered along east side of road, heavily covered with underbrush on private property. Watch for rattlesnakes.

**GUARDHOUSE** is almost hidden by chimneys. It stood at western end of barracks row and was saved from fire by stone construction. Contemporary accounts estimated that more than half million dollars in government property was lost in fire, "yet after pretended investigation, no conclusion was arrived at as to the cause of the diabolical deed."

**COMMANDING OFFICER'S** quarters are marked today only by chimneys. Barracks buildings were in area indicated by distant chimneys. Post was constantly harassed by Indians and one account tells of two soldiers mysteriously disappearing. Searchers found traces a few miles away of fire in which were charred bones, buckles and buttons, apparently remains of where Indians had burned them at stake.

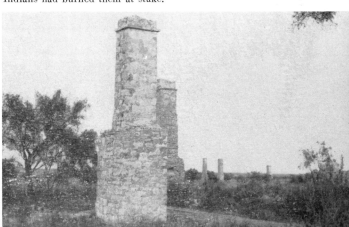

# FORT CHADBOURNE, TEXAS

Many are the tales of the potency of frontier whiskey, but few can top the story that dates from September, 1855, at Fort Chadbourne.

Even the post surgeon said that a truthful recital of the incident would cause him to be branded a liar. Here it it as told by General David S. Stanley in his *Personal Memoirs:*

"One very beautiful, bright moonlit night in September, we were both awakened by some strange noise like someone groaning and calling, and going out we found a soldier by the name of Mattock, who was being helped to the hospital by a soldier who lived with his wife near the creek.

"Mattock had been over the creek to the hut of a Dutchman, who sold liquor. Having filled up, he was on his way home, very happy no doubt, and at the crossing of the creek, which was in deep banks, five or six Comanches waylaid him, and as he passed commenced shooting at his back with bow and arrows.

"Mattock shouted and ran until he met with the soldier, who lived in the cabin and who brought him, moaning and crying, out to the hospital.

"Now comes the incredible part of the story. Mattock had fourteen arrows in him. He bristled with them like a porcupine. Three of these arrows had gone so far through him that the surgeon extracted them by pulling off the feathered part of the arrows and pulling them through the man's body.

"In two weeks' time, Mattock was walking around and his only disability was finally from a superficial wound which had lacerated a nerve."

Whatever the brand of rotgut served by the Chadbourne hog ranch, one Dutchman could have made a million by selling the recipe to the medical profession! Ruins of the saloon can still be seen across Oak Creek from the post.

Founded on October 28, 1852, Fort Chadbourne was one of the outer ring of posts designed to protect the Texas frontier from the Kiowa and Comanche Indians. In this it was extremely active, sometimes serving as a rendezvous for patrols—it was in this function that it worked with Robert E. Lee—but often doing its best just trying to keep the Indians from overrunning it.

**EARLY VERSION** of Fort Chadbourne shown here bears considerable resemblance to present ruins. Barracks and several officers' quarters still remain in varying stages of preservation. In this plan, post was undergoing renovation and many buildings were in poor condition. Both barracks were stone, the left one with a shingled roof, the right had a canvas roof "nearly worn out, requires covering before winter," according to Army inspection report. Most officers' quarters were of logs placed upright in ground with canvas roofs. (Redrawn from National Archives.)

Indians constantly prowled around its outskirts. The storied Cynthia Ann Parker, dressed as an Indian but wearing a bonnet to hide her light hair, often begged bread at the post. She had been captured by Comanches when only nine and had resisted all white attempts to rescue her. Happy as an adopted Comanche she answered all suggestions that she was not Indian with a violent, "No no, me Comanche." One of her sons was Quannah Parker, nemesis of the post-Civil War Army.

The Army decided to end the Indian visits after two soldier mail carriers were waylaid, tied to a tree and burned to death. Major Seth Eastman summoned the tribal leaders, estimated at between 13 and 40 in number, depending upon which source is more credible.

While the post commander parlayed with the Indians, an infantry company drilled on the parade ground, rifles loaded. As the conference continued, the various wheels and turns of the company gradually brought it closer.

The Indians volubly denied anything to do with the killings. Eastman noticed, though, that a blanket on one partly hid a gun lately owned by one of the soldiers. The trooper's name was engraved on a brass plate on its stock.

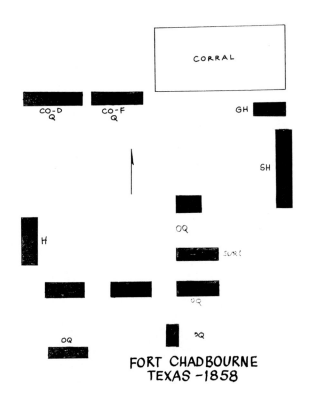

FORT CHADBOURNE
TEXAS –1858

COWS OCCUPY far barracks at Fort Chadbourne. One reason for large extent of remains is that fort was temporarily occupied by Army as sub post during 1870 Kiowa and Comanche campaigns, and El Paso stage line used it as station after Army officially abandoned it in 1867.

He also noticed that a piece of paper used by an Indian to make a cigarette looked suspiciously like a sheet of used note paper. Closer examination showed it to be part of a letter carried by the soldiers.

By this time the "drilling" soldiers were close at hand and Eastman told the Indians they were under arrest. They turned, saw the line of determined troopers, and made a break for liberty.

Nine were shot in their tracks. The chief rushed into Eastman's quarters and barred the door, firing through it at any noise on the other side.

Lieutenant C. W. Thomas ordered his men to ram down the door with a rail and rushed in as the door splintered. He felled the chief with a shot through the head just as the Indian rose from behind a table to fire at him.

TO GET THERE: Fort Chadbourne is part of the privately owned C. O. Richards ranch off U.S. 277 about 32 miles southwest of Abilene, Texas. It is not open to visitors.

OFFICERS' ROW from hospital ruins shows that substantial efforts went into permanent construction at post. Nearest building still is occupied. Parade ground itself has not been touched, is grazing area for cows. Post was a key timetable stop and division headquarters on Butterfield Overland Mail, 1858-61. Indians frequently raided mail stations, on one occasion were unhapy about poor quality of loot. They took all livestock, stripped blankets from beds, and told station keeper that if his stock were no better in 30 days he would be killed. True to their word, Indians returned month later, burned the station to display their displeasure of unimproved conditions, and station crew had to fight their way to safety.

HOSPITAL AT Fort Chadbourne is impressive ruin today. Inspector's description in 1850's could almost apply today: "Hospital stone with shingles. Roof needs repair. Dirt floor. No sashes or glass on windows so that when the weather is cold the interior is in darkness, the windows being filled with canvas."

# FORT INGE, TEXAS

Call it pluck, nerve, or guts, but it was something of that sort when Lieutenant Walter H. Jenifer went Indian chasing from Fort Inge in 1857.

Some people would call it plain lunacy.

Jenifer left the post on March 23 with a small detachment and by April 4 had traveled something like 300 miles. The going got too rough for cavalry, so near the headwaters of the Nueces River he dropped off the horses and a guard. He moved forward hot on Indian traces with only seven men.

After a few backbreaking miles, they came upon a camp of 100 Indians. The somewhat unequal odds did not faze the lieutenant, apparently. He continued to advance until he was attacked by the warriors less than 250 yards from their camp. A second hostile party hit him from his rear.

"He was powerless to make an aggressive fight," the 5th Cavalry historian recorded, "but he repulsed the enemy with a known loss of three killed and wounded."

At dark he was able to sneak back to his horses. Still unfazed by the odds, the next morning he returned to start the fight again. By this time the Indians probably figured they had more than they could manage, and disappeared. Jenifer led his men home but they had to go without rations for the final three days of the 17-day patrol.

This kind of aggressive spirit seemed to be common at Inge. The fort had been established in 1849 right in the middle of Indian grounds, and at the base of 150-foot-high "Mount" Inge. This was a rocky knob that jutted up from the mesquite flats and was used by the Indians for signalling. Until the Army came, that is.

Not long after Jenifer returned from his patrol, Lieutenant Robert C. Wood, Jr., defeated the Indians near the Nueces. A month later, Jenifer was at it again and outfought a band at the same place.

Patrol honors were not confined to officers, either. In the summer of '57 Corporal John Boyden defeated a band of Comanches near the headquarters of the Rio Frio. Sergeant William P. Leverett did the same to a band near the Llano river.

In October, '58, Lieutenant William B. Hazen and thirteen soldiers were joined by 28 civilians in chasing a band of Indian raiders. They surprised the Indian camp, and, with Hazen in the lead, charged the band. The Indians were able to get to their horses and a 20-mile running fight followed.

Reportedly only one Indian survived and when he returned to his tribe he had a broken arm to show for the fight. Hazen was severely wounded by a bullet that hit his hand and ricocheted into his breast. He was taken to Fort Clark, 80 miles away, and survived after considerable hospitalization.

Inge was not much as far as a post went. The 1853 inspection said, "The men occupy two buildings con-

**PARADE GROUND** still is obvious at Fort Inge site, and strewn rocks remain at hospital location. This was at base of "Mount" Inge. Two northernmost officers' quarters also were at hill's base. Site was covered by brush and trash until recent years when Uvalde civic groups started restoration program. Plan is to rebuild fort and make area picnic and tourist center. (Redrawn from National Archives data.)

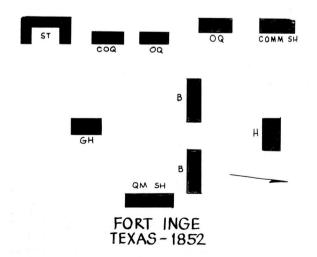

FORT INGE
TEXAS – 1852

**BARRACKS ROW** stood along this point which looks to east. "Mount" Inge is at left, with recently erected flagpole atop it; note marker under tree at base.

structed of upright poles, chinked up, with thatched roofs. These, besides being insufficient, are in a wretched state of dilapidation. Part of the troops also live in tents . . . The building used as a storehouse is in a decayed condition."

Some of the problem was that Inge never was firmly in the Army's scheme. It was started in 1849, abandoned in April, 1851, reoccupied in June, abandoned in 1855, reoccupied in 1856, abandoned to the Confederates in 1861, and then regarrisoned for a short time after the war. None of this on-again, off-again status contributed to stability.

Robert E. Lee passed the post in 1854 with a party that included four camels and a yearling. As described by Carl Coke Rister, Lee found the post "as was usual-

ly the case with border forts, there were no structures for defense, except a stockade of mesquite logs about the stables, which were open thatched huts.

"The post consisted of a dozen buildings of various sizes . . . all scattered about the border of a parade ground, pleasantly shaded by hackberries and elms. The buildings were rough and temporary, some of the officers' lodgings being jacal. But all were whitewashed and neatly kept, by taste and discipline."

TO GET THERE: From Uvalde, Texas, take U.S. 83 (Getty Street) south from center of city to fork with State 117. Follow this to left turn on Farm Road 140. Mile and a half east is sign to fort on right (south) side of road, "Mount" Inge is prominent at right. Follow dirt road about one mile into fort site.

MARKER stands midway between site of barracks and hospital. Leona River is under trees in background, officers' quarters were directly in front of them. In 1853 detachment of 3rd Infantry was located half mile southeast at "Camp Near Fort Inge" after escorting Mexican Border Commission.

# FORT MASON, TEXAS

Ask any Indian around Fort Mason about 1852 and he would assure you, with somewhat fearful looks, that the soldiers' big chief was a medicine man. Or maybe even a minor god. Or a devil.

The man with the somewhat uncertain status, but obvious powers, was Lieutenant Colonel Robert May. As commander of the 2nd Dragoons at Fort Mason, he had not only built the new post but had established a near-voodoo reputation with the redmen.

Any resemblance between the reputation and truth was purely intentional, as far as May was concerned. He had gathered the local chiefs together and informed them that he had magical powers.

When no one would believe his claim that he could resurrect the dead, May announced, "I am depressed by your obvious lack of confidence in my abilities, but perhaps that small dog at your heels may do to prove my powers, and, with your permission, I shall retire and put him to death."

A few minutes later he returned with the dog's apparently lifeless carcass. He clipped off tail pieces as souvenirs for each chief to convince them that the dog was dead. Then May took him into his tent and a moment later the dog reappeared, barking and jumping about.

From that day on, May's reputation was set and the Indians steered a path far clear of the "magic man." They didn't know about one thing: a new medicine called chloroform that had just arrived at the post with which Colonel May anesthetized the dog for his subsequent "resurrection."

May's command did not stay long at the post near the Llano River and it was abandoned in early 1854. Two years later it became the headquarters for the newly organized 2nd Cavalry.

As regimental commander, Colonel Albert Sidney Johnston located himself and six companies at Mason. Finding the fort dilapidated, they resorted to tents, camping in a clearing to the north of the stables. Johnston reserved himself only a single room as an example to his fellow officers and their families. The post buildings served as storehouses and a hospital.

The troops were in tents raised five feet from the

ground on adobe walls. It was not long before stone or wood construction replaced the temporary quarters and the soldiers could concentrate on Indians again.

Their first contact was when part of company C trailed an Indian raiding party for six days, finally overtaking and routing them. Several braves were killed. Two soldiers were severely wounded and arrows passed through the clothing of two others. Before getting back to the fort, the troops were reduced to desperate circumstances and were forced to eat the horses that had to be abandoned.

A year later, Lieutenant John B. Hood—later a Confederate general—met a party of Indians who were carrying a large flag. Any doubts he had about the flag were removed when the Indians dropped the flag, set fire to a pile of brush they had gathered, and a second contingent opened fire. A third party of 10 mounted Indians charged his force.

Hood led his men "with ringing cheers," according to the regimental historian, "and engaged the savages in a hand-to-hand combat."

After being pressed back, Hood "again inspired them with his superb courage, and led them in a revolver charge straight at the enemy, who fell back, unable to withstand the impetuosity of the attack."

Out of ammunition, the soldiers pulled back. Six men were killed or wounded, including Hood who had a severe arm wound. They estimated ten warriors had been killed and 12 wounded.

Indian fights occurred frequently and as the Civil War approached the soldiers began to suspect that

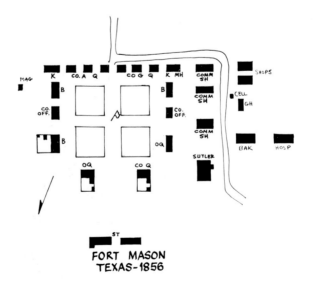

FORT MASON
TEXAS-1856

**ONCE IT WAS BUILT,** Fort Mason had a neat, military appearance. Today only scattered rock walls and foundations remain. Lee's quarters were those marked for the commanding officer. Here he wrote about entertaining at breakfast a newly married lieutenant and his bride. Suggesting that an appetite was essential to enjoying breakfast in Comanche territory, he said, "The lady's, I am sorry to say, was timid, her swain's, bold and soldierly, and he attacked the beef steak, hashed turkey and boiled eggs fearlessly." (Redrawn from National Archives data.)

white men were with the braves. In 1860, an attack on a Comanche camp netted only the horses because the warriors escaped in a thunderstorm. The patrol commander's report suggested there were white men in the party. He said that when the first charge was made he heard two men speaking the English language too fluently for Indians.

Lee was at Mason periodically during his Texas tenure, once enroute to Camp Cooper, once as a member of a court-martial, and then for a short time as its commander. He was serving in this capacity when he was ordered to report to Washington, D.C., to be offered, as it turned out, the command of the Union Army.

When he left Fort Mason, Lee was asked by a company commander whether he would fight for the North or South.

Lee's answer stated his future course. "I shall never bear arms against the United States," he said, "but it may be necessary for me to carry a musket in defense of my native state, Virginia."

TO GET THERE: Take U.S. 87 east from San Angelo, Tex., to city of Mason, 103 miles. Fort site is one mile south of town at state marker.

**FOUNDATION STONES** show outlines of many Fort Mason buildings. Although no elaborate ruins remain, stones and other traces of fort are scattered over area.

**ALMOST A** "Who's Who" of Civil War generals appears on Fort Mason marker. (Modern Photographs by Kilman Studio, Fredericksburg, Texas.)

SITE OF
FORT MASON

ESTABLISHED JULY 6, 1851
BY THE U. S. ARMY
AS A PROTECTION TO THE FRONTIER

NAMED IN HONOR OF
LIEUT. GEORGE T. MASON,
KILLED IN ACTION NEAR BROWNSVILLE,
APRIL 25, 1846

ALBERT SIDNEY JOHNSTON,
GEORGE H. THOMAS, EARL VAN DORN
AND ROBERT E. LEE,
OF THE 2ND U. S. CAVALRY,
WERE STATIONED HERE AT INTERVALS
FROM 1856 TO 1861

EVACUATED BY FEDERAL TROOPS,
MARCH 29, 1861
REOCCUPIED AFTER THE CIVIL WAR
UNTIL 1869

Erected by the State of Texas
1936

**CAMELS** waited patiently while men and mounts crowded water-hole in this version of camel experiment by Narjot in 1867.

(NATIONAL ARCHIVES.)

# THE CAMEL EXPERIMENT

*"And be it further enacted, that the sum of $50,000 be, and the same is hereby appropriated under the direction of the War Department in the purchase and importation of camels and dromedaries to be employed for military purposes."*

—Passed by the 33rd Congress and signed by the President, March 3, 1855.

IF CAMELS can work in the deserts of Africa, why can they not do as well in the American West? That was the question, more or less paraphrased, posed during the Seminole Indian War of Florida by Army Major George H. Crossman and presented ultimately to Secretary of War Jefferson Davis.

From that thought came about one of the strange tales of the Western Army, the Camel Experiment that seemed to have everything in its favor, yet went nowhere.

When these humped-back creatures arrived in Texas, the reaction was akin to the arrival of the first gas buggy many years later. Horses bolted, Indians disappeared into the brush, and strong men rushed to the nearest bar for a liquid bracer.

Tales are told that the camel business failed because the soft pads on their feet could not take the rough rocks and foliage of the American West. Not so. They could march cross-country with the best the Army had to offer, and leave them behind. They could go days without water and tote a load that would have foundered a mule. Their swaying gait presented a smoother platform than a horse's from which to fire a rifle. And in every impartial test patrol they made, they passed with flying colors—and usually, a few riders.

But it all came to naught. Jeff Davis was the man behind the scheme and in post-Civil War America anything with his tag was hopeless. The camels were sold or permitted to "escape." Some wound up in circuses, some in ill-fated private transportation schemes.

51

# CAMP VERDE, TEXAS

"Little Egypt" is the nickname once enjoyed by what could be considered one of the most unusual outposts of the U.S. Army. Camp Verde, Texas, was almost more involved with camels than it was with Indians, and it had both the population and the facilities to prove it.

The "population" started with the first shipment of 34 camels in 1856. A year later a second shipment of 40 more arrived. From that time on, no further camel imports were required because their prolific tendencies took care of the population increase naturally.

Camp Verde was built primarily to be part of the frontier chain of forts. Not long after its founding on July 8, 1856, it was treated to the sight of an awesome barnlike structure being erected within "downwind distance" of the officers' quarters. Actually it was upwind, but when the drafts shifted, so did the officers and their families, camel odors being what they were.

This structure was copied detail by detail from a camel caravansary in North Africa. Timber was shipped in at $125 per 1,000 feet to build this "khan" —for that was what the Arabs called it—and the first and probably only camel barn in the U.S. Army took shape.

It was rectangular, generally speaking, except for the slight angle made by the north wall. Constructed of concrete and timber, known as "pise" work, it measured 150 feet around each side. The north wall was 15 feet high, the southern a little less. A well with an old style Egyptian sweep was in the open courtyard.

The camels must have felt at home in their personal khan, but apparently it offered little security for them. Records show that Indians stole two of them from the khan on one occasion, an uncommon development to say the least. Most other records suggest that the Indians had more fear than love for these ungainly creatures.

The camels ranged throughout West Texas, using Camp Verde as their base. Actually it was the only

place where they were permanently stationed and the only place where experienced personnel could tend them. The expedition that bought them from African sellers also brought with it a dozen Armenian drivers and their families. These were the only camel skinners with the touch required by the fugitives from the Arabian Nights.

The cavalrymen developed an immediate distaste for them. Camels apparently had a fragrance that would drive grown men mad, and the matter of khan cleaning was enough to drive them to desertion. The dumb brutes did not develop a rapport with their riders, as horses and mules did. It is an understatement to say the feeling was mutual.

Despite this, they performed feats to startle even the most experienced packer. When they were unloaded from the Navy's ships at Indianola, Texas, in 1856, one camel patiently waited while four bales of hay were loaded on its saddle. Then it calmly stood up and walked off with its 1,256-pound load.

After arriving at Camp Verde, six camels and two six-mule wagons were sent to San Antonio for oats. The camels made the 60-mile round trip in 54 hours with 3,648 pounds of grain. The mules had to rest a day in San Antonio and returned after 96.5 hours with the 3,700 pounds of grain in the two wagons. The camels had stalked straight across the mountains, the wagons had to follow the longer roads.

Still, the camels were considered a novelty rather than a real part of the Army. They were an expensive novelty, however. The Camp Verde commanding officer considered them his most valuable camp property when the Confederates took over the post in 1861.

Four years of Confederate occupation saw little use of the animals, despite Jefferson Davis' part in the

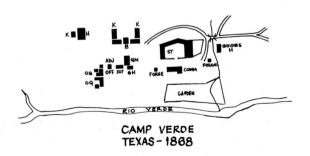

CAMP VERDE
TEXAS - 1868

**STABLES FOR** camels did not follow proportion of building plan but general shape agreed with original design. Parade ground was between river and guardhouse. Barracks consisted of three buildings in this plat, but today have been remodeled into one. (Redrawn from National Archives plat.)

**ONLY SLIGHT MOUNDS** mark site of camel khan at this point. Camp Verde parade ground was to right of near tree. In addition to camel activities, post had its share of Indian fighting. Second Cavalry records show 1st Sergeant Walter McDonald led patrols in February, 1856, and January, 1857, in which Comanches lost six and two tribesmen, respectively. In October, 1857, Lieutenant Cornelius Van Camp chased a Comanche party for six miles, finally killing two and recapturing property they had stolen.

original scheme. This did not seem to harm the camel breeding situation, though. Not counting animals that were lost, strayed, stolen, or otherwise appropriated by the settlers, the herd had increased to 100 by the time the Union Army returned for a temporary two-year stay in 1865.

TO GET THERE: From San Antonio, Texas, take U.S. 87 north past Comfort about 55 miles to intersection with County 480 to Center Point. Go through Center Point to intersection with County 689, turn right about two miles to town of Camp Verde. At general store, continue on county road. Camp Verde site is about two miles, right (north) side of road. Marker and officers' quarters can be seen from road on privately owned ranch of Ray P. Lewis.

**BARRACKS** of Camp Verde have been corrected and still are occupied. Building burned in 1910, killing one occupant, but construction was so solid that with new roof and floors it could be used again. Design on chimney includes architect's credit line: "Pise Work—Poinsard—1857." Post was abandoned by Army 1867 after remaining 66 camels were sold to San Antonio transportation speculator for $31 cash.

**SIDE OF QUARTERS** shows wing extending to rear of main building. Present owners use Camp Verde as vacation house but ranch manager insures that American flag flies there every day.

# CAMP HUDSON, TEXAS

The Devil's River region of West Texas is today almost as remote and wild as it was more than a hundred years ago. That was when Camp Hudson was established and camel caravans saved the lives of men and mules alike.

Despite its almost lost place in history, and the scarcity of records, Camp Hudson once was a major post on the frontier line.

First known as Camp on San Pedro, the site was selected in 1854. It was renamed after Lieutenant Walter W. Hudson who had been killed by Indians in 1850. The first site was close to the Devil's River, but turned out to be too close. The first rainy season washed the camp away and the soldiers hastily selected a spot a few hundred yards to the north and several feet higher in elevation.

When Robert E. Lee took charge of the Texas Department, he determined to test in detail the capabilities of his imported beasts of burden. In 1859, Lieutenant William H. Echols took 24 camels and an equal number of mules from San Antonio and struck out toward Hudson. At Hudson, Lieutenant Edward L. Hartz and an infantry company joined the caravan for a 75-day patrol through the West Texas back country.

Hartz reported later that, in spite of their complete inexperience with camel chaperone duties, generally the troops caught on. The matter of pack saddles was a problem. The regulation ones would not fit the camels' non-regulation humped backs and loads frequently were loosened and fell off. They overcame this handicap and were able to carry 300 pounds on each female and 500 on the males.

Hartz wrote later: "The patience, endurance, and steadiness which characterize the performance of the camels during this march is beyond praise, and when compared with the jaded and distressed appearance of the mules and horses, established them another point of superiority."

Lee wanted an even more stringent test. In 1860, Echols took another detachment through Camp Hudson, this time heading toward Fort Stockton. It was the acid test and almost fatal.

"I never conceived that there could be such country," wrote Echols of the desolate Big Bend country of Texas. His 20 camels carried barrels of water which saved the lives of both men and mules, but hardly drank any themselves.

Lee's official report spoke highly of the experiment, pointing to the "camels, whose endurance, docility, and sagacity will not fail to attract the attention of the Secretary of War, and but for whose reliable services the reconnaissance would have failed."

In April, 1859, Captain Albert G. Brackett marched his cavalry company from Camp Hudson via Fort Lancaster and the Great Comanche War Trail. At the Rio Grande, on the Mexican side, he intercepted a Comanche raiding band, killed two and captured their supply of dried horsemeat.

He had been away a month and his rations were exhausted. His exhausted patrol passed through the State of Chihuahua to San Carlos where they rested and were asked by the Mexicans to help them capture an Indian looting party. Without mentioning their previous border-jumping expedition, Brackett refused, aware that it would be impossible to keep secret a second such affair.

His arrival at Presidio del Norte threw the town into a turmoil. The 66-man detail was first believed to be bandits, and the Mexicans could not understand how the Americans could be coming from the interior of Mexico.

The 600-mile expedition aroused a momentary flurry of talk in the American press, but the San Antonio paper stopped any criticism with: "The facts in the case are simply these: Captain Brackett has done what several officers could have done long ago, and which, had they done it, would long since have cut short these marauders who cross the river, take their plunder, and flee into Mexico."

TO GET THERE: From Del Rio, Texas, take U.S. 90 north to Comstock. Turn right on State 163. Marked Camp Hudson site is 20 miles north on the right side immediately after crossing the Devil's River.

**DESOLATE, ROCK-STREWN** field is site of Camp Hudson. State marker and tiny gravestone of a baby are its only memorials. Post was used during Civil War by company of Texas Mounted Rifles who were prohibited by state regulation from horse racing, gambling, whiskey drinking, and rifle firing, "except in case of actual necessity." U.S. troops reoccupied it after the war, but abandoned it in April, 1868. It was a sub-post manned by single companies that rotated monthly during 1871 Indian campaign.

# FORT DAVIS, TEXAS

The Davis Mountains of West Texas rise gradually from windswept, arid plains. Grassy canyons and meadows, occasional peaks, groves of oak trees, sparkling mountain streams all give an oasis-like aura.

It is so today and was so more than 100 years ago when the Army marched from San Antonio and established Fort Davis in 1853. But the oasis appearance was deceiving. As one of the frontier's most active posts, Fort Davis knew its full share of combat and the mountain streams saw the mingled blood of soldier, settler and Indian.

Even when enroute to establish the post the Army found the going would not be easy. Following a report that Apaches had run off a wagon train's stock, half of the patrol was sent in pursuit. Under Lieutenant Eugene A. Carr, they pursued the trail into a canyon and collided head-on with 40 Mescaleros. A 70-lodge camp lay behind them.

In the hand-to-hand fracas that followed, Carr was severely wounded. Only the arrival of the remainder of the patrol held back 150 more warriors hiding behind rocks and on the ledges of the canyon's sides.

The Indian opposition was armed principally with bows and arrows. Their few rifles were fired with poor aim and poorer results. One soldier was killed when the combined patrol withdrew from the canyon. The Apache casualties were at least six dead and a dozen wounded.

Carr survived his wound to become a General and a leading Indian fighter 15 years later.

When the patrol joined the six-company expedition, they found that no time was being wasted in establishing the post. First called "Painted Camp on the 'Limpia,'" after the bubbling mountain stream nearby, it became Fort Davis as soon as all of the troops had arrived. The orders were to make the command "as comfortable as circumstances will permit for the winter." With the prospect of an immediate campaign against the Mescaleros in the offing, there was no delay.

The post was deep in a canyon surrounded by 300-foot palisaded rock walls on three sides. The open side looked across an open prairie that stretched to the southern horizon.

The location within the canyon was intended to be temporary. The commanding officer, Lieutenant Colonel George Washington Seawell, hoped to build farther south at the mouth, but in his absence an over-eager captain built six stone barracks. This pretty well fixed the location of Fort Davis.

These permanent-type buildings were surrounded by more than 50 miscellaneous planked and thatched affairs which deteriorated rapidly. The wood had been green when it was used. The general rickety condition of the quarters kept a pair of carpenters continually busy repairing what were termed officially as "altogether very uncomfortable and insufficient quarters."

Fort Davis was three years old when it played host in 1857 to Lieutenant Beale's 25-camel survey expedition. Although a camel was bitten by a rattlesnake east of the fort, and all had gone four days without water, no ill effects were noted. The humans in the expedition did not fare as well.

After the dust-eating journey from Camp Verde, the men descended upon the post sutler's bar. A diary of one of them tells that some of the camel chaperones had "a gait that denoted a slight indulgence in alcoholic stimulants" and later "the whole party who were in the fort after dark got very funny."

Camels came twice again to Davis. An 1859 expedition to find a shorter route to Fort Davis was fielded by 24 mules and 24 camels. The camels came through without difficulty; the mules were almost completely worn out.

An 1860 expedition went 120 miles in five water-

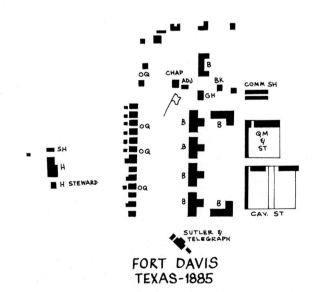

FORT DAVIS
TEXAS-1885

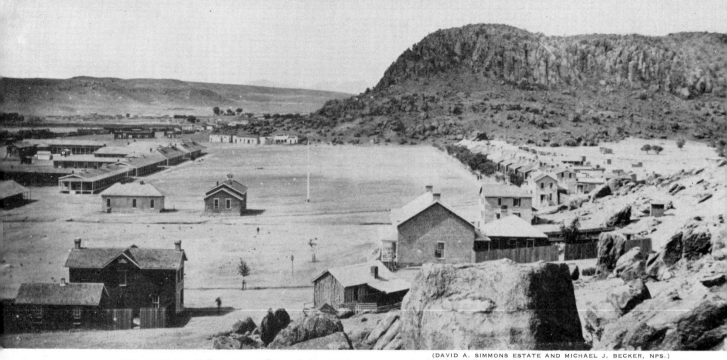

FORT DAVIS in 1886 had reached the peak of its construction. Officers' quarters are at right, barracks at left. Town is in distance beyond barracks. Legend is told locally of mountain near fort where Mexican girl, Dolores, burned fire every Thursday in memory of fiance who had been killed shortly before their wedding. Until as late as 1893, mourning Dolores climbed mountain that now bears her name. Until recently, charcoal remains of fires could be found atop it.

(DAVID A. SIMMONS ESTATE AND MICHAEL J. BECKER, NPS.)

less days. The infantry escort and 20 mules were saved from disaster by the 25 camels which carried water but consumed none.

But camels and mules were some of the lesser of Fort Davis' problems. The heights that surrounded three of its sides permitted Apaches to approach unnoticed almost to the edge of the post. On more than one occasion the beef or horse herds were scattered by raiders. Despite quick pursuits by patrols, the Indians usually were able to lead the herds through hidden passes and got them away clean.

The monthly Santa Fe stage made Fort Davis a regular stop in 1853, and the Butterfield Overland Mail built a stop a half mile northeast in 1859. These coaches fell frequent prey to ambushes. In 1859 a mail run was waylaid, the guard killed, and the mail stolen. While examining their loot, including a bundle of illustrated newspapers, the Indians were surprised by the Army and lost 14 men. Convinced the picture papers were responsible for this disaster, the superstitious Indians thereafter avoided them.

When Fort Davis was abandoned at the start of

FORT DAVIS in 1957 had many reminders of past. This shows officers' quarters with edge of barracks at far left. Sutler's buildings have disappeared but town of Fort Davis had increased in size. Many modern photographs appearing here were taken by author in 1957 before National Park Service ownership.

the Civil War in 1861, two stagecoach drivers took charge. The Confederates manned it periodically until its supplies were gone and it had all but collapsed.

Nearby, a 14-man detachment led by the fort's Confederate commander, Lieutenant Reuben E. Mays, was ambushed by upwards of 100 Mescaleros. Only a Mexican guide lived to bring reinforcements back to the canyon. When he did, the troops could find the littered debris of the battle but no bodies. Mysteriously, the Indians had taken all of them away and they were never found. Today even the site of this massacre is unknown.

Davis was abandoned by the South with the approach of Union troops in 1862. The U.S. troops found the body of a scalped soldier in one of the buildings, apparently the victim of Indians after he was left sick in the makeshift hospital. After reoccupying Davis for three days, the token United States force again left it to the care of the coach drivers.

It was not long before a 250-Indian force swept down on the abandoned buildings, burning and looting. Unknown to them, nine settlers had hidden behind the parapets of one of the flat Mexican-style adobes. While the Apaches caroused below, this tiny group stayed on the roof for 48 hours, hoarding a cask of water and eating blobs of dough they cooked on a tiny smokeless fire. Fortunately some one had thrown wagon-wheel spokes on the roof and this provided fuel for the fire.

The Confederates passed through Fort Davis again in 1864. Legend says that the defeated Sibley column buried two brass cannon and other equipment some 16 miles from the open end of the Fort Davis canyon, but they have never been located.

Earlier dreams of a post at the mouth of the canyon were realized when the Army returned in 1867. General Wesley Merritt began a 200-man garrison at this point, rather than try to rebuild the wrecked fort. It was 1880 before the dream was completely realized. The ruins of today date from this post-Civil War period, for the most part.

It was here that between 200 and 400 men defended the Texas frontier during General William R. Shafter's campaigns across the Staked Plains and into the Big Bend country of Texas. Militarily, these expeditions drew little blood, but they opened country that previously had been considered inaccessible.

General Benjamin Grierson operated from Fort Davis during the Victorio War in 1880 which finally settled the frontier. It was settled so effectively, in fact, that when Grierson retired from the Army he returned to Fort Davis and built his retirement home on the plains at the mouth of the canyon facing the fort.

**LEGEND OF** Indian Emily lives in gravestone near fort, though National Park Service research cannot back it up. Local tale is that Emily was Apache girl who worked at fort, fell in love with an officer and left when his fiancee arrived from East. While with her tribe later, she overheard plan to attack fort. She went to alert lieutenant, but was killed by sentry when she tried to enter post at night. With her dying gasps, she told of impending attack and prevented massacre the next day. Or so the story goes.

Davis was a combat post throughout most of its years. In 1878, its scouting average was the highest for the Department of Texas: 6,724 miles.

To relieve the monotony of Indian-fighting, the post had the nearby "hog ranch" of Chihuaha. This tiny hamlet next to the reservation not only provided corn at about $3 a bushel, but had available the diversions unavailable at the post.

These unpoliced entertainments were not without their drawbacks. In 1870, a pleasure-bent soldier died of a pistol shot in the stomach. A few months later, two soldiers disagreed in a Chihuaha saloon and one fell dead stabbed with a butcher knife. The officers occasionally found the diversions too much for them and one captain appears in the records as having died "of acute inflammation of the stomach produced by intemperance."

Diversions on the post, other than the library, band, school and chapel, included the ups and downs

**PARADE GROUND** was 500 feet wide, provided plenty of room for mounted drills. Officers' quarters had covered porches across front of each building, but these have disappeared. Four buildings were of limestone, remainder of adobe.

TO GET THERE: Town of Fort Davis is at intersection of State 117 and 18 in West Texas. Fort site is on State 17 on east edge of town, north side of road.

of military discipline. Major Zeno R. Bliss, once a lieutenant at the pre-war post but 20 years later its commander, forbade gambling on the reservation and prohibited enlisted men from carrying concealed weapons, "especially knives, razors, sling-shots and pistols."

The same Major Bliss vented his ire at chickens and in 1874 announced that "no fowls will be kept within the limits of this garrison."

When the Texas Pacific and the Southern Pacific railroads came to West Texas in the 1880's, their routes by-passed the fort. Although thoughts were entertained of making Fort Davis a government hospital "owing to its salubrious climate," its troops left it in 1891.

The abandoned buildings served as summer homes for West Texans, then in the 1920's a movie colony headed by Jack Hoxie tried to resurrect it as a resort. After the 1929 depression doomed this, the ruined fort saw frequent attempts at restoration.

Finally in 1963 it became a part of the National Park Service. Today the uniforms of Park rangers are in evidence among the tourists and a new Fort Davis era is in the making.

OFFICERS' ROW in 1957 resembled early appearance, mainly because of residential use after fort's abandonment. Author visited fort again in 1964, found National Park Service had replaced roofs and porches along entire row.

# FORT DEFIANCE, ARIZONA

For the commanding officer of Fort Defiance, Arizona, it was almost a prediction of his future when the Camel Experiment clattered into his post in 1857.

The camels were under the command of Edward Fitzgerald Beale, a former Naval officer who was surveying a wagon road across northern Arizona for the Secretary of War. His charges had come from Camp Verde, Texas, and in this expedition were to prove themselves sure-footed, trail ready, and desert fit.

Upon nearing Fort Defiance, Beale dismounted from the mule he had been riding, and climbed atop one of his dromedaries. This was not the usual procedure for the expedition—the camels usually carried supplies rather than men but Beale felt he must make the right impression on the post commander.

Aboard his swaying white ship of the desert, the ex-sailor evidently created an impression that was far more lasting than expected. Colonel William W. Loring, a one-armed Mexican War veteran, commanded Defiance and later became a Confederate general. Even later than that, he joined the Egyptian Army and became a general of division, a pasha, a holder of all of the highest Egyptian medals, and, it is assumed, the possessor of untold numbers of camels, white and otherwise.

Despite the uncommon impressions the caravan created along the way, it probably excited little more than amusement at Defiance. The troopers at this embattled outpost were used to almost anything, whether it be two-legged or four.

The classic *Massacre of the Mountains* describes Defiance as "simply a group of barracks, stables, and offices around a parade ground 300 by 200 yards in extent. There were no stockades, trenches, blockhouses, or other fortifications. The buildings were principally of pine logs with dirt roofs, though a few of them were of adobes. There was one stone building for the officers."

The garrison had been established in 1852 with the idea it would keep the Navajos quiet after several treaty attempts had been miserable failures. Just three miles inside the eastern border, it was the first United States fort in the boundaries of present-day Arizona.

The records of Defiance fit its name in reference both to Indian and Army. Colonel E. V. Sumner termed it such to show his attitude; the Indians reacted against it in like fashion.

On two occasions their feelings took on a grotesque sense of humor, each time with an innocent Mexican as the deadly butt of the joke.

In 1854 after a soldier had been killed by a Navajo, the Indians agreed under pressure to surrender the guilty brave. Contrary to their usual custom, the Indians requested and were granted permission to hang the culprit.

After a redman had been strung up before a formation of soldiers, the truth came out: the now dead culprit was not the Navajo murderer, but one of their Mexican slaves!

The same trick was tried again in July, 1858, with the murderer of "Little Joe." What started out with a bit of humor, ended in blood.

It seems a Navajo chief had a wife who preferred to attend a dance rather than the festivities of his choice. He followed her and, as *Massacre of the Mountains* tells it, "reduced her costume to an ultra-fashionable style by tearing every stitch of clothing from her. This failed to bring her to a sense of her conjugal duty, and it was about as far as Navajo

FORT DEFIANCE
ARIZ. - 1853

WHEN ARMY INSPECTOR visited in 1853, he found post "in a high state of discipline, and every department of it unexceptionable and highly creditable to the distinguished officer in command" and complimented "the great labour that had been performed in erecting quarters in this locality where everything had to be originated." (Redrawn from Mansfield report 1854.)

**FORT DEFIANCE** in later years bore basic resemblance to early ground plan, mainly because post became Indian agency after abandonment in 1861. Large three-story building lasted until 1960 and was still a solid structure when torn down. Other barracks and officers' quarters agree with plat. Bonito Canyon, site of 1858 ambush, is the slash in mountain behind barracks.

**FORT DEFIANCE TODAY** shows changes wrought by remodeling and tree growing, but post outline and Bonito Canyon remain. Picture was taken from site of blockhouse erected in 1858. Although tribal history states that Fort Defiance was original site of Fort Canby used in 1863-64 Canyon de Chelly expedition by General Kit Carson, simultaneous references to both in official records suggest otherwise. Latter post probably was 28 miles southwest.

customs permitted him to go in the way of direct coercion."

The alternate step, it seems, was for him to kill an outsider. Little Joe, a handyman of the post commander, was the victim.

The day after the killing, the Army demanded that the murderer be surrendered. After a great deal of haggling, the tribe was given an ultimatum to give up the man or else. The "or else" took place on August 29 when six Indians were killed in the so-called Battle of Bear Springs.

The post was reinforced, a blockhouse was built on the steep hill east of the fort, and the Indians were informed that the time for talk had ended.

On September 8 they announced that they had found and wounded the murderer and, alas, he had died enroute to the fort. When the corpse was produced, it was obviously another ringer. It was recognized as that of a Mexican frequently seen around the fort, and the post surgeon determined that the wounds had been inflicted only that morning.

The fighting became intense. Three hundred Navajos ambushed an Army detail in nearby Bonito Canyon. Patrols alternately killed or captured Navajos and were spared high casualties only because the Indians had abandoned their traditional bows and arrows in favor of rifles, and did not know how to handle them.

Finally on December 4, the Navajos sued for peace. It did not mean much—the post underwent and almost lost a siege by several thousand Navajos in 1860—but the record shows that the Indian with the defiant wife never was surrendered and his spouse returned to his wigwam, for better or for worse.

TO GET THERE: From Gallup, N.M., go north on U.S. 666 eight miles to left turn on State 68 (Arizona 254 or Navajo 3) to intersection with Navajo 7 at Arizona border east of St. Michaels. Take this past Window Rock to modern agency of Fort Defiance, about seven miles, the site of old fort.

**POST CEMETERY** has this lone grave marker from Army days of Sylvester Johnson, killed in raid by Navajos in April, 1860, when several thousand assaulted fort. Why this was left when other bodies and markers were moved after post abandonment cannot be explained.

# FORT TEJON, CALIFORNIA

Fort Tejon was started as an early experiment in Indian management. It was not long before that term was changed to mis-management, and painted pantaloons were partly to blame.

The post began in association with Edward Fitzgerald Beale before he became involved with camels. As California's Superintendent of Indian Affairs, Beale had recommended that his charges be placed within reservations where they would work under the supervision of government agents and be protected by the Army.

Beale's tenure in the job lasted only a year. He was able to get several reservations established—including Fort Tejon in 1853—but the political wrangling got the better of him and he was removed. Under him, the Indians were pictured by contemporaries as "perfectly happy" to the extent that they "could not be driven away with a 'Big Stick,'" from the reservations. He and his assistants were credited with transforming "a wilderness into a peaceful home, and wild men into quiet and contented cultivators."

His successor was a politician who had more concern with the problems of committee rooms than Indian councils. That was when the Federal government decided to step in. It found that Beale's enlightened administration had been replaced with a corrupt ring that issued blankets and clothes that were so thin they were almost transparent. Food was inadequate

and half-starved cattle were sold to the Agencies at prime prices.

And during the summer at Tejon, the agent did not bother to issue trousers. He suggested that the Indians paint green or red pantaloons on their legs, mainly out of respect for the sensibilities of settlers who passed by. One government inspector suggested facetiously, but in anger, that striped blue shirts painted on their bodies might be c o o l, economical, and picturesque.

During this time, the Army was a curious and usually helpless observer. At the fort, it could do little to help the Indian situation and its time was spent in shepherding settlers through the reservation. The post was near Tejon Pass, a critical entrance on the road to the Pacific, and keeping the peace was a full-time occupation.

Tejon was one of the most pleasant garrisons in the mid-century Army. "All of the quarters are furnished in the best style and it is generally acknowledged to be one of the finest, if not the best post on the Pacific coast," an 1857 visitor described it. "There are 15 buildings in all, in the garrison. You can form no idea of the beauty of this place until you visit it."

As headquarters for the 1st Dragoons, Fort Tejon figured prominently in the military operations of the West. It was a major training ground for Civil War

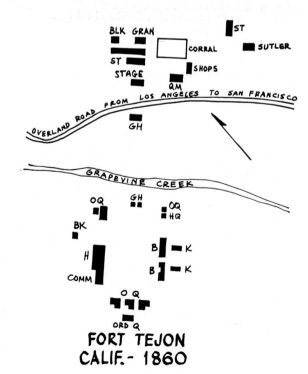

FORT TEJON
CALIF.- 1860

**CAMEL OCCUPANCY** of Fort Tejon might have accounted for fact that stables were located across creek from less odorous activities of post. Visitor in 1857 described sutler's store as "a fine commodious adobe building, plastered on the outside and whitewashed." Ruins of many of these buildings dot site today, although only three have been restored. (Redrawn from California Beaches and Parks system plat.)

**FIREPLACE** inside orderly quarters has been rebuilt by historians, but original plaster-covered adobe walls are evident. Each room had fireplace which used single common chimney. Flooring was laid on top of dirt.

(LOUIS WAKEFIELD AND KERN COUNTY MUSEUM.)

**FORT TEJON** was part of Beale's Tejon Ranch when this picture was taken in 1885. Buildings were used for ranch purposes, but military arrangement around parade ground was evident. Barracks were at far side, officers' quarters at right side of parade, and remains of hospital at near side.

**FORT TEJON** today, as seen from same vantage point as in 1885, shows only one barracks is left, along with one officers' quarters and the orderly building to its rear. Once peaceful valley, left rear, now is split by high-speed, divided modern highway. In 1858, route was used by Butterfield Overland Mail and a Butterfield station was located at fort.

generals—15 of its officers attained this rank, almost equally divided between the North and South.

The camels came here in 1857 when Beale took his expedition to the scene of his earlier reservation experiment. There were 28 of the humped creatures at the post at this time, and camel detachments operated from here until 1861.

The post was abandoned temporarily at this time,

**FROM ORDERLY'S** quarters, Fort Tejon probably looked similar to this in its early days. Edge of officers' quarters is at right, barracks in center; ruin at left is of middle officers' quarters.

**EIGHT MEN** died at Fort Tejon, seven of them memoralized by tiny marker at base of this stone. Family of eighth, First Lieutenant Thomas F. Castor, 1st Dragoons, placed marker in his honor after his death in 1855. Cemetery was in canyon to rear.

**BARRACKS** were considered comfortable contrasts to usual shelters of frontier forts. This one is the southernmost barracks and has been restored.

but in 1863 California Volunteers re-garrisoned it. They brought with them 1,000 Indians from the Owens River valley. This time no one suggested painted pantaloons, but the difficulties of feeding and clothing such a number was a major undertaking for militiamen who had the same problem to solve for themselves.

The Volunteers used the Tejon buildings only occasionally, usually rushing there from some other fort whenever the peace was threatened. Finally in 1864 the post was abandoned because the Indians had left. Beale returned again, but this time as a private citizen.

He added the post to his ranch, using its buildings for ranch operations. Ultimately, the Beale Ranch included more than 200,000 acres and is still in operation today. Appropriately, it is named, "Tejon Ranch Company," in honor of an earlier day when it was the military and political center of the interior of Southern California.

TO GET THERE: Fort Tejon is now part of California State Beaches and Park system and restored buildings are on west side of U.S. 99 about 36 miles south of Bakersfield.

**FORMER USE** of this building has stumped local historians. Because of its location behind officers' row, it is assumed to have been occupied by officers' orderlies or servants. Building has been restored, original adobe requiring support by steel braces and step-like brickwork at right.

# THE POSTS AT BENICIA, CALIFORNIA

To the Army of the West, Benicia, California was truly "a many splendored thing." It was more a geographical entity than just a simple fort or cantonment; in fact, it was at least four different things and not one at a time, but simultaneously.

When the Army Inspector visited it in 1854, the place was five years old. He found that there was Benicia Barracks, which was headquarters for the 3rd Artillery, "in a good state of discipline . . . well quartered, a good hospital and bakery . . . and all public property in a good state of preservation." He spelled it with an "e" instead of the first "i".

Then he noted there was a Benicia Arsenal, sort of brother to the Barracks, commanded by an Ordnance Department officer. Things were not as rosy here, no fault of the commander, though. The Arsenal was in the process of construction, and had been for several months, but with one complication. The powers in Washington decided that the bills for the

work were not quite legal, and refused payment. The C.O. found himself $9,044.66 in debt to the government for work already underway.

The contractor continued the projects, including a 100- by 40-foot stone storehouse, in order to finish before the rainy season. He figured he would take his chances on being paid.

A third element of Benicia was the Benicia Subsistence Depot, headed by an Artillery officer and charged with providing food for the West. The problem: by the time it got by sea around the Horn or across Panama, there was more that needed condemning than could be kept. The recommendation was,

**CASUALTIES FROM INDIAN WARS** were brought to original post hospital which was built in 1856. Among officers who have served at Benicia were U. S. Grant, W. T. Sherman and, in later years, General James Doolittle who obtained his Tokyo bombing raid ordnance here.

**SEPARATION** of various elements of Benicia is obvious in ground plan. Depots were in top left-hand corner, Barracks to right, Ordnance Depot at bottom. Bulk of post was built after this early-day version. (Redrawn from Mansfield report, 1854)

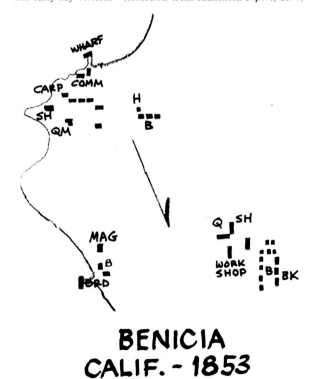

BENICIA
CALIF. - 1853

**FIRST MILITARY BASTILLION** in California, built in 1859 this was a stone fort with two crenelated towers and port holes for heavy gun firing. After explosion and fire in 1912, building was rebuilt with one less than its previous three stories, and one less tower.

**LAST STOP FOR CAMELS** were these two storehouses built in 1853 and 1854, respectively. Known locally as "The Camel Barns," here is where the camels were kept until auctioned in 1864. Sandstone for all buildings at Benicia was obtained locally, a reason for its permanence.

**BUILT TO FIGHT FROM,** "Clock Tower" building's entrance shows rifle slits, to right, and large ports through which cannon could be fired, right of door.

STILL IN USE until Benicia was deactivated, guardhouse dates to 1872, has seen troublemakers of many generations.

IN DEATH, modern soldiers rest with those of yesteryear. Benicia post cemetery includes recent graves along with those of men who died as early as Thomas Reilly, foreground, in 1853 at age of 31. His Army branch is uncertain: Ordnance Corps bursting bomb is one end of tomb, Artillery Corps crossed cannon is at other end.

buy foodstuffs locally where "they can be obtained to any desireable extent and where they can no doubt be had at less price."

The tour of Benicia was not over . . . Benicia Quartermaster's Depot was under the charge of a Quartermaster Captain and had on its rolls a diverse variety of items. The good captain was "commodore" over a fleet of one sailing brig and a schooner, both used in moving supplies between San Diego and Puget Sound, and a sloop, used in moving supplies between Stockton. He employed 26 civilians, including a ship captain at $5 a day, and spent just under $100,000 a year in supplying the Pacific Army.

Benicia apparently was the goat of all work on the Pacific coast. When the Civil War broke out, it rushed 30,000 muskets by ship to the East via Panama . . . then had to supply a company of troops to guard the ships when the Navy did not have enough Marines to go around. It had to send another Army company

to guard the powder magazine at Mare Island Navy Yard for six months until a Marine detachment from the *USS Lancaster* could relieve them.

It had a role in the Camel Experiment, too, although a final one. Many of the humped creatures who were veterans of the Beale expedition were herded from Fort Tejon and Camp Drum, near Los Angeles, to Benicia in 1863. Here they were sold at auction on February 26, 1864.

It was a major recruit camp for California Volunteers and was enlarged with new barracks just in time to beat the snows and heavy rains of California's 1861-62 winter. This same winter brought misery to the many less fortunate camps that shivered under tents elsewhere in the state.

Battles as such never were fought from here, but the Civil War was close. Sentries fired at a ship that violated the 200-yard boundary line. Sentries watched in expectation when two other ships collided

PROOF OF ITS AGE is displayed over entrance of magazine. Originally used to store gunpowder, modern-day contrast is shown by "fallout shelter" sign. Its walls are three feet thick.

CONSIDERED ONE OF California's finest examples of stone-cutter's art, original magazine was built in 1857 by French craftsmen recruited just for this purpose. Building today looks almost new.

SHOWPLACE OF area was commandant's house, scene of many social events. Its interior railings supposedly were brought "around the horn."

near the wharf, not accidentally but apparently in good commercial rivalry.

And the troops gathered in July, 1863, to witness a tragic ceremony, the firing squad execution of a private found guilty of murder and desertion. Formed in three sides, the soldiers watched while the prisoner was blindfolded and seated on his coffin. He fell backward into it as 11 bullets found their mark; one of the 12 muskets had a blank cartridge so that each man could feel he did not fire a fatal shot.

When the war ended, Benicia still had a role. Companies were sent out by sea to Southern California to cross the deserts and outpost the forts of Nevada and Arizona. To Benicia, the end of a war meant only a reduction in activity, not a cessation. So it had been in the 1890's, the World Wars, the Korean War. Unlike most other western forts, Benicia had a role to play that remained long after the frontier and been settled.

TO GET THERE: Benicia, California, is a city north of San Francisco and west of San Pablo Bay. The post is adjacent to the city. It was scheduled for deactivation by the Army in 1964 and plans were to convert it to an industrial park, the State of California assuming responsibility for the many historical structures.

HILLY TERRAIN of Benicia is shown by this early view.
(HARPER'S ILLUSTRATED WEEKLY.)

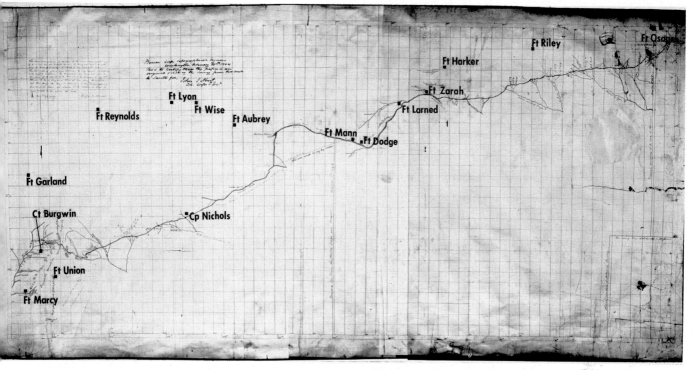

SANTA FE TRAIL earliest representation was this map drawn
in 1820's. The later locations of Army posts along trail have
been superimposed on it.

# ROAD TO SANTA FE

*"The wagons marched slowly in four parallel columns, but in broken lines, often
at intervals of many rods between. The unceasing 'crack, crack' of the wagoners'
whips, resembled the frequent reports of distant guns."*

—Contemporary description of moving westward on the Santa Fe Trail.

It STARTED at Fort Osage in Missouri and ended at the public square 775 miles away in Santa Fe,
New Mexico. Across Kansas, through corners of Colorado and the Oklahoma Panhandle, and into
New Mexico it moved between 1821 and 1880, bringing trade goods, emigrants and soldiers.

Dusty, sun-baked, Indian threatened, and dry, the Santa Fe Trail was the key to the Southwest.
From 30 men and $300 in goods in 1821, in 1864 it carried $40,000,000 and 12,000 persons. Maps
show it only 775 miles long, but its real eastern terminus was Europe and the ports of the Atlantic
coast, the western terminus, Mexico City and the Pacific.

Unlike other trails, the Santa Fe was primarily for commerce. Emigrants used it, but most of
them preferred more northern routes. The businessmen used it to move their goods to the profitable
markets of the Southwest. The first trade train in 1824 realized a 2,000 per cent profit. Later trips
did not fare as well, but still the profits were enormous . . . especially whenever the Army could
guarantee free passage by providing protecting escorts.

Slowly the life of the trail was cut away. The railroad moved along its route and the wagon
train portion became shorter and shorter. They ended completely on February 9, 1880, when—
appropriately enough—the first Santa Fe train steamed into Santa Fe.

# FORT LARNED, KANSAS

Fort Larned may have been the most important post on the Santa Fe Trail, but it also was one where the generals miscalled the shots with an uncomfortable regularity.

In 1867, when the fort was eight years old, General Winfield S. Hancock fielded a 1,400-man force there to impress the Kiowas and other tribes with the might of the United States Army. Instead, he was so impressed with the avowed peaceful intentions of Chief Satanta that he presented the Kiowa chief with a major general's coat, complete with epaulets and stars.

A few days later the word came from Fort Dodge that their livestock had been stampeded by Satanta's band. The good chief proudly wore his general's costume as he directed affairs.

Perhaps the gift did pay off, though. Only a few years before, Satanta had done the same thing to Fort Larned, killing a sentry and capturing the horseherd. To make sure credit was placed where credit was due, and to improve the stock, Satanta sent word back to the post quartermaster that the horses were inferior and he hoped the Army would do better next time.

General Phil Sheridan's *Memoirs* tell that Hancock was not the only general bamboozled by the redman at Larned. When Sheridan took command of the Department of the Missouri in 1867, he sent General Alfred Sully to Larned to quiet unhappy Kiowas and Comanches camped around it.

They were indignant that the Indian Bureau had suspended the i s s u e of arms because of a recent Cheyenne raid on friendly Indians.

"The Indians came to see him," Sheridan wrote about Sully's arrival, "and protested that it was only a few bad young men who had been depredated, and that all would be well and the young men held in check if the agent would but issue the arms and ammunition."

Sully decided the Indians spoke truthfully and he advised the Indian Agent to issue the arms, "the Indians this time condescendingly accepted."

Sheridan considered "this issue of arms and ammunition was a fatal mistake; Indian diplomacy had overreached Sully's experience, and even while the delivery was in progress a party of warriors had already begun a raid of murder and rapine, which for acts of devilish cruelty perhaps has no parallel in savage warfare."

The Indian War of 1868 had begun, only to be ended by the introduction of Sheridan's winter campaign and the "scorched earth" Battle of the Washita by devil-may-care General George Armstrong Custer.

Another incident is told of when the post commanders were less than sterling and infallible leaders of their men. The story dates itself in the period when state troops were garrisoning the fort, so its disrepute does not rub off on the Army.

Reportedly the Mati Hari trick was tried wholesale on this occasion. Step one was to get the commanding officer drunk, which was done. Step two was for the Indian women to entertain soldiers with a dance, distracting all attention to their duties. This was done.

At which point step three took place: the braves silently moved in and made off with 240 head of horses and mules.

According to an Indian Bureau report, the soldiers were more than a little guilty in the matter. It accused them of selling whiskey to the Indians and demoralizing their women.

FORT LARNED
KANSAS – 1875

MOST OF THESE buildings remain and can be identified. Blockhouse, the guardhouse, was torn down after 1886, had been built in 1865 at same time entire post was surrounded by an earthen breastwork. It was connected with adjacent buildings by a tunnel. (Redrawn from Division of Missouri Report, 1876.)

(KANSAS STATE HISTORICAL SOCIETY.)

**OFFICERS' QUARTERS** in 1879 look little changed from today. Center set was for post commander, the near and far set were for other officers. Four families were in each flanking building, two captains and their families having two rooms apiece and sharing a kitchen. Lieutenants fared even worse. Their families had to get by with single rooms each, and no kitchen. Later wooden wings were added so that each two lieutentants could share a kitchen, dining room, and servant's room.

"Dissipation, licentiousness and venereal diseases prevail in and around to an astonishing extent," the Bureau inspector reported in 1864.

This condition must have cleared up when the regular Army returned at the close of the Civil War. The post surgeon's 1868 statistics show that there was not a single venereal disease case that year, from a total of 215 men. The following year, only four were reported out of a strength of 184.

It may be the doctor was more concerned with his hospital problems than statistic keeping, though, for an 1870 report from him describes the place as "an old adobe building erected in 1860 . . . improved in 1866 by a shingle roof, which leaks. One end fell in a storm in the winter of 1869 . . . the ceiling is of canvas."

Two years before, this had been predicted in a letter which said the hospital "is about worn out, and

**OFFICERS' QUARTERS TODAY** have been renovated to early appearance. Interiors of some rooms show typical furnishings of living and office spaces. Post commander's house, right, still is occupied by Robert Frizell whose family has owned site since 1902. Fort Larned was abandoned in 1878.

**SOLID CONSTRUCTION** of commissary and quartermaster storehouses causes them not to look their age, regardless of 1866 date over near door. Double-story connection between two buildings is recent farm addition. Opposite side of these buildings faces broad Kansas plains, is only side not protected by meandering Pawnee Creek, and has gun slits piercing its sandstone walls.

**ESCAPE TUNNEL** officially dug so that water could be hauled during sieges, leads out of fort from under eastern storehouse. Local Explorer Scout troop re-dug it with help of mechanical ditch digger. Fort had good reason to have escape route: more than 100 Indian skirmishes were fought by Larned soldiers and more than 500 troopers, plainsmen, and Indians were killed and wounded within 30 miles of post.

in a condition which renders it liable to fall down on the sick at every storm that comes. It has already given way in one wall, and has been propped up."

With one end of the roof collapsed and one wall fallen in, it is pleasant to note that by 1875 a new hospital had been installed in half of the northeastern barracks. This was probably not due to any sympathy for the surgeon and his wards; the garrison was so undermanned the doctor got some of the vacant rooms.

In spite of its internal problems, Fort Larned had a military record of continued activity. It was besieged by Indians at least five times, fielded several expeditions and countless patrols, and beginning in 1864 provided armed escorts for Santa Fe wagon trains. This was the rendezvous point where the trains waited until they were large enough to proceed under military guard.

Not long after the policy of military escorts was established, Fort Larned found itself almost swamped by hundreds of loaded wagons, all waiting to head west. Dwindling supplies and even more dwindling patience finally caused the wagons to be formed up, four abreast. More than a thousand wagons moved together that time, a sight never again equalled.

The end of the Trail was not long in coming to Larned. Five years after the Civil War, troopers from the fort guarded railroad construction workers. In 1872, the Atchison, Topeka, and Santa Fe reached the valley of the upper Arkansas River and the days of the wagons and their guardians were no more.

TO GET THERE: From Larned, Kansas, take U.S. 156 west for six miles. Post is on left (south) side of highway. Although set back 100 yards or so, post has a marker and road-side park next to highway. Fort Larned is privately owned as a stock ranch, but old fort buildings are managed by non-profit Fort Larned Historical Society and about 40,000 persons a year take tours, at a small fee, through post.

# FORT ZARAH, KANSAS

Almost 280 miles out of Independence, Missouri, after the first buffalo had been seen and shot at and the prairie had turned to stubby buffalo grass and cactus, the Santa Fe traveler saw what appeared to be a strange mirage rising before him.

It was no optical illusion, however. In fact, it was more of an optical treat. For it was Fort Zarah, a sandstone edifice that seems to have been the figment of some engineer's flight of fantasy, a duplicate of which probably does not exist anywhere else in Army history.

A single building 120 feet long and 52 feet wide, it had towers at two diagonally opposite corners. There was room inside for soldiers, horses, kitchen, storehouse, and well. It was built to withstand the best the Indians could offer.

As the easternmost post in the chain of Santa Fe forts, its appearance was worthy of its unique location. Fort Zarah afforded protection for the Old Walnut Crossing of Walnut Creek, a favorite stopping place for the wagon trains. From the day it was founded in 1864 and until abandonment in 1869, it also stood in the middle of favorite Indian marauding grounds.

It was not a year old when Fort Zarah troopers of the 2nd Colorado Cavalry reported the massacre of four Mexican herders right from under the noses of a 25-man military escort.

As First Lieutenant R. W. Jenkins, escort commander, reported it, he had met the train seven miles from Fort Zarah the day before, camped for the night near it, "and gave orders to the wagon master of train not to move until daylight . . . I prepared for the march at sunrise, and then found that the train had moved between 1 and 2 a.m.

"Proceeding immediately down the road about nine miles, I found the loose stock belonging to the train near the road and the herdsmen (four Mexicans) killed and scalped."

Apparently in their urge to get moving, the train had figured it could make better time away from the Army. They pulled out quietly—or the soldiers slept soundly—and kept moving until reaching nearby Plum Buttes. Here they built a fire, a beacon for the Indians as it were, and 15 accepted the invitation.

Only the herders with the cattle were victims. The men at the fire did not see "the transaction," as Jenkins writes, "and no one of the herders escaped alive to tell the tale."

The heaviest attack on Zarah came in 1868 as part of the Indian War of that year. A newspaper reporter with General Sheridan wrote in *Troopers on the Border*, "A body of 1,000 Kiowas attacked Fort Zarah on the Arkansas, but were driven off after a brisk fight."

Historians must have demanded a recount on that one because the official marker at the site states with considerably less exaggeration: "Attacked by 100 Kiowas October 2, 1868."

When the Army left in 1869, Fort Zarah was dismantled but the engineer's fantasy remained. An officer's wife's diary tells of camping near it in 1872:

"Our camp tonight is near the ruins of a very old fort, and ever since we got here the men have been hunting rattlesnakes that have undoubtedly been holding possession of the tumble-down buildings many snake generations . . ."

With somewhat less than engineer accuracy, she added, "The old quarters were evidently made of sods and dirt, and must have been dreadful places to live in even when new."

TO GET THERE: From Great Bend, Kansas, take U.S. 56 east three miles. Site is now a state park on left (north) side of road. Camping facilities.

FORT ZARAH
KANSAS-1867

EXCEPT FOR MAGAZINE and blacksmith shop, Fort Zarah was self-contained. Magazine had tunnel connecting it with cellar in main building under storehouse area. Second cellar was under kitchen. Main story was 10 feet high, walls were between 24 and 20 inches thick. Loopholes in walls were slanted downward, were 10 by 26 inches on the outside, narrowing to a three-inch slit a foot high closed with a three-inch oak door inside. (Redrawn from plat in National Archives.)

**FORT ZARAH** as pictured by an 1891 artist probably did not look quite like this. Plans in National Archives give it a single-and-a-half story appearance only 20 feet from ground to roof peak and with parapets only 17 feet high. Windows and doors faced outward along all exterior walls, but had shutters in which rifle slits were cut. Rifle slits also were every three feet along walls, but slightly over four feet from ground. Second story was a loft reached by ladder. Hospital space was there, 50 feet long, 18 wide, and 7 high, not matching porportions shown here.

**FORT ZARAH** today has disappeared completely but is memorialized by state park on site. After fort was abandoned, settlers hauled its sandstone blocks away and all traces were gone before turn of century. Post was named by General Samuel R. Curtis for his son, Major H. Zarah Curtis, killed in Baxter Springs Massacre in 1863.

# FORT MANN AND ATKINSON, KANSAS

Many were the ways tested to stop Indian attacks, but history records only one time when sugar was so employed. And it worked.

It was at Fort Atkinson, nee Mann, in July, 1852. William Bent, the same Bent of the Colorado forts, had just arrived at the stockaded post when a courier rode up in a cloud of dust and lather. He announced that Kiowas and Comanches were trying to stampede a nine-wagon train that was a little behind Bent's.

The Indians were running back and forth, screeching and waving buffalo robes, it seems. They were setting the scene for someone to get hotheaded and precipitate a real shooting incident.

Bent gathered his crew and rushed to the rescue. Yelling at the top of their lungs, they broke through the Indian demonstrators and formed a ring around the wagons. Bent and his men carried on a running exchange with the Indians of insults and uncomplimentary gestures until they got the wagons into the fort.

This did not seem to have helped. The troopers were so nervous—the Indians had surrounded them for several days angling for presents—that Bent realized they would be of small aid.

He lined the Indian chiefs up, knocked the head from a sugar keg, and fed them its contents, spoonful at a time. He was waiting for the reinforcements he knew had been summoned.

The Indians still were going through the line, licking their lips and jostling for position, when two companies of riflemen marched up on the double. The redmen figured their sweet tooth had been satisfied and beat a hasty retreat across the Arkansas.

As a military site, this spot four miles west of modern Dodge City, Kansas, was one of the earliest in Santa Fe Trail history. The government was uncertain in the early 1840's whether forts were needed and finally put up two to give the theory a try. Fort Kearney was started near Nebraska City, Nebraska, and Fort Mann was built 26 miles below the "Cimarron Crossing" of the Arkansas. Mann was supposed to be a rest stop and repair station midway between Leavenworth and Santa Fe.

It was started as an adobe stockade in 1847 by Lieutenant Colonel William Gilpin and his Indian Battalion. On his way to Colorado, he left off three companies to build it. One of the men wrote later that it "was simply four log houses connected by angles of timber framework, in which were cut loopholes for the cannon and small arms. In diameter the fort was about sixty feet. The walls were twenty in height."

One thing the soldier did not mention: in 1847, Fort Mann had its own temperance society and observers announced "the beneficial tendency was not unfelt."

The post lasted only a couple of years and was almost immediately succeeded by Camp Mackay at approximately the same location on August 8, 1951. On June 25, 1851, the name was changed to Fort Atkin-

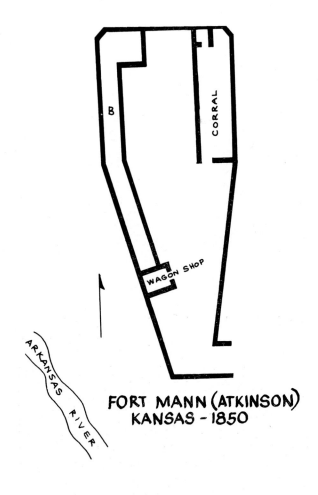

FORT MANN (ATKINSON)
KANSAS - 1850

LOGS WERE PLACED on end and packed with sod to make stockade which was 355 feet from end to end and 150 feet across. Sod walls made up interior buildings. Whether this was Fort Atkinson or Mann is uncertain since original drawing was made by James P. McCollom from tradition and memories of pioneers. In 1870, local residents found three or four graves in area, and two lime kilns. Road to timber reserve also was visible then, reports indicating it was as wide as Santa Fe Trail and had signs of heavy use. (Redrawn from plat in Boot Hill Museum, Dodge City, Kansas.)

**ONLY THIS MARKER** is left of Forts Atkinson and Mann. When Fort Atkinson was abandoned, New Mexico legislature protested because it was only protection for 600 miles. The Caches, noted on marker, were series of jug-shaped holes in which 1822 caravan cached their trade goods after their horses died from cold. The men walked to Taos for more animals and returned following spring to recover their property and proceed on to Santa Fe. No traces remain.

son, but legend says the soldiers called it "Fort Sod" or "Fort Sodom," apparently because of its unsanitary condition and the overabundance of vermin.

A draft of Army recruits passed it in 1850, and one of them recorded in his diary, "Arrived Fort Atkinson, garrisoned by one company for the protection of travelers from the Indians. The camp is in constant fear of an attack from a nearby camp of 1,500 hostile Indians. This company has to send 35 miles for firewood and are obliged to send 12 or 15 men in company to get it."

The fear was well-founded. Not too long after,

the post was besieged by a large body of Comanches and Kiowas. Only the timely arrival of a 1st Dragoon detachment prevented serious results.

Atkinson was abandoned in 1853 after a treaty was signed there with the Comanche, Kiowa and Apache. It was temporarily reoccupied for four months in 1854, then destroyed so the Indians would not be able to use it.

TO GET THERE: Take U.S. 50 west from Dodge City. Marker for fort is on right side of road after about four miles; original site was between road and Arkansas River, left (south) side of road.

# BENT'S FORTS AND FORT WISE, COLORADO

History came twice to Fort Wise, Colorado, once to bring a measure of peace, once to ignite the flames of war.

Both the geography and genealogy of Fort Wise are confusing. It is in southeastern Colorado, so close to the Kansas border that its first troops thought they were in Kansas.

It has been known by so many names, and relocated so many times, that it is hard to tell the players without a datecard. The earliest ancestor of Fort Wise was Bent's Fort, usually called "Old" Bent's Fort, north of modern Las Animas, Colorado. Built in 1828 by the four Bent brothers (Charles, Robert, George, and William) and their partner Ceran St. Vrain, it had an ancestor of its own. This was a stockade between Pueblo and Canyon City, Colorado, built two years earlier.

First known as Fort William, and then as Bent's Fort, the second stockade became one of the most prominent landmarks along the Santa Fe Trail. It was of adobe, ran 180 feet long and 135 feet wide, with 15-foot high walls that were four feet thick. Cannons were in the bastions at the southwest and northwest corners. Cactus was planted on the tops of the walls to discourage climbers.

This trading post was a rendezvous for Fremont's expedition to the Rockies, Kearney's march to Santa Fe, and Price's Mexico column. It lasted until 1852 when William Bent, bitter over his unsuccessful attempts to sell it at his price to the Federal government, moved his gear out in 20 wagons and blew up the place.

The chronology continues with Bent's "New" Fort, 30 miles to the east and on a bluff overlooking the Arkansas. Here he built a smaller version of his adobe establishment. It stood on a point so that it could be approached only from the north. The 16-foot high stone walls surrounded a dozen rooms and a large central court. A 55-foot long warehouse was inside. Although it had no bastions, it retained the cannon of the earlier fort and these were mounted on the corners of the roof.

Bent's reputation of fair dealing followed him and his trade kept up. Then in 1859, the Army moved nearby and hinted that it might like to stay. Noting the damper that this put on his trading, Bent suggested that the Army might like to buy him out. Major John Sedgwick concurred.

"I would strongly suggest that it be purchased," Sedgwick wrote in reference to the fort, "both for the convenience and the economy. It is offered for sale for $12,000, and I do not think that the government can put up such a work for that money."

Later Sedgwick watered down his opinion a bit. "We could build one that would answer the purpose for much less," he reported. "Whether some consideration is not due to Colonel Bent for locating the fort near him and injuring his trade with the Indians is not for me to say."

In 1860, Bent's New Fort became Army, but only on a lease basis: at $65 a month. Contrary to some historians, the Army never bought the fort. It paid the rent for a couple of years, then determined that Bent was only a squatter on Indian lands without legal title.

The Army first re-named the place Fort Faunterloy, after a Dragoon officer, then Fort Wise, after the governor of Virginia. It used the stone stockade principally as a commissary and quartermaster storehouse. The center of Fort Wise was built by Sedgwick's 350 men on the low ground next to the Arkansas a mile away.

FORT WISE at start of Civil War was described by occupant: "Quarters and stables are ranged on the sides of a square plat of smooth level ground, containing perhaps 20 acres. The other necessary buildings are grouped in the background, giving the whole that neat appearance so pleasing to the military eye. Colonel Bent's new fort, situated on a rocky ridge running to the water's edge a short distance below, furnishes a good commissary."

It was during this time that history was made here by William Bent. The rumblings from the south were aggravating both settler and Indian alike, and the tribes were receiving overtures from Confederate commissioners. Dreams of loot, booty, and prizes were dangled before them if they would join the rebel side —although the Confederate Commissioners claimed they merely wanted to insure their neutrality.

Trusting in Bent's wisdom, Cheyenne and Arapaho chiefs visited him while he was settling the matter of leaving his "New" fort and erecting another stockade at the mouth of Purgatory Creek. Had he followed the lead of his brothers—who had joined the Confederacy—and recommended in that direction, assuredly the tribes would have agreed. But he did not. Stay out of the white man's war, he advised.

The effect of this was almost immediate. When Sibley invaded from Texas, the Indian help he counted on was missing. It could be argued whether with this support Sibley could have pursued his campaign to a successful capture of the entire West and changed the course of the Civil War, but that is one of the many "if's" of history.

Fort Wise, below Bent's new fort-turned-storehouse, was described by a Colorado militiaman. "The buildings are stone laid in mud, with dirt roofs and floors," he wrote in his reminiscences. "Inside of the loose stone corrals no furniture was seen—nothing

but bare walls and dirt floors. Decreasing snowbanks marked the deficiencies in the roofs, and there was not a foot of lumber within 200 miles with which to remedy the defects. Nice quarters, were they not?"

The Colorado militia exercised their talents to improve their lot. As reported in the memoirs, "We divided into messes, occupied some deserted rooms, stole and cut up wagon boxes for bunks and tables, bought a set of dishes and some cooking utensils and lived to suit ourselves while we remained there."

They also broke into sutler's store, rationalizing their action by his "outrageous prices and the fact that he was secesh in principle." They regretted the petty thievery, "especially since it had been found out," but were saved from court-martial by their officers. The latter chipped in to make up the sutler's losses and ended the incident by "reading us a severe lecture on our dishonorable proceedings, which we could but acknowledge we richly deserved."

Fortunately their Fort Wise experience did not dull the Coloradans' fighting spirit. Not many months later they marched into New Mexico and helped stem the Confederate advance in the Battle of Glorieta Pass near Santa Fe.

Fort Wise's genealogy continues to June 25, 1862, when it lost its name—what Federal fort could continue to be named after a Confederate governor at this late date? It was renamed in honor of General Nathaniel Lyon, killed in Missouri in 1861.

In later years, the Fort Wise tag was retained in referring to the site in order to avoid confusion with its direct descendant, the Fort Lyon near Las Animas to which it moved in 1867. That is another story covered elsewhere under the Fort Lyon banner.

The time for history to strike again came to the post on November 29, 1864, with one of those affairs that are called "battles" or "massacres," depending upon the point of view. In 1861, the government had entered into a treaty with the Arapaho and Cheyenne which guaranteed peace along the Santa Fe Trail in the area. By the summer of 1864, this had deteriorated to the point that officially the area was considered in the throes of a general Indian war.

The governor of Colorado announced t h a t all friendly Indians, depending upon their tribe, were to go to Forts Larned, Wise, or certain northern forts. The Cheyennes under Chief Black Kettle went to Sand Creek, 40 miles north of the fort. They raised the American flag over Black Kettle's tepee and waited for the Army's representatives.

**BENT'S OLD FORT** looked like this when Army Lieutenant J. W. Abert visited it in 1846. Archaeological remains mark site today. Considerably larger than Bent's later stone fort, this adobe stockade was impressive sight along Santa Fe Trail.
(NATIONAL ARCHIVES.)

At dawn of the 24th of November, the Army came, but to fight not to talk. Their commander, Colonel John Chivington, the hero of Glorieta, had been instructed by the district commander: "I want no peace until the Indians have suffered more."

Chivington had 750 cavalrymen and his cannons were loaded with grape shot. The cannon razed the village before a defense could be organized. The cavalry charged in, shooting, slashing, burning.

"I at daylight this morning attacked a Cheyenne village of . . . from 900 to 1,000 warriors," Chivington dispatched to headquarters. "We killed between 400 and 500."

Chivington's figures were high. Even counting women and children, there were no 900 Indians in the camp, and the dead were later estimated at 163, including 110 women and children.

A hero's welcome greeted Chivington in Denver. Then word began to leak out that the Sand Creek Battle was really a massacre.

A Congressional investigation was held at Fort Wise and the government publicly repudiated the affair, paying reparations to the tribe. Chivington, a hero with a besmirched escutcheon, tried newspapering and politics in the East, then returned to Colorado where he died a condemned or admired man, depending upon the point of view.

The defenders of Sand Creek have cited the bloody record of the Cheyenne prior to their arrival there, and the presence of fresh scalps and a coat supposedly made completely of scalps, found there. The real settlement has never been reached, and never will be.

In 1866, Fort Wise was flooded by the Arkansas and a hasty evacuation to the new site was made. Two years later, Captain George Armes passed the site and "found the old fort or buildings on fire and plenty of fresh signs of Indians all around us. We . . . arrived just in time to put the fire out. The post having been abandoned, the Indians concluded to burn the buildings, but our arrival was just in time to save them."

TO GET THERE: Take U.S. 50 west from Lamar eight miles to Prowers sign. Turn left a mile to a dead end, turn left, go half a mile, turn right for another half mile. Bent's New Fort is on rise to the right, located by marker. From this point, look to the southwest. Between the marker and the river is Fort Wise site. For Bent's Old Fort, from Las Animas take U.S. 50 for 10 miles west of Las Animas, to State 194 branching to northwest. Site is jointly administered by National Park Service and Colorado State Historical Society.

**DEFINITE OUTLINE OF** Bent's New Fort can be seen in rock remains strewn on ground. This is due mainly to historical and archaeological studies which have unearthed area. View is to north and shows area of eastern wall of fort.

**VIEW OF MARKER** looking south toward the Fort Wise site.

# BARCLAY'S FORT, NEW MEXICO

When the Mountain Route and the Cimarron Cut-off became one again in northeastern New Mexico, the Santa Fe Trail travelers knew they were on the last lap of their journey.

Here at the junction of the Mora River and Sapello Creek and not too far from the future Fort Union, enterprising traders established what was to be known as "Barclay's Fort."

In the strictest sense, this was not a military fort. The government never owned it, troops never manned it. But troops passed in and out all day long, and escorts guarding the trains knew it as the first settlement worthy of the description for more than 700 miles. Military or not, when the troops arrived at Barclay's Fort, they stopped, rested, sampled Alexander Barclay's wares and wines, and let off steam.

Barclay himself was an expert at the armed trading post business. An Englishman, he learned his profession under the tutelage of William Bent, and was Bent's factor or manager at Bent's Old Fort for four years. After a fling at operating his own post to the west of Bent's for awhile, he headed south where he could profit from trading with trains from both branches of the Santa Fe Trail, not just the Mountain Route.

An 1853 visitor described Barclay's Fort as "a large adobe establishment" which housed "both men and animals. From the outside it presents a rather formidable as well as a neat appearance, being pierced with loop-holes and ornamented with battlements."

Once inside, however, the visitor found that the rooms "were d a m p and uncomfortable," he complained, "all the surroundings looked so gloomy, the hour being twilight, that it reminded me of some old state prison where the great and good of former times have languished away their lives."

The design of Barclay's Fort was not accidental. It matched the standard for the major trading posts of the west. Built the way Barclay's was, as Captain Hiram Chittenden of the Army engineers wrote, it "was really very strong and was practically impregnable to an enemy without artillery.

"A host of savages armed with bows and arrows or with the indifferent firearms of those days could make no impression upon it, and the garrison could look with indifference upon any attack, however formidable, so long as they used reasonable precaution and were supplied with provisions and ammunition."

To prove the case, Chittenden added, "There is no record of a successful siege of a stockaded fort in the entire history of the fur trade west of the Mississippi."

**BASED ON MEMORY** of Francis W. Cragin, who drew original plat in 1904, Barclay's Fort had double stories along northern side, and eastern row of rooms also were double-storied, both reached by six-foot-wide stairways. Between latter group of buildings, corral and sheds for horses were located. Western row of rooms was single-storied. Cragin remembered, "The two-story part had a two-story porch in front of it, both of the porch stories roofed over." Bastions had small iron cannon "with three portholes on each of the three low stories of the bastions; the portholes had iron doors at the outer end." There was a watch tower over the gate. (Redrawn from Cragin's plat now in Denver Public Library Western History Collection.)

TO GET THERE: Take U.S. 85 north from Las Vegas, New Mexico, about 20 miles to Watrous, turn left on County 160 (before crossing Mora River). About one mile north, and just before road turns sharply to left, is site of Barclay's Fort on right side of road between it and river. It is unmarked, but rock foundations from fort are strewn in pasture.

**FOUNDATION LINE** of Barclay's Fort runs up middle of picture, as shown by row of foundation stones. In this area there was also an adobe walled corral. Mora River flows under trees. Army apparently considered buying fort in 1850, and report of inspector suggested Barclay would accept $15,000 for it. Official description said "outer walls are square of 64 yards, with some circular bastions or towers at two opposite corners . . . The buildings, either for quarters or storehouses are one room deep, about 15 feet in the clear."

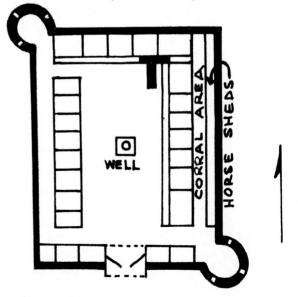

WELL

CORRAL AREA

HORSE SHEDS

**STARS AND BARS** flew over Alamo after General Twiggs surrendered it to Texas troops.

(HARPER'S WEEKLY, MARCH 23, 1861.)

# GRAY CLOUDS FROM THE SOUTH

*"The people may now rest assured that the era of anarchy and misrule . . . has passed away; and that now, under the sacred banner of our country, all may claim and shall receive their just rights . . . Let them once more pursue their avocations with the full confidence that protection will be given them."*

—The California Column's General Order 15 in New Mexico, 1862.

WHEN Robert E. Lee arrived in San Antonio in 1862, the Stars and Bars were flying from the Alamo. State troops were in command. On February 1, Texas seceded from the Union.

Despite vigorous efforts by the Confederates, most of the Southwest did not follow Texas. Arkansas seceded in May, 1861; Missouri had both rebel and Union governments; New Mexico, Oklahoma, and Arizona all had a paper status within the Confederacy at times, but without much effect. Nevada and California had Confederate scares, but these were put down quickly.

The South moved into New Mexico rapidly at first. After continued success, they met defeat at the Battle of Glorieta near Santa Fe. The secession movement lost ground after that. In Arizona, a Confederate state was set up south on the 34th parallel, extending from California across the bottom of New Mexico to Texas.

"We will not recognize the present Black Republican Administration," declared the first Confederate convention for the Territory of Arizona in 1861. Neither did the United States recognize them. When the column of California Volunteers arrived in 1862, the supremacy of the Union was quickly restored.

The question was not solved so easily in Oklahoma. The forts were abandoned and the garrisons consolidated to the north.

The Confederates attempted to administer the Fort Cobb Indian Agency. The Indians usually did not take sides in the "white man's war," but the Cherokee Tribe in Oklahoma signed an alliance with the South.

Stand Watie, a mission-schooled Cherokee and co-editor of a Cherokee newspaper, led a home guard company. Then, as a colonel and later a brigadier, he commmanded a regiment that was mustered into the Confederate Army. Although in 1863 most of the Cherokee had repudiated the South, Watie remained loyal. His was one of the last Southern units to surrender.

The Civil War's effects were far-reaching in the Southwest. The most important effect was to create a restless air in the East and a curiosity about the West. After the war, the Easterners moved West to see for themselves.

# FORT FILLMORE, NEW MEXICO

Two distinctions set Fort Fillmore aside from its contemporaries. It was the first Federal Fort to surrender lock, stock, barrel and without a fight during the Civil War. And it appears to have been the only Army fort to be commanded, even unofficially, by a woman.

These items in themselves might indicate that Fillmore was a strange or at least, unusual, installation. In appearance it was unlike the stalwart fortresses of the East, but no more so than the bulk of western posts.

As it commander, Major Isaac Lynde, wrote departmental headquarters on July 7, 1861, "This fort is very badly situated for defense. It is placed in a basin, surrounded by sand hills, at least half the circumference of the circle, and they are covered by a dense growth of chaparral. These sand hills completely command the post, and render it indefensible against a force supplied with artillery. A force of a thousand men could approach it within 500 yards under perfect cover."

The post had not been built for a siege, but as a resting place for soldiers between Indian campaigns. It was a series of small square adobe buildings, each of which had a parapet because its walls extended higher than the roof. The post surgeon complained that a cannon had been mounted atop his quarters, and would topple the whole business with the first shot.

When Mrs. Lydia Spencer Lane accompanied her soldier husband to Fort Fillmore in 1860, her opinion was less than enthusiastic. "Such a dreary looking place I have seldom seen," she wrote later in *I Married a Soldier*. "The stiff line of shabby adobe quarters on three sides of a bare parade ground suggested neither beauty nor comfort, and for once I felt discouraged when we went into the forlorn house we were to occupy. It was filthy, too, and the room we chose for a bedroom must have been used as a kitchen.

"The woodwork was rough and unpainted; the modern method of oiling pine was not known in Army quarters then . . . There was a hospital, but no doctor nearer than 40 miles, for whom we once had to send; on another occasion the doctor was at a fort 80 miles away when summoned; relays of mules were posted along the road to bring him in as rapidly as possible."

It was this same lady who served as the unofficial commander of the post. All of the garrison was ordered on a patrol and "a sergeant and ten men, all that could be spared from the little command, were left behind to guard the post and our small family, and they were picked men. Those in the guardhouse were taken on the scout.

"I was left in command of Fort Fillmore. All public funds were turned over to me, and the sergeant reported to me every day. He slept in our house at night, heavily armed, which gave us a sense of security."

She said the money gave her considerable uneasiness "and I hid it away in what I considered a secure place; then it seemed to me that would be the first place searched, and I found a safer one. I was determined no one would have the money while I was alive to defend it."

Noting the bare flagpole on the parade ground, she had her husband obtain a flag before leaving on the patrol.

"I knew I would feel safer to see it floating above us, and it was run up at reveille every morning through the summer before the post was abandoned," she recorded.

Headquarters recalled the patrol and began to reinforce Fort Fillmore when rumors of a Confederate advance got stronger. Garrisons of other forts were pulled out and moved to Fillmore, and Major Lynde became its commanding officer. Despite his criticism of the location and design, he wrote headquarters that as soon as the remainder of the troops

FORT FILLMORE
N.M. - 1852

"FORT FILLMORE IS a large and pleasant military post, and is intended to garrison a battalion of troops," a contemporary description said. "The form is that of a square, the quarters of the officers and men inclosing the open space within on three sides, while the south is open toward the river. The buildings are adobes, but comfortable . . . There is also a well-selected library for the use of the officers and men, which is an evidence that the government does not overlook the mental wants of her soldiers." Official Army inspection in 1853 claimed, "the quarters for this post for both officers and men are the best in the Territory." (Redrawn from Mansfield Report, 1854.)

arrived, "I shall then have very little fear of the result of any attack that will likely to be made from Texas . . .

"With the force that I shall have at this post in a few days I do not think that the enemy will attempt to attack us, but if they do, I think we shall give them a warm reception."

Lynde's orders were to secure "the interests of the United States against attack from any quarter" but to destroy the fort and its property if threatened by a force that could not be resisted. Apparently these orders never were known by Lynde's officers. The few Union men among them complained bitterly about his refusal to throw up breastworks, strengthen the guard, and evacuate the families to the safety of Santa Fe.

The night of July 24, Lynde was awakened by two men sneaking into the post. They were soldiers who recently deserted to join the Confederacy, but announced they had reconsidered. The pair told Lynde they were part of a Texan 250-man force that was camped only 600 yards from the fort, ready to attack at sunrise. The idea of firing at their old comrades was too much for them.

Fort Fillmore was alerted. The Texas troops realized that surprise was lost, so they skirted the post, crossed the Rio Grande, and captured the pro-Southern town of Mesilla (which is today on the Fillmore side of the river because of a shift in its course.)

Lynde decided to test the Texas strength. He marched 380 men and a howitzer to the outskirts of the town, fired two ineffective cannon rounds short of the place, then fell back. The Texans had been waiting and with the first round from the howitzer, they let loose with fire from every house, corn field and corral.

Suspicious of the allegiance of the command, Lynde and some of his loyal troops later claimed that they received fire from within their ranks. He began to feel the rumor was true that not more than a couple of his officers were loyal. "From the moment he appears to have lost all confidence in his officers and men; to have suspected treachery, of which he was to be the first victim," the department commander wrote later.

The troops returned to Fillmore and hastily began fortifying it. An hour later, Lynde announced that Fillmore was to be abandoned and the troops were to march northward to Fort Stanton. First, all property was to be destroyed.

Here the final and fatal error occurred. The destruction reached into the hospital stores, and the soldiers sampled the medicinal whiskey. It appears that many emptied their canteens, refilling them with stronger stuff than water.

The next day the New Mexican sun beat mercilessly on the 750 men in the retreating column. When the Texas force met them east of Las Cruces, they found 500 men gasping for water and stretched out along the road for five miles. Lynde saw the Confederate force approaching and tried to form a defense.

"I could not bring more than 100 men of the infantry battalion on parade," he wrote later. "Under the circumstances . . . it was worse than useless to resist; honor did not demand the sacrifice of blood."

The Texans took over the public property, accepted those men who wanted to join the South, and paroled the rest. Lynde was ousted from the Army, but after the Civil War quietly reinstated and retired out of deference to his 34 years of honorable service.

A year later, California Volunteers rode into the Rio Grande valley and Fort Fillmore. Department headquarters was set up at Mesilla, the Overland Mail route was reopened, and New Mexico's loyalty was confirmed, despite the earlier poor showing.

TO GET THERE: Take U.S. 80-85 south from Las Cruces. About five miles south, site of Fort Fillmore is on right between this highway and State 487, paralleling it. State marker is in vicinity, but not on actual spot. There are no traces. Loose sand makes driving off road to site inadvisable. Watch for rattlesnakes.

**FORT FILLMORE** today has fallen victim to shifting sands. Only traces of adobe and slight mounds suggest location of fort, but artifact hunters frequently locate buttons and other souvenirs of military occupation. Center of old fort was where power poles stand in right center of picture. Organ Mountains, and retreat route of troops, are in background.

# FORT BLISS, TEXAS

It took more than 40 years of shopping around before Fort Bliss found itself a permanent home. When oldtimers talk about the fort, it is necessary to determine how old the oldtimers are in order to decide what one of five Forts Bliss is involved.

Things in early day El Paso were not the calmest, what with Mexicans raiding settlers, settlers raiding Mexicans, Indians raiding both, Confederates raiding Northerners, and desperadoes and crooked politicians taking from all without regard to race, nationality, politics or any other niceties. Except when it was involved in its frequent shifts of location, Fort Bliss brought to the area a certain degree of respectability and order.

The post first began in 1850 when a battalion of the 3rd Infantry settled down at Smith's Ranch, opposite El Paso del Norte, Mexico. The garrison built an adobe fort and was known variously as the "Post at Smith's Ranche" and "Post Opposite El Paso, New Mexico." The latter was more common because El Paso numbered several thousand inhabitants while Smith's Ranch included only three ranches and a mill.

The troopers hardly had time to build a fort and guard a few supply trains before they were moved. In 1851, the policy was to take the soldiers out of the cities, and most of the El Paso force was shifted to Fort Fillmore.

When the Army Inspector passed the site in 1853, his report had a lot to do with returning soldiers to El Paso. "A post is indispensable opposite the town of El Paso," he reported. "These few families are exposed at all times to the depredations of the Indians, and since the troops were removed in September, 1851,

many depredations have been committed . . . By a post here, the bottom lands of the river to Isleta, and a trading town would soon spring up with an Americn population capable of self-defence."

Soldiers returned to El Paso when the facts made it obvious they were needed. In the two years they were away, there had been 23 Indian attacks and 18 men killed, and the need for Army protection was obvious.

Site number two then came into being: at Magoffin's Ranch not far from the first location. Four companies of the 8th Infantry garrisoned the place beginning in January, 1854, first calling it "Military Post Opposite El Paso, Texas." In April this was changed to Fort Bliss to honor General Zachary Taylor's chief of staff during the Mexican War.

Commands shifted back and forth at early-day Bliss and it rotated between being an infantry and cavalry camp. Its patrols roamed the entire territory and three companies fought in the Battle of the Gila, 1857. Here they employed the hunter technique, the mounted troops flushing the Apaches and driving them toward the infantry positions. Although most of the Indians escaped, 24 were killed and 26 captured.

The friction between infantry and cavalry was pronounced at Bliss. After the 1,339-mile, 124-day Gila expedition, a cavalry lieutenant wrote in his diary that he had "hopes of being comfortable for a few days, though between escort duty and the annoyances of a post commanded by an infantry officer I do not hope for much military pleasure."

The same officer had comments about the daily routine. "Life at the post was dull enough until the fiestas commenced," he said, "then bull fights and billiards, bailes and monte, intrigues and crimes, made gay and noisy scenes where but an hour before all was monotonous as the desert."

Secession fever ran high in the area in 1860. Anson Mills, later a general, was a civilian at the time and wrote in his reminiscences that when the vote for secession came he publicly displayed his ballot. "My vote was one of the two cast against secession in El Paso county, where there were over 900 cast for secession," he wrote. He added that the majority of the votes were cast by Mexicans across the river and were illegal.

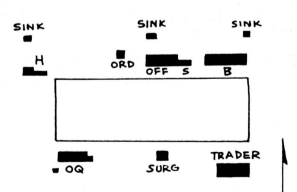

FORT BLISS
TEXAS – 1875

"THERE IS NO fortification whatever here," wrote surgeon in 1870. "The barracks are in the two large buildings on the north side. There is capacity for 200 men. The buildings are warmed by fireplaces and ventilated by windows and doors." This ground plan is of third site of Fort Bliss, 1868-77, the Concordia location. (Redrawn from Division of Missouri report, 1876.)

**FORT BLISS** was a cluster of adobes in earliest versions. This was fort of late 1850 era. In 1857 Beale's 28-animal camel expedition passed through this location, but fortunately for sensibilities of cavalrymen and their mounts most troops were away from fort on expeditions.

Mills went to Washington with the Fort Bliss commander's request for permission to take his troops and property away from El Paso. The commander had told Mills that "he did not want to obey Twigg's order to surrender to the Texans because he has large government stores, which would be of great value in case of war to either the government or the Confederates."

While Washington stewed, the Confederates moved in on March 1, 1861, and the post was surrendered. Although the troops were permitted to march out, they were taken prisoner near San Antonio in May and spent almost two years as hostages.

The post saw the Confederate column move northward in July, 1861. It received the battered and starving remnants the following May. It was burned by the Confederates when they abandoned it soon after.

California Volunteers were stationed at two locations near El Paso for the rest of the war. Attempts to rebuild the post were made, but the flooding of the Rio Grande created more havoc than Confederate action. In 1868, the garrison shifted to the third Bliss site a mile to the northeast.

This was called Camp Concordia for a year until the Bliss name was resumed. The post surgeon had few good things to say about it. "The present loca-

**FIRST FORT BLISS** today is a replica at modern Fort Bliss. It was built by El Paso Chamber of Commerce and is major visitor attraction. Its buildings serve as a chapel and museum.

tion presents no advantages of a military character that is not afforded in as great, or greater degree, by almost any 40-acre lot that borders on the Rio Grande," he reported in 1870. "There is no water nearer than the river . . . No trees grow in the vicinity . . . Cows, sheep, &c., cannot be kept, on account of the scarcity of water and grass."

He said that mail communication was irregular "as wagon trains only start when a full load of freight is obtained." He found "the inhabitants of the vicinity of the post are . . . agricultural and industrious; thieving and lewd, as a general thing, among the lower orders. The exceptions are said to be few, and, therefore, more honorable."

The fort was abandoned in 1876 and the lawless elements in El Paso broke loose. "Gambling, especially among the Mexicans, was soon a leading amusement on both sides of the river, and the saloon and red light districts for many years gave the two cities the just reputation of being among the most disorderly and lawless in the country," Mills wrote.

"No mayor could be elected unless he harmonized with and fostered all three of the above mentioned elements—some mayors lived in the red light district," Mills added. "Many cruel murders were committed, but it was impossible under the dominance of the three bad elements to procure convictions."

The Army decided to make Fort Bliss a permanent base after the governor of Texas appealed for help at El Paso. The Concordia post was nothing but a collection of ruins, so troops were billeted in rented warehouses in El Paso. The public square was used as a parade ground.

After three years of this makeshift situation, they were moved to the east of the city at "Hart's Mill." Here on a 135-acre reservation next to the actual El Paso del Norte, the Army finally occupied a strategic location.

But it was too strategic. When the railroad arrived in 1881, the tracks were laid right across the parade ground. Although the troops spent much time away from the post in Indian campaigns, it was obvious that they could not fare happily at a fort bisected by both the Southern Pacific and the Santa Fe. In 1893 the fort was moved again.

Five miles northeast of El Paso, Fort Bliss found its final home. From this site it fought the border troubles of the early 20th century. Today it is a major training command but within its shadows is a startling contrast: a cluster of adobes which are a replica of the first Fort Bliss.

TO GET THERE: Take U.S. 80 from center of El Paso, turning north at the overpass for U.S. 180-62 (Chelsea Avenue). Stay on Chelsea when it branches away from U.S. 180-62 at Montana Avenue. Turn right at Pershing Drive which leads directly into modern Fort Bliss. Hart's Mill site of fort is at west edge of El Paso at intersection of the U.S. 80 (alternate) overpass and Doniphan Street. Buildings can be seen on west side below overpass. There are no remains at other fort sites.

BARRACKS at Hart's Mill probably are little changed from earlier days. Adobe bricks are evident through cracks in plaster. Site parallels Rio Grande and hillside in background actually is in Mexico.

OFFICERS' QUARTERS at Hart's Mill fort now serve as apartments. Site is next to U.S. 80 (alternate) and shadows of cross-country highway overpass are in foreground. Parade ground of 1880-1893 fort was at this point until railroads put tracks along right-of-way now shared by highway. Many buildings of former fort are huddled next to overpass.

# FORT SMITH, OKLAHOMA AND ARKANSAS

When soldiers at Fort Smith did not like the post sutler, they took action into their own hands; no official channels for them!

It was back in the period of the post's second occupancy—1833 to 1838—that it happened. The reason for it has not been preserved, but the soldiers' actions have.

One morning before sunrise, unnamed and later unidentified troopers inserted into the muzzle of the sunrise cannon an assortment of shot, scrap iron, rocks and other miscellany. When the sun came up like thunder, so did the cannon. Its contents smashed through the sutler's house, careening just over his bed and barely missing him.

Local legend states from that time after, the post sutler was the most polite man around Fort Smith. He had taken the hint.

Action was typical of the occupants of this post, one of the first established in the Southwest. When it was founded in 1817, it was far beyond the frontier and activities with both Indians and settlers were continuing affairs.

"To prevent the encroachments of the white settlers upon the lands still held by the Indians," was the official reason for its being, but it had many other tasks. Arkansas River traders and trappers stopped at Belle Point, its site, to rest. Missionaries, surveyors, explor-ers—that early day tourist—, and soldiers all passed this landmark.

The first Fort Smith was on a sandstone point about 35 feet above the junction of the Poteau and Arkansas Rivers. No one was quite sure at the time, but it was completely within what is Oklahoma today. An 1858 marker for the boundary remains today about 100 yards east of the site.

This post was a stockade typical of the early 19th century. Squared timbers were driven into the ground closely together. The wall was about 10 feet high and eight inches thick, good enough against bow and arrow, anyway. Two blockhouses were at opposite corners, north and south. A ditch, six feet deep and eight feet wide, was outboard of the palisade.

The post was two years old when it was the scene of a peace meeting between the Osage and Cherokee Indians, with Major William Bradford, post commander, as the referee.

The Cherokees had captured some Osages and had no desire to return them. With chiefs of both sides present, the Osages affirmed their desire to regain their lost tribesmen. The Cherokees were equally firm that this would not happen.

Finally an ultimatum was given the Cherokees: return the prisoners in 10 days, or else.

On the eleventh day, the Cherokees had not produced the prisoners but five of their chiefs were at the fort. It was suggested that the Osages take the five

**TWO FORT SMITHS** and two different states; Belle Point stockaded fort (left) had most of its activity inside, although some minor buildings were outside. This plan called for stockade to be 132 feet square. Second Fort Smith (right) was built nearby—note outline of first fort's approximate site—and edged over state border. Today only Commissary storehouse and the center barracks remain. (Redrawn from plats courtesy Fort Smith Chamber of Commerce and Thomas Norris, National Park Service).

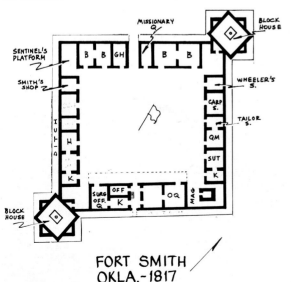

FORT SMITH
OKLA.-1817

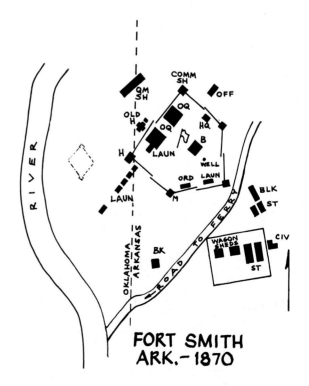

FORT SMITH
ARK.-1870

as hostages. No, the Osage chief said, if he did his people would kill the hostages out of spite, if nothing else.

A more-than-subtle summons went from the Army to the Cherokees: come back and talk, now. And the next day the Cherokees sat around a council fire with the Osages and Major Bradford. His umpiring became less a suggestion and more a demand. The Cherokees relented, the hostages were returned, and what could have been a bloody Indian war was settled over the Army's version of the peace pipe.

The same Osage tribe returned to Smith three years later 400 strong. They stood across the river yelling, waving their weapons, and making suitable gestures to the fort.

By this time Colonel Matthew Arbuckle (he of the many Oklahoma forts of that name) was in command of Smith. Telling his men to "cover me," he paddled a small boat across. The Indians stopped their racket when he approached alone, agreed to send a few spokesmen with him to talk, and moved back into their camp. Some influence may have been exerted by the fact that Fort Smith's artillery was on the opposite bank, its ranges set for point-blank fire.

The stockade site was abandoned in 1824. The Indian pressure had become so great that the government decided to move the troops closer to the tribes. An Indian Agency was to be set up in the buildings in 1826, but this had to be cancelled. When he arrived, the agent found the fort in shambles because the troopers had taken with them the floors, doors and windows.

The post was used for a season in 1833 to keep the Indians in line, but it was not until 1838 that the government bowed to Territorial pressure and returned the Army to Fort Smith.

This time, it was Fort Smith, Arkansas, but again, no one was quite sure. The border had shifted back and forth several times and was finally stabilized in 1905. The "no man's land" created by the shifts was even in recent years a lawless strip for questionable activities because it was on the Arkansas side of the river, but was within Oklahoma.

Actually, Fort Smith was both. Most of it was within modern Arkansas. As the plat shows, a tiny segment spilled over into the Choctaw Nation, the early-day name for Indian Territory—the early-day name for Oklahoma.

This second fort was to be a real fortress. It is said that the French fortifications expert Marshal

**"HANGING JUDGE PARKER,"** on whom much of Fort Smith city's fame rests, held court in this building. Seen through gate in restored wall, building on right was once barracks at Fort Smith. After Army left it in 1871, fort was used for various purposes, then Federal Court took it over. Judge Parker's court was only law in Indian Territory, tried 13,490 cases in 21 years, sentenced 161 men to die; 79 were hanged. Despite these cold numbers, Judge was considered fair and honest, most citizens agreeing his justice was necessary. Second story, and jail wing (left), were added after Army left.

**FIRST FORT SMITH** foundations have been unearthed by National Park Service. This is probably part of northern blockhouse, although at time of excavations identity could not be certain. River is through trees in background.

Vauban had a hand in its design, or at least it was after the style of his works. It was to be an early-day pentagon, 450 by 600 feet, with cannon and bastions at each angle of the wall.

When General Zachary Taylor arrived at Fort Smith in 1841, he found the post still incomplete, $120,000 spent, and the men living in squatter-type huts in a temporary "Cantonment Belknap" next to the post. He decided that he could keep order without an elaborate stone fort and halted the extravagant designs. He settled for finishing what had been begun, but nothing fancy.

Two bastions became storehouses, one became a magazine, and two never really were finished. Construction finally ended in 1845. It was not long before Mexican War volunteers were drilling at the fort and living at it and Cantonment Belknap. The town of Fort Smith gave one company to the war. It reached Vera Cruz with 128 men, but only thirty returned. Disease rather than battle had taken the rest.

War came to Fort Smith in 1861, but it was bloodless. Only a company of U.S. forces were stationed there and they tactfully withdrew on April 23, 1861 when 300 Confederates and 10 artillery pieces threatened it.

"After supplies were cut off by the State of Arkansas," explained Captain S. D. Sturgis, the commander, "the post would be untenable. We could have occupied it in any case but a few days more . . . To have contended against this force . . . would have resulted in our being taken prisoners and loss to the government of all arms, horses, means of transportation, etc., at the post."

Confederates used the fort for awhile. One unit was the "Hempstead Hornets," 80 strong, who were armed with double-barreled shotguns and fearsome long-bladed knives. Its men fought in the Battle of Wilson's Creek and Pea Ridge. After the Union returned to the fort, displacing a tiny garrison in a manner similar to Sturgis's departure, United States forces used it as a toe hold in Southern territory.

Five square earthwork fortifications were erected around the fort. Troops fought one battle nearby, Massard Prairie, in which 5,000 federals were surprised and defeated by 2,000 mounted Confederates.

TO GET THERE: From downtown Fort Smith, Arkansas, take Second Street one block southwest of Garrison to Roger Avenue. On the southeast corner is the former barracks and Judge Parker's courtroom; former Commissary building is down hill on right. Go one block farther to dead end; first fort site is directly west across railroad tracks. Now National Park Service National Historic Site, markers indicate points of interest.

**ONCE PART OF FORT** wall, as the northern bastion, this building became Commissary storehouse. It has been defended since end of Fort by Fort Smith Museum Board, small group of ladies who zealously preserved traditions and history of post. Its walls and interior woodwork, doors, hinges all are original.

# FORT TOWSON, OKLAHOMA

Fort Towson might have been one of the handsomest posts on the frontier, but it was not until after it was abandoned that it attained its most important role.

The U.S. Army chronology for Towson might read: established by the 7th Infantry, May, 1824, as Cantonment Towson; abandoned June, 1829; re-established as Camp Phoenix, November, 1830; renamed 1831; abandoned June 8, 1854.

More dates, but not as dry because of the image they suggest, might be found in the Confederate records. Here it was in 1864 that General S. B. Maxey conducted Southern affairs for the Indian Territory. And here it was in June, 1865, that Cherokee General Stand Watie surrendered his Confederate force, said to be the last organized unit to surrender.

Thoughts of Civil War probably were far from the minds of the soldiers when they built the first post in 1824. Marauders "are in the habit of committing the most outrageous acts of robbery, violence and murder," wrote General Winfield Scott, referring to a site on the banks of Gates Creek, seven miles from the Red River.

This became Cantonment Towson, a temporary place of wooden shanties and tents. There were so few men that Indians could come within four miles of the post and, as they did, make off with the officers' horses.

Two soldiers were killed in 1825 about 10 miles away, and the Army called upon civilian help to form a military-citizen posse. This pursued the killers successfully.

After the Army moved out and then returned in 1830, Fort Towson began to take permanent shape. When an officer's wife described it in 1849, she found it a beautiful place marked by "many trees within the enclosure which add much to the beauty of the place."

The soldiers' reputation for construction activities must have got around. No sooner were the buildings finished than two companies were detailed to build a road through Choctaw country . . . a matter involving bridges, ferries, and felling countless trees. It also meant keeping it open once it was built.

The fort maintained its fighting status, however. Indians and white men worse than bad Indians kept the frontier busy. The Mexican War found Fort Towson the center for 800 men of the 6th Infantry before they headed to the border.

The garrison was down to a single company when the post was abandoned after the war. It was not too soon: two days before the company left, a storm slashed across the post, toppling trees, unroofing buildings, and generally creating "a very dilapidated condition," according to its last commander's report.

The Indian Agent, Colonel Douglas H. Cooper of Fort Arbuckle fame, used the buildings and it became the seat of the Choctaw Nation. In later years a fire destroyed all but a single barracks and the hospital.

When the Confederates took it over, orders for much of the last months of the Western war came from here. Early-day psychological warfare was used here, too, when General Maxey set up a printing press and ground out propaganda aimed at keeping the Indians on his side.

TO GET THERE: From the town of Towson, in south central Oklahoma, take U.S. 70 east across the bridge and turn left at first crossroad. About 1 mile north, beyond a farmhouse on the left, and about 500 yards west of the road is the fort site. This is privately owned property.

FORT TOWSON
OKLA. - 1840

FORT TOWSON shown here is based on earlier plat than that from which painting was made. Quadrangle does not show same number of buildings. Cholera hospital was used during frequent epidemics that struck soldiers, citizens and Indians impartially. (Redrawn from National Archives data.)

**WHITE BUILDINGS,** shade trees, gravel walks contributed to Fort Towson's claim to beauty. Officers' quarters were along northern edge, were of logs on limestone foundations, story and a half in height. Buildings left and right of officers' row were used for bachelor officers, offices, "amusement parlor" and schoolroom. Nearest buildings were barracks. Each building had stone fireplaces nine feet wide, four feet deep, six feet high. They were large enough to accommodate entire steer at one roasting, but probably were not too efficient for heating.

**EAST ROW OF** buildings is marked by walls like this. Although much of fort was hauled away by settlers after it was finally abandoned, these elaborate but overgrown ruins remain. When Towson was active, it had "highly moral" reputation, temperance society to which half of garrison belonged, Sunday School, bi-weekly prayer meetings sometimes conducted by post commander personally. Missionary commented: "I have never seen a place where there was a more decided religious influence." Reputation did not hinder 1838 4th of July celebration where soldiers drank 13 "regular" toasts and those still standing added ten more, including one to "the cardinal virtue of the soldier—fidelity, courage, and a decided contempt for all humbugging."

**BARRACKS TODAY** are vine-covered walls, all but hidden by jungle-like growth. This wall is probably the 9-foot-high foundation of barracks building in foreground of painting. Because of sloping ground, foundations were built up from three feet at north end to this 9-footer, two basements deep. Basement excavation is within ruined walls, filled with brush and sizable trees.

# FORT SCOTT, KANSAS

When it came to taking sides on the secession question, Fort Scott was just about the unsafest place in pre-Civil War Kansas.

That was during the interim period in the military fort's life. Started in 1842 and closed up by the Army in 1855, until the Army officially reclaimed it in 1862 the old fort was a hotbed of secession and of Free Staters. Its biggest days of Army celebrations never equalled the activity that went on across the former parade ground after the Army left.

On one side, the Free State Hotel occupied one of the former officers' quarters. It was a stopping place for John Brown and company, and even the New York papers publicized it as the headquarters from which raids were conducted on pro-slavery sympathizers.

Directly across the parade ground stood a former barracks that was attached to the old hospital. In 1856, this became the Pro-Slavery Hotel. The Civil War, on a smaller scale but porportionately almost as bloody, had begun as far as Fort Scott was concerned.

The post first came about when it was decided in the late 1830's that a garrison should be located between Fort Gibson, Oklahoma, and Fort Leavenworth, Kansas. Daniel Boone's son, Captain Nathaniel Boone, was in the party that selected the site in 1837.

In 1842 two companies of the First Dragoons dismantled Fort Wayne, just over the border in Arkansas and five miles south of the Missouri line. They brought with them to Fort Scott the movable furnishings and building material they salavaged. Considering that Fort Wayne had only a partly finished barracks, two unroofed officers' quarters, and the famework for a hospital, there was not much they could bring.

So the first Fort Scott was a hastily erected scattering of tents and huts northeast of the final site. Detailed plans for an elaborate post were received and work began immediately using native materials and soldier artisans.

A wooden stockade came first, and this completely surrounded the post. This was pierced at only one point and here at the southwest corner an iron gate controlled all movement into and out of the post.

Headquarters House came next. This was completed in 1843 and from it commanders controlled troop movements as distant as Wyoming and Denver. In 1844, five Dragoon companies marched 2,200 miles from Fort Scott in 90 days to the Platte river in Wyoming, down past Denver to the Santa Fe Trail, and back to Fort Scott.

The Mexican War and the constant war to protect the Santa Fe Trail occupied the Dragoons until the post was vacated in 1853. This signalled "open season" for the various political sides and frequently the Army had to be called back to calm things down.

The infamous Marais des Cygnes massacre was an outgrowth of these troubles. Occurring about 30 miles north of Fort Scott, apparently 11 Free State Settlers were captured by a group which included several Fort Scott townsmen. They were driven cattle-style into a dead-end ravine and so badly beaten that five died.

The Army came in full force on the heels of this nationally publicized and condemned affair. The boiling point had been reached and by the start of the Civil War the entire countryside was an armed camp. In 1860, a Missouri militia force headed toward Scott to attack it, but after four days on the march they heard about the U.S. troops at the post and about faced.

When that war started, General William S. Harney established his Department of the West headquarters here. In 1862 Ohio and Wisconsin Volunteer regiments officially reestablished Fort Scott as the headquarters for the Army of the Frontier.

And at the same time, the Pro-Slavery Hotel took for itself a new, and more politic, name: the Western Hotel.

EARLY DAY FORT SCOTT can still be seen today. Traces of most of these buildings remain although it does not appear that center officers' quarters and southeastern building ever were built. Apparently a raised walk extended along entire front, though plan for porches to surround buildings was not followed. Fort Blair, Civil War blockhouse, is directly north of Headquarters House, easternmost building in officers' row. When Civil War came, most of these buildings were occupied and entire area was dotted with fortifications, tents, temporary buildings. (Redrawn from plat courtesy Robert E. Galvin, Fort Scott.)

FORT SCOTT
KANSAS - 1860

**OFFICERS' ROW** includes these two buildings that still stand today. These are the westernmost quarters. Headquarters House, the Free State Hotel during Border Wars of 1850's is at left. It was restored in 1939 as WPA project. Furnishings are of Border period and include memorabilia of Fort Scott area. On top floor is small room once used as cell for disciplining minor infractions by officers.

**HEADQUARTERS HOUSE TODAY** is exact image of its early years. It was occupied by General James G. Blunt when he moved out on offensive strike into Arkansas. Series of successful actions fought by Fort Scott troops in this campaign included Battle of Cane Hill, Ark., and seige of Van Buren, Ark. Building has 19 fireplaces, also a mystery souvenir: a Confederate States Navy Yard plaque dated 1861-1865, source unknown.

TO GET THERE: Fort Scott, the city, is in eastern Kansas 85 miles south of Kansas City on U.S. 69. From the center of town, go north to Wall Street. The post is off Wall Street, on historic Carroll Plaza, the former parade ground. City of Fort Scott maintains a museum and many fort buildings remain, although privately used (the city jail was once the guardhouse, for instance). Nearby is U.S. National Cemetery No. 1, established in 1862.

**CANNON FROM FORT** Scott were used to good advantage after Civil War Battle of Mine Creek. Confederate General Sterling Price was routed by Scott troops, then headed toward fort. Attack was repulsed by fort's artillery fire. This remaining piece stands in front of Headquarters House, privately owned throughout period. Railroad construction guarding caused "Post of South Eastern Kansas" to be established in 1869, centered at Fort Scott, for three years.

**FORT BLAIR,** behind Headquarters House, was one of several earthworks, or lunettes, established during Civil War. Entire area bristled with them, bearing such names as Fort Insley, Henning, and Lincoln—the last an extensive log structure. This blockhouse was restored in 1958 by Western Insurance Companies. It was originally on corner of 1st and Scott Streets, was moved to present site near original location of similar blockhouse.

# FORT GIBSON, OKLAHOMA

Goldbricking apparently is not a modern-day invention of the military—the soldiers at Fort Gibson had it refined to a near art and that was back in 1833.

When the first Fort Gibson was built in 1824, it was placed on the low ground east of the Neosho or Grand River. Not only did this make it subject to seasonal floods—the bakery, stables and several small buildings were carried away in 1833—but the malaria situation in the low grounds was almost impossible.

During the summers the garrison moved temporarily to the slopes of the hill overlooking the site. It was cooler and the malaria situation improved, but it had one drawback. Water had to be carried all of the way from the fort.

In 1833, General Arbuckle decided to dig a well at the summer camp. The officer of the day was directed to put two guardhouse prisoners to work. The progress of a foot, a few inches, or some estimate was made and dutifully recorded by the Officer of the Day, month in and month out for 18 months.

When the total was added up, the still unproductive well was officially sunk to a depth of 465 feet. The Officer of the Day finally was ordered to inspect it . . . and hit rock bottom at 15 feet. Here he found a hollowed-out room and the guardhouse tenants calmly playing cards, well protected from the summer heat and winter cold!

Well they might find an excuse to while away the time, however, for Fort Gibson was both the most important post in the territory and the dullest. It was easily the largest, having more men than all of the others at times. In such a situation the individual soldier and officer felt himself lost.

Stories still persist that the quadrangular stockade construction of the first fort was less to keep Indians out than to keep the soldiers in. Local "hog ranches" were operated by mixed-blood Cherokees next to the reservation. Gambling and drinking went full blast as long as soldiers and their money were available.

The post commander strictly forbade the troops from remaining outside of the reservation after retreat had been sounded. He reinforced the order with 10-foot-high pickets on two sides of the stockade. "Where there were no pickets, the windows are grated with iron thus giving the barracks the appearance of a dilapidated Arkansas jail," the post quartermaster reported.

Jefferson Davis was stationed here as a lieutenant and it was here that he was court-martialed in 1834 and left the Army. A lieutenant at the time, he was accused by the Dragoon commander of failing to attend the reveille formation. When pressed for a reason for his failure, the official court-martial record charged that "the said Lt. Davis did in a highly disrespectful, insubordinate, and contemptuous manner, abruptly turn upon his heel and walk off saying at the same time, 'Hum.'"

Apparently the court did not agree that "hum" was disrespectful, insubordinate, and contemptuous. It found Davis not guilty. This seems to have been the

**FIRST FORT GIBSON** was a stockade but many buildings were on outside. Stockade was 230 feet square and contained both officer and enlisted quarters, though some officers owned and lived in their own homes on other side of stockade. (Redrawn from NPS plat.)

**NEW FORT GIBSON** was on hill overlooking fort. This ground plan does not hint at the two different levels on which forts stood. Most of the buildings of second post are in evidence today, many of them occupied as private residences.

FORT GIBSON
OKLA.-1840

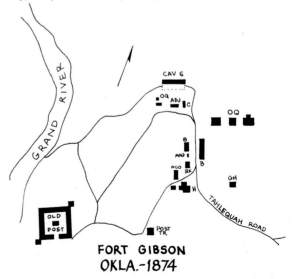

FORT GIBSON
OKLA.-1874

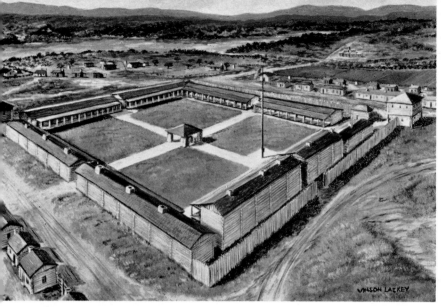

incident that pushed him into resigning, although General Arbuckle held his undated resignation for months in an effort to dissuade him.

The site on the bottomlands drew continual complaints. The Army Inspector in 1840 reported that it was so run down it could not be "defended against any force we could not meet in the open field . . . The stores of all kinds are in houses outside of the garrison . . . the magazine is inside the pickets, but is not large enough to contain more than half the powder. The rest is left in the block houses and one of the barracks rooms, at the hazard of blowing up the whole concern."

An 1837 newspaper article complained, "Fort Gibson is beyond question the most unhealthy post within our borders, and has been kept up at sacrifice of life greatly exceeding the advantages which have resulted from its location . . . All the officers who have visited it . . . view it as the 'graveyard of the Army.' "

In 1834, 163 Gibson Dragoons d i e d, including those killed in skirmishes and by disease.

Finally after 20 years in the old fort, work began in 1845 on the new site. By March, 1846, a two-company barracks was near completion when the sawmill burned, stopping all work. Then the steamboat bringing a new

mill upriver sank far downstream, causing further delay. The barracks walls stood for 10 years and were still unfinished when the post was abandoned in 1857. Only a commissary storehouse was finished by this time.

The Cherokee tribe claimed ownership of the land and buildings under an old treaty and took possession.

With the Civil War, in 1863 the hill above the fort was occupied by a total of 3,150 soldiers and six cannon. Earthworks were extended one and a quarter miles long embracing 15 to 17 acres. Originally the name "Fort Blunt" was attached to the new defenses, honoring Major General James G. Blunt, commanding the Union forces in the District of the Frontier. Later the Gibson tag was resurrected.

The post was the most fortified in the territory, served as its headquarters, and by mid-1863 had 6,014 men and 18 cannon. The post was manned almost continually until 1890 and temporary camps used the buildings in 1897 and 1901.

TO GET THERE: In the town of Fort Gibson, take its Main Street north and it will run right into stockade reconstructed by state. Second site is on hill to east, winding road from in front of stockade goes up hill.

ROTTING OF LOGS at Fort Gibson took place faster than they could be replaced. This view is of the outside of the stockade facing the river.

**FORT GIBSON** today is reconstructed stockade built by state and WPA. Double-storied officers' quarters are across parade ground, right, blockhouse is in center, enlisted barracks at left. Magazine was a base of blockhouse. Edge of well house is at right. It was here that Sam Houston stayed in 1829 and married a Cherokee girl. He was here until he began his work in Texas.

**PARADE GROUND** at old Fort Gibson today does not hint at high death rate in fort's early days. In its first 11 years, the toll was 561 men and nine officers. Despite this, times were lively at fort. An 1842 inspection tells of a race track where wagers sometimes included high stakes. It also mentions nearby "hog ranches" managed by "pretty Indian women bootleggers."

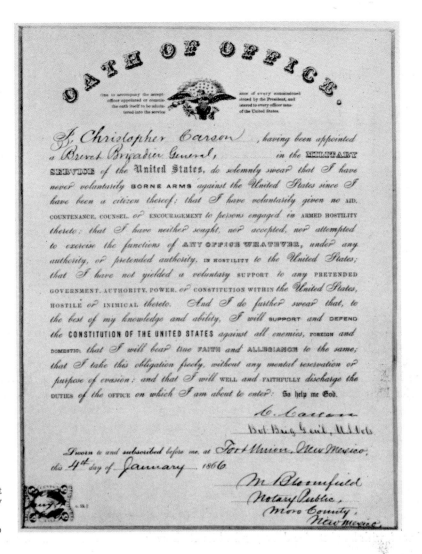

**HIS APPOINTMENT** as a brevet brigadier general was taken by Kit Carson in January, 1866.

(NATIONAL ARCHIVES.)

# THEY CALLED HIM "KIT"

*"He is small-sized with blue eyes and sandy hair, but has a heart of first magnitude. He is ever ready to sacrifice his all for a friend in need, and his name is a terror to the Indians."*

—Ex-Dragoon Sgt. James A. Bennett writing of visiting Kit Carson in 1854.

LEGEND SURROUNDED him even in his own lifetime, so that the real Kit Carson was lost somewhere between cold logic and campfire tale telling.

He came to the west from Kentucky and Missouri, a teenage saddler's apprentice who listened enraptured to the stories of the trappers and traders. Sixteen years old, he joined a Santa Fe caravan in 1826 and quickly impressed the unimpressionable by amputating a wounded man's arm to prevent gangrene.

His contacts with Indians were close. He killed his first one in 1835, it is said, fought them in Canyon de Chelly in 1864 as a colonel. He married two of them, saw one die soon after their child was born. His second wife was the belle of the Indian village, but her extravagant ways taxed his resources. He was uncomplaining when she divorced him by throwing his equipment and him out of their quarters at Bent's Old Fort.

He married again, this time to Charles Bent's sister-in-law, and became the father of eight children. He lived a full life up to the end and less than a month before his death he made a trip to Washington to help the Ute Indians. At the same time he became a father again. He was 59 when he died, a legend of the frontier of the old West.

97

# CAMP NICHOLS, OKLAHOMA

An unlikely place for a honeymoon, but that is what Camp Nichols was to Mrs. Marion Russell in 1865.

The new bride of Lieutenant Richard D. Russell, Mrs. Russell had been married three months when her husband was ordered from Fort Union, New Mexico to "Cedar Bluffs or Cold Spring, on the Cimarron route to the States."

Here, by departmental order, Colonel Kit Carson was to "select and establish a camp . . . to have troops at that dangerous part of the route in order to give protection to trains passing to and from the States."

This was just the description to convince a 20-year-old girl that here was a fine place for a wedding trip!

Carson left Fort Union in early May, 1865, and Mrs. Russell followed in two weeks. Cautious Kit had refused to let her accompany the first contingent, but sent back a wagon train shortly. Lieutenant Russell headed it. He had orders to complete his business at Fort Union and return to the new post. The "business" came back with him.

The honeymoon suite was a tent similar to the others occupied at the new camp. Later the tents were replaced by stone buildings described by Mrs. Russell as being "half in the ground and half above, and had dirt roofs supported by logs."

She wrote that these buildings were outside of the fort while "the soldiers, some 300 in number, slept in tents and dugouts within the enclosure . . .

"Our house consisted of two stone rooms, dirt floor and roof, with blankets for doors, and white cloth over the window frame in place of glass. Our water was brought from the stream some 600 feet away, in buckets, and a soldier in our company was assigned us as cook."

The furnishings were of the same decor as the rustic building, she remembered: "simple." She added that "our bed was made from a log six feet long slit in two and laid on the floor, then covered with boughs and blankets. A folding Army table with no chairs completed the list."

The post was so short-lived that latter-day comforts did not have time to arrive. It was constantly on the alert and every night mounted pickets were sent two miles east and west to give the alarm in the event of Indian attack. Indian-wise Carson kept sentinels roaming between the post and the horizon on a 24-hour basis, and no Indians dared attack. They wisely decided it was safer to do their raiding against targets more poorly defended.

Mrs. Russell's tent was about 50 feet from Carson's. She once wrote her impressions of the 15 days he spent at Nichols before he was summoned back to Fort Union on legal matters, not returning in time for the camp's abandonment in the fall of 1865.

"He was exceedingly kind and courteous to me," she remembered, "a man short of stature, slow of speech, and sparing in conversation, though ever solicitous of our comfort. He visited much with us, and I remember his crude English, 'whar' for where and 'thar' for there.

"I do not recall that he superintended to any great extent the work of the soldiers, which seemed to go on with the regularity of clockwork."

She said he spent most of his time in his tent. The sides were usually rolled up and she remembers that often he was lying on his bed scanning the horizon for Indians.

Shortly after her arrival, Mrs. Russell rode out an Oklahoma rainstorm without difficulty, but not so her famous neighbor. Carson's tent collapsed about him and "he had to call the sergeant of the guard to come and get him out," she added.

**CAMP NICHOLS OKLA.–1865**

**MOUNTAIN HOWITZERS** were placed at corners in Camp Nichols to command approaches. Fort was on a ridge that gave it excellent defense. Cannon were fired only once, however: during Fourth of July celebration in 1865. Flagpole was 100 feet south of gate; Kit Carson's tent was left of it. A grave south of fort was of a New Mexican Cavalry Volunteer who died in 1865 and sandstone cross, three feet high, lasted until turn of century. Stockade was 200 feet square, had 20-foot-wide flagstone walk in center on which horses were hitched. (Redrawn from plat courtesy Jack C. Johnson, Jr., Boise City, Okla.)

**NORTHERN SIDE** of Camp Nichols, looking from howitzer position toward western corner. Low walls still remain and area of corner "blockhouse" still is built up. Contemporary reports also says that 12-foot-wide ditch surrounded stockade on three sides, giving it a moat effect.

Camp Nichols brought a touch of security to the desolate stretch from the Arkansas to Fort Union. It fielded 50-man details to guard wagon trains and the usual orders were to stay with the train if attacked, corral the wagons, and fight back. This tactic replaced the previous policy of roving patrols. These were intended to keep the Indian on his toes and to remind him that he would have to answer to the Army for his transgressions, but they did not accomplish what was desired.

The Indians attacked trains whenever the Army was gone. The answer was to form large trains and have soldiers go along. The attack rate plummeted.

The Army Quartermaster Inspector recommended in 1865, "A permanent camp or post should be established on this route at or near the present one of Colonel Carson's where fuel and water can be procured in sufficient quantities."

Despite the suggestion that a cavalry and two infantry companies be stationed permanently at Camp Nichols, nothing came of it. Camp Nichols was abandoned in November, 1865.

**ONLY THREAT** to Camp Nichols was this ridgeline to northeast. Howitzer could rake it with grapeshot and longevity of any Indian snipers there would be short. Rock ruins are of house built outside of wall.

SANTA FE TRAIL ruts pass a mile south of Camp Nichols. This was Cimarron cutoff, abandoned due to westward advance of railroad which also doomed the post. Shallow trough running up center of picture is 40 feet wide.

TO GET THERE: Take blacktop road that runs straight west from Boise City, Oklahoma, for 15 miles. It turns left, then one-half mile later, right, to Wheelus, seven more miles. One mile past Wheelus turn right on dirt road marked possibly by temporary sign erected by Boy Scouts. Take this dirt road a mile north, go through gate (close it after!), and follow tracks bearing left. They will cross Santa Fe Trail ruts. In three-quarters of a mile, track dips into ravine, then out. Bear right to stone mounds, Camp Nichols. Access in fair weather only.

AN INDIAN ATTACKER would have this view of Camp Nichols from southeast. In foreground are ruins of a rock house; to rear is hospital corner of fort proper.

# FORT STANTON, NEW MEXICO

If there was one thing that Fort Stanton was not, probably the word for it was: "quiet."

From the day it began back in 1855 almost to when it became a hospital in 1896, this relatively isolated post saw the comings and goings of a variety of malcontents, Indians, characters, and the like.

Proof that it started with a bang appears in a soldier's diary of the period, under an entry for March 19, 1855: "Arrived at an encampment of United States Soldiers, 300 men under the command of Lieut. Col. Dixon S. Miles. They are here for the purpose of building a fort to be called Fort Stanton in commemoration of the captain who was killed three months ago. General John Garland selected the site for the fort today. The officers all got drunk."

With this auspicious beginning, it is almost surprising to note that an entry for August 13, five months later, records considerable progress for the fort. "The fort is now going up fast," he wrote. "Quarters are already built for eight officers, one company of men, a guardhouse, the commissary and quartermaster's store rooms, etc. Soldiers are all at work."

Haste might have had something to do with it—or the quality of materials—but the guardhouse proved something less than satisfactory. It was five weeks old when two prisoners casually dug through the wall and escaped.

Although at first it had two blockhouses, Fort Stanton never was a fortified post. Indians and settlers had fairly free passage around it. In 1856 a supposed Mexican girl was able to receive shelter in it after claiming she had escaped from eight months of Apache captivity. After being cleaned up, she was housed with one of the laundresses.

The next morning she was gone, along with most of the laundress' clothing. It was assumed that she had been put up to the trick by her Indian allies.

When the Civil War came, Fort Stanton was abandoned. The capture of the Fort Fillmore garrison caused the soldiers at Stanton to move to Albuquerque. Confederates burned the post on their arrival, and only the corrals and the building walls were left.

Colonel Kit Carson brought his volunteers to Stanton in 1862. It was his headquarters during expeditions against the Mescalero Apaches. He also put his men to rebuilding the post, but they settled for

mere utilitarian occupancy. The post surgeon in 1870 reported upon arrival, "These dilapidated walls were rudely and temporarily repaired on the reoccupation of the post, and with earth floors, earth roofs in the barracks, constituted the quarters of the troops until the present time."

Things were too active for fort building, apparently. Carson conducted a vigorous campaign against the Mescaleros. Despite the departmental commander's order to kill all the braves "whenever and wherever they can be found," Carson granted them sanctuary at Stanton. In the Battle of Dog Cañon, 500 Apaches—including 100 warriors—were routed by California Volunteers. They fled to Fort Stanton and surrendered to Carson.

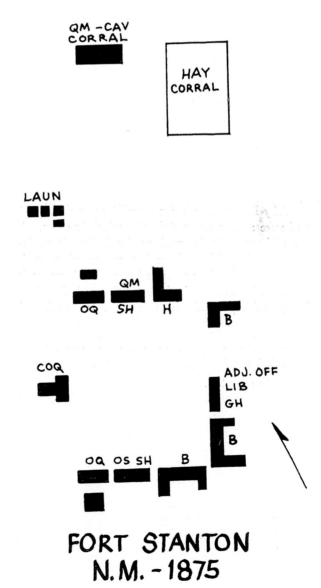

FORT STANTON
N.M. - 1875

**REBUILT FORT STANTON** dates from 1868. Stone buildings replaced adobe and log affairs of Civil War period. Ultimately officers' quarters filled row where commanding officer's house is shown. Sites of these buildings exist today, although modern hospital construction now covers south end of parade ground. (Redrawn from Division of Missouri Report, 1876.)

**PARADE GROUND IN 1885** was scene of dress parade by 6th Cavalry and 13th Infantry. Commanding officer's residence is at right, officers' quarters and storehouse to rear. Thirty years before, Stanton was considered to have best quarters in the Army at the time.

As the Civil War continued, Indian forays against the post also continued. The horse and mule herd from the fort was stolen in 1864. The mail runner was ambushed and had to take to the hills, leaving his mules and mail to the Indians. Another time two soldiers' bodies were found, one tied to a stake where apparently he had been roasted alive.

Fifty Indians attacked a 15-soldier patrol in 1864 and were able to sweep right through their camp. A several-hour fight followed as the Indian force increased to 200. When the soldiers ran out of ammunition, they broke their rifles in half and split up, each making his own way back to the fort. A few days later, an Army detachment chased the Indians for 45 miles, finally captured eight livestock and plunder but no Indians.

After the war, Stanton was host to General Lew Wallace, of *Ben Hur* fame, General (then Lieutenant) John J. Pershing, and a William Bonney, alias Billy the Kid. The "Kid" stayed overnight in the fort guardhouse. It is one of the few jails from which he did not escape—obviously it had been rebuilt after the walls were punched out in 1855.

TO GET THERE: Take U.S. 380 west from Roswell, N.M., for about 66 miles to turnoff (left) marked for Fort Stanton State Tuberculosis Hospital. Fort site, location of hospital, is about five miles south alongside of road.

**PARADE GROUND** today has trees and bushes virtually hiding old buildings. This view is similar to that of 1885; commanding officer's residence and officers' quarters at far end of parade ground still can be recognized.

**"OLD BARRACKS"** noted on plat at eastern corner looks like this today. Basic construction and shape remain, even to the wing to rear, but building now serves as headquarters for state hospital. Post was garrisoned into 1890's to keep watch on Mescalero and Jicarello Apaches living at reservation nearby.

# FORTS MASSACHUSETTS AND GARLAND, COLORADO

Kit Carson was a peacetime soldier and a brevet brigadier general when he took command of Fort Garland in 1866. That did not mean there was no Indian and bandit fighting to do, but now the North and South were doing it side by side. And the old guide and Indian agent had mellowed enough that he stayed with the Army, at least for a time.

Fort Garland was not new to him, nor he to it. The post dated from 1852 when, as Fort Massachusetts, it had been located six miles to the north. It was "placed too near the spur of the mountain for a good defense against an enterprising enemy," as the Army inspection report in 1853 commented. In 1858 it was relocated and renamed.

At the new site, the post quickly took on the appearance which was to remain until the present day.

**MANY OF THESE** buildings remain today, most of them restorations although civilian owner after 1883 conscientiously tried to retain Army appearance. Three of the five officers' quarters remain. Only major element missing from parade grounds is western barracks on northern edge; plans to place a replica here await funds. (Redrawn from Division of Missouri report 1876.)

Unlike most other forts, Garland underwent a minimum of changes and the same flat adobe buildings served from 1858 until it was abandoned in 1883.

Until the Civil War, Garland was involved in Indian chasing and parlays with chiefs over poor rations from the Indian agents. The war brought volunteer forces to the post. Almost the entire garrison was involved in stemming the Confederate advance in the Battle of Glorieta Pass in 1862.

While the militia was at the post, the regular soldiers found it hard to accept these unmilitary and untrained near-civilians. It seemed that not a complete uniform was shared by the entire company, and one unit could lay claim to only a single overcoat.

Legend has it that the company commander noticed this same coat always on the guard. Not knowing it was passed from man to man, he accused the first sergeant of keeping the same man on permanent sentry duty.

"No, be jabers," the sergeant answered, it was not the same man "but the same coat kivers the whole company now."

One of the nastiest affairs encountered by Fort Garland was the 1863 chase of Felipe Nerio Espinoza. He was a crazed bandit who had sworn to avenge the

**NOT ACTUALLY A FORTRESS,** despite blockhouse and apparent wall, Fort Massachusetts had fences connecting buildings, giving degree of security. This did not prevent Indians from firing into it from surrounding hills. Post was built by soldiers and about 125 usually were stationed here between 1852 and 1858. (Redrawn from Manfield report, 1853.)

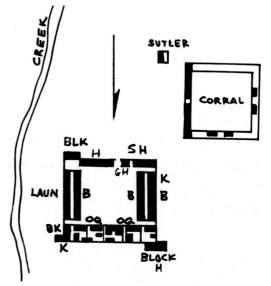

## FORT GARLAND COLO. - 1875

## FORT MASSACHUSETTS COLO. - 1853

FORT MASSACHUSETTS suffered more from isolation and sickness than from Indians. Its location on low ground caused much disease. Distant location meant that soldiers had to buy shoes and clothes from sutler at exorbitant prices because Army wagons could not get through. Nor could paymaster: Army inspection in 1853 revealed five-month gaps between paydays.

deaths of six of his relatives in the Mexican War a hundred times, 100 white men for each of his kin.

The Fort Garland area became his area of operations. He had passed the 40-killing mark when the Army was asked by the governor for help. Fifteen soldiers, a lieutenant, and Tom Tobin, veteran Indian scout, picked up his tracks from where a man and a girl had been ambushed and the girl raped.

After the large detachment scared Espinoza away once, Tobin managed to "lose" most of the soldiers and three days later came upon the bandit camp.

"I took a step or two in front and saw the head of one of the assassins," Tobin later wrote. At this time I stepped on a stick . . . he heard it crack and looked and saw me. He jumped up and grabbed his gun. Before he turned around fairly, I fired and hit him in the side . . .

"I tipped my powder horn in my rifle, dropped a bullet from my mouth into the muzzle of my gun while I was capping it. A fellow came out of the ravine, running to an undergrowth.

"I yelled, 'Shoot him, boy!' The others fired and missed him. I threw up my gun and broke his back above the hips."

To prove Espinoza was dead, and for evidence so he could collect the $2,500 bounty, Tobin whacked off the both bandits' heads with his hunting knife. Espinoza is said to have yelled after Tobin's first try with the knife, "Hurry! The knife you have is very dull."

The heads were taken to Fort Garland where they were pickled in alcohol and sent to Pueblo to await the Territorial Legislature's session and payment of the reward. The bottles broke enroute and, to preserve the heads, Tobin had to substitute bar whiskey. Ultimately he received $1,500, a handsome rifle and a buckskin suit.

When Carson arrived at Garland he found that the main concern was in keeping the peace with the Ute

FORT GARLAND in its final years reveals most buildings from plat. Hospital, large building at right edge, was condemned in 1870 by surgeon because adobe bricks in it were improperly dried and ceiling beams were placed too far apart. "In the wards, kitchen and dining room," he reported, "the majority of the beams are broken, requiring supports to be placed under them, and in the largest ward no less than five of these supports are required." One wall also needed braces.

Indians. Their chief, Ouray, had been to the White House and was convinced that the Indian way would have to change, but he was almost alone in his stand. General W. T. Sherman and Carson parlayed with Ouray at Fort Garland in 1866, and the combined influence of Carson and Ouray kept the peace. Finally almost 15 years later the Ute War occurred and more than 1,500 soldiers were at Garland, but this was long after Carson.

During Carson's stay at Garland, the post saw the tensions of the Civil War relaxed to those of an Indian War garrison. Carson prohibited the sale of liquor on the post, one of the less well-received of his decisions.

One of his captains waited until Carson was absent for a few hours one day. Proclaiming himself "acting commanding officer," which technically he was, he told the sutler to open up the liquor sales. He bought a 10-gallon supply for himself.

When Carson returned, the captain explained that he had no copy of Army Regulations with him so he had proceeded according to common sense. And besides that, if Carson did not like it, well, he could countermand it . . . there was not any more liquor left.

**SOLDIER'S THEATER** is inside rebuilt eastern barracks, and backdrop is original. Although faded, it was visible when restoration started, and modern methods brought out its colors. This is inside former cavalry barracks, and is little known facet of frontier soldier life.

TO GET THERE: Take U.S. 160 east from Alamosa, Colo., 25 miles to town of Fort Garland. Post site, now a Colorado State Historical Monument, is just south of the intersection with State 159 in the center of town. State 159 passes within 20 yards of the post. Massachusetts site is reached by dirt road two miles west of town and six miles north of U.S. 160.

**FLAGPOLE AND** its man-high flag, dwarf commanding officer's house at Garland. Kit Carson lived in this building, and here he and General Sherman met with Chief Ouray. Mount Blanca, in background, is same mountain that overlooked Fort Massachusetts, six miles north.

**OFFICERS' ROW** has been restored but original adobe-making methods were used in reconstruction. Local women spent countless hours working mud into crevices between adobe brick to give walls smooth appearances, the same method of 100 years ago.

# FORT LYON, COLORADO

The road had been a long one for Kit Carson. Trapper, trader, guide, Indian agent, general, and sage . . . Christopher Carson had come a long way, accomplished a great deal, lived a full life. He came to Fort Lyon to die.

In 1868, his wife died in giving birth to their seventh child. His failing health found it hard to accept her death. Leaving his six children and the baby with relatives in Boggsville—where he had located so he would be near the doctor at Fort Lyon—he moved to the fort. It was across the Arkansas and almost opposite Boggsville.

The post surgeon examined him and announced he had pneumonia. The great scout knew the end was near. In a tiny cabin behind the barracks, he had his last meal and died while smoking his last pipe.

"The flags at the fort were lowered to half mast and preparations were made for the last rites," according to the official history of the post. "The wife of one of the captains stationed at the fort contributed her wedding dress to line a rough board coffin, and other officers' wives removed flowers from their bonnets to provide a covering for the casket.

"Friends at Fort Lyon and Boggsville provided a funeral with full military honors and he was buried beside his wife in the garden of relatives in Boggsville." Later, the bodies were moved to Taos, New Mexico, as he desired, and today are buried in the Kit Carson Memorial Park . . . appropriately at the end of Dragoon lane which extends north from Kit Carson Avenue.

The house in which Carson died was one of the temporary officers' quarters erected hastily when Fort Lyon was built in 1867. The earlier post, also known as Fort Wise and Bent's New Fort, was flooded out and the move, long contemplated, became a matter of necessity.

The temporary quarters, one of which Carson occupied, were of limestone and mud, with board roofs, measured 24 by 54 feet and nine feet high. By 1875 when permanent officers' quarters were built, the temporaries were turned over to the laundresses who were employed by the cavalry companies at the post.

The fort was on a sandstone bluff 36 feet above the Arkansas. About 2,000 feet wide by 1,500 long, the bluff was surrounded on its southern and eastern edges by the river, an objectionable matter when the spring floods left stagnant water on the lowland below, but an advantage from the viewpoint of a water supply.

Energy marked construction of the post and the enlisted men were pressed into duties as carpenters, bricklayers, stone masons and general handymen. This occasionally backfired as when, for example, sandstone and adobe used in the bakery collapsed and the entire place had to be rebuilt.

The post surgeon was impressed with the Arkansas as a water source, but his pet project was to tap the river about six miles upstream. A canal from that point would have sufficient flow to bring water right into the fort, he theorized, but almost as quickly discarded the idea.

"In order to dig the ditch, a full garrison would be required," he decided, "and the men detailed on ditch-digging would, in all probability fail to see the future benefits enjoyed by their successors."

Fort Lyon was on the outskirts of the Indian War of 1868 and never really got into active fighting. Patrols from it "indicated that the regiment had maintained its well-earned reputation for dash and bravery in Indian warfare," according to the 5th Cavalry historian, however.

One of these was a battalion-size expedition led by General Eugene A. Carr which had originated at Fort Harker, Kansas, in October, 1868. It spent three

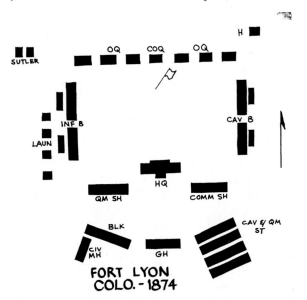

FORT LYON
COLO. - 1874

**OFFICER'S WIFE** wrote that in 1870's Fort Lyon was unlike Eastern posts because "there is no high wall around it." She said, "It reminds one of a prim little village built around a square, in the center of which there is a high flagstaff and a big cannon. The buildings are very low and broad and are made of adobe—a kind of clay and mud mixed together—and the walls are very thick. At every window there are heavy wooden shutters, that can be closed during severe sand and wind storms." Another item she noted was the reveille formation, "when a big gun was fired that must have wasted any amount of powder . . . then three or four bugles played a little air, which was impossible to hear because of the horrible howling and crying of dogs." She later asked post commander "Why soldiers required such a beating of drums and deafening racket generally, to awaken them in the morning?" (Redrawn from Surgeon-General Circular No. 8, 1875.)

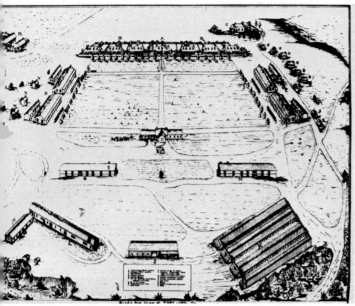

(SURGEON-GENERAL CIRCULAR NO. 8, 1875.)

**FORT LYON** in 1875 was almost complete. Kit Carson's final residence, one of the buildings behind barracks at top right, was now occupied by laundresses. Today most of the officers' quarters and the two storehouses, on opposite side of post, remain. Son of Army officer living at Fort in 1885 wrote later that their quarters were "adobe with walls two feet thick. We had a tin lined bathtub in the house and the water was heated by a water barrel back of the kitchen stove."

days at Fort Lyon, then on December 2 left on a 79-day march into New Mexico, Texas and Oklahoma. One company marched 75 miles in 26 hours during a blinding snowstorm.

The historian had good comments on this movement, even though it ended "without having encountered hostile Indians or accomplished any material results . . . the companies were conspicuous for their energy, untiring pursuit, and rapid movements."

TO GET THERE: Take U.S. 50 east from Las Animas, Colorado, to County road 183. Turn right, road runs into Fort Lyon Veterans Administration Hospital, one mile.

**FLAGPOLE** at Fort Lyon has unusual bell at its base—unusual, that is, for a fort. Commemorating use of post by Navy between 1906 and 1922, it is a ship's bell inscribed "U. S. Naval Hospital, Fort Lyon, Colorado, 1907." Commanding officer's former residence is in background and, now remodeled, is occupied by superintendent of hospital. In 1956, hospital was honored by American Psychiatric Association as the one in U.S. and Canada that contributed most toward care and treatment of neuropsychiatric patients.

**EARLY DATE** and construction of commissary building is shown by this marker, still in building. Kirk served in Department of the Cumberland in Civil War in charge of transportation in Chattanooga and Nashville, and was breveted major for meritorious service.

**KIT CARSON DIED HERE**. Marker in foreground came from Fort Wise apparently, considering its 1860 date. Building now is chapel used mainly for funeral services.

**ORIGINAL STORE HOUSES** still serve same purpose. These show on old view and plat south of parade ground. Commissary department used near building, quartermaster was in far warehouse. Except for occasional bricked-up window, buildings look exactly like those in early sketch. They are 100 feet long, 42 wide.

# THE COMMANDERS

*"It was in these posts in quiet seasons that the Western soldier was formed—a strong, brave man of many resources and vast endurance, loyal to his country and his officers, willing to follow not only where they led, but to stay with them to the end, no matter how hopeless the end looked."*

—Forsyth's *The Story of the Soldier*, 1905.

MOST OF the Southwestern forts were garrisons of a company or two. They had short careers and small areas of influence. When their job was done, or when they were found wanting, they were abandoned and the troops went elsewhere.

Some forts had a permanence and importance they extended far beyond the limits of patrols. These were the places from which the campaigns of the Southwest were directed. Here the plans were devised, the supplies gathered, the commanders briefed, and the orders promulgated.

Many could claim the title "headquarters" for varying periods during their existence, but some carried it almost throughout their existence. Some carry it even today.

The brains and the breadbaskets of the Southwest Army were at these headquarters forts. Sometimes they looked just like any other fort, but usually they were larger, more impressive, more comfortable, and always more influential. These were the commanders in the winning of the Southwest.

# FORT LEAVENWORTH, KANSAS

Uncertainty marked the early days of Fort Leavenworth. At first it was 12 miles north of the present location. Even after it found a home, its unhealthy condition was such that the Army considered using it as a camp for winter use only.

One thing above all else weighed in its favor. Its location as the portal to the West, and midway in the frontier chain of forts, caused it to become the most important military fort in the westward movement. This gave it a longevity and permanence virtually unmatched.

The tent camp pitched by Colonel Henry Leavenworth in 1827 was a far cry from today's modern post. It was on the west bank of the Missouri near the mouth of the Little Platte River. Evidence of it remains today in remnants of a stone wall built in 1827. Intended to defend against Indians, this wall has slits from which muskets could be fired.

Disease struck the founders of Fort Leavenworth. Of the 200 men in its garrison, only 92 could turn out for inspection on August 26, 1827. On another occasion, of the 174 men at the post, 65 were taking care of the 77 sick. Only 32 were left for post duties. It was at this time that many of the men were sent to Jefferson Barracks, Missouri, for the summer and thoughts were entertained of making Leavenworth a post for use only in the winter.

But the press of military requirements dictated otherwise. The post was too busy for part-time occupation what with Indians, marauding bandits, wagon trains, and whiskey runners.

This last occupation kept Leavenworth soldiers especially busy. All Missouri river steamers had to stop for inspection at Leavenworth. Troops scrutinized all baggage carefully to insure that no alcohol was being smuggled into Indian lands.

Prince Maximilian of Weid was subject to this search in 1832 and later he wrote, "We were stopped at this place and our vessel searched for brandy, the importing of which into Indian Territory is prohibited; they would scarce permit us to take a small portion to preserve our specimens of natural history."

Apparently the whiskey problem was not confined to smuggling attempts. A post tradition began early that all returning patrols received a speech before being dismissed, the speech being equally divided between compliments on their patrol behavior and warnings about the use of alcohol.

Not long after the post began, Zadock Martin received a license to operate ferries across the Missouri and Little Platte Rivers. He supplemented his income by also operating a two-room saloon next to the Little Platte ferry. A few years later he asked that civilian contractors be allowed to farm the fort's gardens to relieve the soldiers of such chores. The commanding officer suspected it was a plot to move the saloon closer to the source of demand and turned him down.

The Army took definite steps in 1837 to end the illicit hog ranch-type business that had surrounded the post. A reservation of 6,000 acres was declared. This meant that such places as the "Rialto" would have to be vacated. This was a notorious place near Weston, Missouri, where the ferry landed. It had a counterpart on the other side, nearer to the fort. Both had to be vacated when the reservation boundaries were approved in 1838, and the saloonkeepers and their associates had to move out.

Almost every western expedition and western trail had something to do with Fort Leavenworth. From the soldier point of view, probably one of the best was the Dodge expedition of 1835. This took three companies of Dragoons 1,600 miles in three and a half

**FORT LEAVENWORTH KANSAS - 1869**

LACK OF DEFENSES caused early Army Inspector to complain that there was "as much propriety in calling this place Fort Leavenworth as there would be in calling an armed schooner a line of battleships." Post did have wall located north of sutler in this plat, and blockhouses were erected here and opposite corner of parade ground. First tent camp of 1827 era was north of Arsenal area. Plat exaggerates size of hospital; actually this shows entire hospital compound of nine buildings. (Redrawn from Surgeon General report, 1870.)

months, covering as far west as the Rockies without losing a single man. What is more, when it returned, the colonel was presented with a sword, the officers with a brace of pistols apiece, and every enlisted man got a month's extra pay.

One of its earliest expeditions was that of Major Bennett Riley to the Mexican border in 1829. On this trip he first proved the value of the oxen, the beast of burden for many later westward wagon trains. The border at this time was at the Arkansas River, but on one occasion Riley answered calls for help on the other side and forded across to Mexico to fend off an Indian attack. There was no thought of diplomatic action by either country.

When Riley reached Choteau's Island on the Arkansas, he waited for the Santa Fe train he was supposed to protect. When it appeared, it was accompanied by a Mexican Army escort, commanded by the Army's Inspector General himself. Everyone sat down to an exchange of international courtesies.

"Seated cross-legged around a green blanket in the bottom of the tent," later wrote Philip St. George Cooke, "we partook of bread, buffalo meat, and as an extraordinary rarity, of some salt pork, but to crown all were several large onions for which we were indebted to our arriving guests. A tin cup of whiskey which, like the pork had been reserved for an unusual occasion, was followed by another of water."

He said there were Creoles, Spaniards, a company of Mexican Regulars, several tribes of Indians, many Mexicans, Frenchmen, "and our 180 hearty veterans in rags but well equipped for any service. Four or five languages were spoken. To complete the picture must be mentioned the 2,500 horses, mules and jacks which kept up an incessant braying."

The Mexican War put an end to border tete-a-tetes and Leavenworth was in the middle of it. General Kearney outfitted his Santa Fe expedition here and, as part of it, Colonel A. W. Doniphan mustered his Mounted Riflemen. In what was to become famed as "Doniphan's Expedition," his men were gone from Leavenworth for a year, going deep into Mexico on a 3,600-mile round trip and fighting two battles.

The Missouri Mounted Volunteers left Leavenworth in 1847, but only after considerable friction between their commander and the post commander. The latter refused to supply what the Volunteers needed so the former, Major William Gilpin, challenged him to a duel. Apparently this form of requisition was effective and the equipment was issued.

When Kansas was opened to settlers in 1854, Leavenworth found it was no longer an Army post in the wilderness. Now it was surrounded by farmers, eager land grabbers, speculators, and politicians. The Territorial governor preferred its protective defenses

**HEADQUARTERS OF FORT LEAVENWORTH** actually is f o u r buildings. Center arch building was erected in 1916; Grant Hall with clock tower dates from 1904. Buildings flanking archway are named after Generals Sherman and Sheridan, were built in 1859 as shops in Leavenworth Arsenal. Cannon is one of four Civil War 12-pounders marking site of first encampment.

(NATIONAL ARCHIVES.)

**EAST SIDE OF** parade ground in 1860's shows barracks torn down in 1905 and the so-called "Syracuse Houses" built in 1855 by workmen brought from Syracuse, New York. These two houses are left of barracks. Except for barracks, the other buildings remain today. Parade ground is still almost 495 feet square.

**SANTA FE AND OREGON** Trails both went up this route from Leavenworth's landing. Post also was on routes for Pony Express, Holliday Overland Stage, California Military Road or the Salt Lake Trail, and Butterfield's Overland Stage. It was also headquarters for Russell, Majors, Waddell transportation line that moved Army supplies to West. In 1858 more than 6,000 teamsters and 45,000 oxen were in their employ.

"TOO THIN TO SLICE, too thick to drink" was contemporary description of Missouri river at this point where it flows below Fort Leavenworth. Its course has shifted several times since fort was built. Original landing is now well within wooded bottomlands.

and conducted the first business of the territory in a building northeast of the parade ground.

The town of Leavenworth sprang up, using that name because the promoters thought people would buy lots under the misimpression they were purchasing fort property. Some Army officers bought into the town company despite the jealous protests of latecomers to the territory. Accused of using soldiers to build houses and of steering Army business to their town properties, the officers took their cases to an investigating committee which cleared them of any wrongdoing.

Robert E. Lee visited Leavenworth as a member of a court-martial in 1855. About the same time, civilian lawyer William T. Sherman—said to have lost the only law case he tried in town—contracted with the Army to assist in a road project.

The Civil War came close to Leavenworth. A lieutenant wrote home in 1856 that social affairs were segregated by pro- and anti-slavery factions, but the Army officers usually attended both, being considered neutral. He had definite opinions of the outcome of the political situation: "The fact is that the free-state

OLDEST BUILDING is the "Rookery," dating from 1831 but built on 1828 foundations. It still is occupied as officers' quarters, has some original interior construction. First governor of Kansas Territory lived in it in 1854. Rookery shows behind trees to left of Syracuse Houses in old photograph.

settlers outnumber all others five to one, and there is about as little chance of this being a slave state as there is of my flying in the air."

Both sides complained that the Army was helping the other, but the sentiment in the town was obvious. On April 18, 1861, when a river steamer flying the Confederate flag docked at the levee, the townspeople rushed to the wharf. They dragged up a rusty cannon and forced the captain to replace his colors with the Stars and Stripes. Three militia companies were soon mustered, and in all the town of Leavenworth sent 18 companies to the Union cause.

General Sterling Price's rebel force in Missouri threatened Leavenworth at one point and earthworks and an artillery redoubt were built at the post. Price was repulsed at the Battle of Westport, the so-called "Gettysburg of the West," and pursued south and east by Leavenworth troops.

Railroad protection, supplying the forts of the West, and commanding their tactical moves were the main postwar activities at Fort Leavenworth. The former Leavenworth lawyer, General Sherman, declared at this time:

"Fort Leavenworth is the most valuable military reservation in the West. It will always be the most appropriate depot and headquarters for a department, and should have barracks for a battalion of infantry, a regiment, and suitable buildings for headquarters."

Apparently Sherman's prediction is true. Leavenworth today is one of the Army's leading posts and the location of its Command and General Staff College, one of the world's foremost courses of military instruction.

TO GET THERE: Fort Leavenworth is immediately north of the town of Leavenworth, Kansas. Its entrance is at Metropolitan and Grant Avenues.

# FORT RILEY, KANSAS

Death and mutiny stalked the first days of Fort Riley. The courage of a few men, some of them civilians, stands out in a story of a post that almost died before it was born.

It was on May 17, 1853, that the site of Fort Riley was designated an Army post. Because it was near the geographical center of the United States, its first name was Camp Center. A month later it was renamed to honor Major General Bennett Riley, commander of the Santa Fe Trail's first escort and a hero of the Mexican war.

Building materials were freighted in from the East and in 1855 almost 500 laborers were brought in to erect the post. Unlike the forts that depended upon soldier labor, Riley was to go first class! The soldiers were sent off on an expedition and only a few remained at the post to supervise the work.

By July, 1855, one double-story stone building had been finished and work was progressing rapidly on several others. Suddenly on August 2, cholera struck the place. Major E. A. Ogden, the commanding officer, became ill. Panic spread.

The next day, death took nine workmen, Major Ogden, his orderly, two officers' wives and two children. That night, a gang of workmen broke into the post sutler house and helped themselves to a barrel of whiskey.

"When well liquored up," according to Percival G. Lowe, then first sergeant of the Dragoon troop, "and led by a big stonemason, some of them broke open the building used for the post ordnance department and armed themselves with guns, pistols, and ammunition."

About 25 of the ringleaders gathered on the parade ground "with their leader inside, while all sorts, drunk and sober, looked on." The men demanded their pay. The civilian contractor played for time by passing the request to Lowe, the senior military man not ill.

With an umbrella over his head because of the hot sun, Lowe approached the men. "I saw most of this valiant chief's followers were hopelessly drunk," he remembered. "I stepped into the circle and said to the leader, 'What is the matter?'

"He sprang back and leveled his pistol and if it had been at full cock I would have been shot. Up to this time I had no definite plan of action—had no arms and no fixed notion of what I would do . . . Dropping the umbrella, I seized his pistol, gave him a trip and a quick jerk and he fell so heavily the breath was knocked out of him.

"I had his pistol and threatened to kill him if he moved . . . With my left hand I jerked a gun from the nearest man, who was so drunk he fell over. Throwing the gun on the ground, I told the others to pile their guns and pistols on it.

"I never saw an order more promptly obeyed. The mutiny, or rebellion, so far as these men were concerned, was over."

The workers were divided into details, some tending the sick, others making coffins, others digging graves. The Army surgeon had hastily abandoned the post in fear of his own life, but a civilian doctor appeared and voluntarily took charge of the hospital. A newsparper correspondent passed by to check the rumors of the epidemic, and stayed to nurse the stricken.

The evening of the 4th and 5th, burning tar was placed around the post in the hope the fumes would serve as a disinfectant. By the 6th, the cholera seemed to have run its course.

More than 150 workers had deserted, between 75 and 100 more had died, but those left were reliable and responsible men. Lieutenant E. A. Carr and an Army doctor arrived on the 6th and took charge. The sickness was cleared up, and work on the post got underway with a vengeance. By mid-November, the work was so far along that the workmen were paid off and sent back East.

This first post was built around a parallelogram

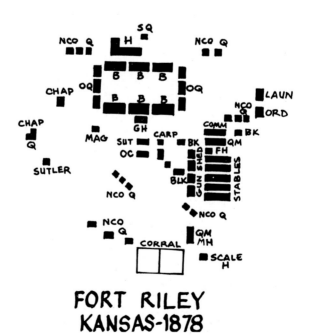

**FORT RILEY
KANSAS-1878**

LIMESTONE was used for most buildings that surrounded parade ground, 553 feet by 606. Barracks were double-storied, 88 by 40 feet, planned for one company apiece. Orderly room, kitchen, dining hall, storerooms were on first floor, while second floor was a one-room dormitory. Porches ran along front and rear of both stories. (Redrawn from Price, *History of Fort Riley*.)

FORT RILEY in 1885 showed construction work in progress at end of barracks row. Officers' quarters there were moved behind those at opposite end of parade ground. Except for this new construction, this photo matches plat of post 10 years earlier. General Sheridan visited Riley in 1885, and decision to expand and renovate it came at that time.

553 feet by 600. It included six two-story barracks, 40 by 88 feet, six two-story officers' quarters, five stables, a hospital, ordnance building, two-story guardhouse, and a brick magazine.

A ghost story grew up around one of the quarters, especially after occupants reported hearing the noise of chains being dragged down the stairs at night. One night, a woman's face was seen pressed against the kitchen window. A servant took immediate action: she heaved her iron through the pane, and quit her job.

The haunt supposedly was a former occupant of the quarters who had drowned herself in the well because of unrequited love. With the tales and incidents increasing, finally the residents had a Junction City priest perform the ancient rituals to "cast out" the spirit, and no further sightings were reported.

Although Riley's troopers were occupied with most of the Indian affairs as far west as Santa Fe, they also were concerned with politics. The Kansas of the 50's was torn by the anti- and pro-slavery forces. This affected the fort reservations, and the survey lines were shifted back and forth at political whim.

The first Kansas capitol was built at Pawnee next to the post, then Pawnee was torn down when the boundaries changed. Official action of the capitol was short—it had only one session, four days long. The capitol remained although its neighboring houses were taken apart, most of the material going into buildings at other settlements.

These settlements were the source of concern to the post commander and area law officers. At one of them, in 1862, a contemporary report states, "Thirteen barrels of whiskey were spilled, either by order of the provost marshal or someone else." The same report noted that at so-called "Whiskey Point," a fight netted two soldiers dead and one wounded, after which "the provost marshal, with a squad of men, went around and closed up every saloon in which intoxicating liquors were sold."

"Whiskey Point's" official name was West Point, but a traveling preacher gave it the first title, and the name stuck.

It had a longer life than most hog ranches. Ten years later, the post records note that on January 4, 1873, a fort detachment raided the Point "and succeeded in capturing a quantity of government property held by the venders of whiskey at the Point, as collateral for their wares."

Realizing that the place could not be legislated away, the post commander recognized the facts of life about this time. He had a rough bridge made between the fort and the Point. This reduced the danger of soldiers being drowned while returning to the fort after a saloon visit.

Junction City was the biggest town near the post. It went through its lurid phases, but a five-foot, nine-inch sheriff named Tom Allen kept things pretty much under control. Tales are told of Allen's besting a half-dozen soldiers in head-knocking sessions. He was impartial in his justice, imparting it freely to all law-breakers, military and civilian.

The "red-light" area of Junction City was well policed by Allen. He suppressed all outside displays and in at least one case took direct action when crossed. It seems that one new recruit at infamous "Madame Blue's" resort decided to advertise by swinging on the madam's front gate. After warning her twice, Allen went into the house and threw her trunk out of the second story window, sash, glass, and all. She was on the next train, having learned that the lesson in Junction City was that it did not pay to advertise.

Riley's official activities in the Civil War were first involved with asserting the local supremacy of the United States. Junction City's southern element decreed that the U. S. flag should not be flown. Captain J. R. McClure settled this by running up the colors himself and then making an impassioned speech for the Union in the town square. He also recruited one of Kansas' first militia companies, and commanded it later.

Some Confederate prisoners of war were kept at Riley. The post's main concern was keeping Indian hostilities at a minimum, a mission that it pursued until the end of the frontier. After the war, the 7th Cavalry was organized at Riley. Later, as the Army's cavalry center, it played major roles in all western incidents, directly or indirectly.

Despite all of this, not everyone was impressed. Or at least that is the tenor of a story told of a new private at Riley during the Civil War. The private was accosted by the post commander one day when he failed to salute. In trying to explain the matter of saluting, and who he was, the major identified himself as the commander of the post.

The private, a chip off the Blarney stone, was hardly impressed. "An sure," he said, "It's a damned good place av yer a mind to kape it."

WOUNDED KNEE affair is memorialized by this marker. Battle in 1890 was fought in South Dakota by 7th Cavalrymen from Fort Riley and was final major engagement with Indians. Thirty officers and men and 200 Indians died in what most accounts have termed a "massacre." Monument was erected in 1893 by fellow members of 7th Cavalry.

TO GET THERE: From Junction City, Kansas, take State 18 directly into the fort, about four miles.

FIRST TERRITORIAL capitol of Kansas is on Fort Riley reservation. Its claim to political fame is tenuous. Only a single session was held here, from July 2 to 6, 1855. Then Free Staters were ousted by proslavery majority and session adjourned to Shawnee Mission. This is rear of building; front faces on river, right rear.

CUSTER LIVED here when he was second in command of Fort Riley in 1867. His reputation as teetotaler is upheld in old records of post store. Charge accounts show purchases of whiskey by most of garrison but Custer's name does not have any liquor tab. Building is 60 by 40 feet and still is a duplex. Kitchens were in rear and building had a cellar.

# FORT SILL, OKLAHOMA

From the blockhouse atop Signal Mountain, a detachment doublechecked the cloud of dust 20 miles to the south. Their field glasses confirmed their suspicions. They heliographed on to Fort Sill: "General Sherman's party sighted."

With this opening, the most dramatic 17 days in the history of Fort Sill were about to start. They would be days to overshadow all that had come before and, in their contribution to the lore of the West, all to follow.

At the time, Fort Sill was but a small fragment of the modern Army post of today. Guided missiles and computer-operated artillery were unknown at the time and Fort Sill's role was that of a cavalry post and Indian peacekeeper.

It had been founded by the freezing troopers of Sheridan's command in 1869. Alternately washed and frozen out of their Fort Cobb camp 30 miles north, Sheridan had moved his forces to this site near Medicine Bluffs. His 19th Kansas Volunteer Cavalry regiment laid out a tent camp nearby, decorating it with brush and trees—which did not last long considering they were chopped off above the roots and merely inserted in the ground.

They also boasted a race track but spent most of a month at the spot grumbling about the scant ration of unsalted meat and 10 crackers a day. When it came time to name the place, the Kansans suggested "Camp Starvation."

The 7th Cavalry was closer to the fort site and, under Custer, was more favored in the matter of tentage and food. Their recommendation for a name was Fort Elliott, after the major killed in the Battle of the Washita.

But Sheridan selected the name of a classmate killed in the Battle of Stone River, although the place also had been going under two other names for a short while: Camp at Medicine Bluff Creek and Camp Wichita.

Sheridan and Custer took their troops away on March 2, 1869, shortly afterward finishing the Winter Campaign after considerable parlaying with the Indians. General Benjamin Grierson was left in command of the new post with the first order of the day being to build a fort.

The canvas-covered wooden frames quickly were replaced by low log or slab buildings reminiscent of a hundred other frontier posts. Grierson was given more elaborate quarters made of pickets. A cottonwood log building served as a storehouse and General Hazen lived in an adobe building.

By the following year, these were replaced by stone structures built of local material. The limestone, lime, plaster and sand ingredients all came from within a mile of the flagpole. Civilian and soldier artisans turned to enthusiastically when it was obvious that this was to become a permanent post where they would be for a long time.

The Indians were not content to let the builders work in peace, however. The Indian agent, Lawrie Tatum, had bowed to the objections of his Quaker leaders and rejected the Army offer of military protection, a step enthusiastically approved by the Indians. So pleased were they by the absence of troops from the Agency, in fact, that at the first beef issue they carted off 30 more beeves than was their ration.

With impunity, the Kiowas and Comanches harassed the Agent and the nearby fort. One night they crawled into the Sill mule corral and shot at the two soldier guards. The latter made the mile run to the guardhouse in record time while the Indians proceeded to steal the entire herd.

To prevent any reoccurrences of this, Grierson built a fort-like stone corral. The walls were loopholed in the event it had to be defended, and this picturesque landmark remains to this day.

By 1871 the Indians were so wild that most Agency

FORT SILL
OKLA. –1874

**ALMOST ALL OF** these buildings are in use today, although modern headquarters is located at site of cavalry stables. Main post was on half-mile square plateau. Each barracks, 200 by 30 feet, housed two companies with kitchen, supply room, and messroom in wings to rear. Redoubt was built in 1872 to defend post against sudden Indian rushes from southwest. Chapel was added after date of this plat and is at northeast corner of parade ground. (Redrawn from National Archives data.)

**FORT SILL IN 1880** as it looked from hospital shows officers' row on left, rear of barracks, right. Guardhouse in which Satanta, Satank, and Big Tree were imprisoned is at right edge of picture. In later years Geronimo spent nights here for safekeeping while he slept off hangovers. In 1881, Fort Sill was scene of Great Silver Rush as officers and men suspended Army business to prospect and file claims throughout post. When mining claims intruded on Indian reservation, agent had to appeal to departmental commander before silver fever was stopped and soldiering resumed.

employees had left. Tatum saw the folly of trying to deal with the Indians without Army backing. Thereafter, troops were present at the ration days but, in deference to the Quaker thinking, they kept out of sight. In a basement under the commissary they could huddle around a stove and not be seen, but still be ready.

At the same time Tatum wrote his Quaker supervisors that he felt it necessary to treat Indian murderers in the same fashion as whites. Although they did not agree with him, their disapproval was unnoticed in the furor raised over the so-called "Jacksboro Incident."

It was immediately after this merciless massacre of a wagon train near Fort Richardson that General Sherman came to Fort Sill. As the leader of the United States Army and a potential presidental candidate, his visit was the occasion for hurrying the work on the post. Much of it was still unfinished in May, 1871, but Sherman was not really interested in inspecting buildings and supplies. He wanted to get the men responsible for the killings near Jacksboro.

Not long after Sherman had begun his rounds of Sill visiting, word came from Tatum to Grierson:

"Satana, in the presence of Satank, Eagle Heart, Big Tree, and Woman's Heart has, in defiant manner, informed me that he led a party of about 100 Indians into Texas and killed seven men and captured a train of mules. He further states that the chiefs, Satank, Eagle Heart, and Big Bow were associated with him in the raid. Please arrest all three of them."

The Indians were summoned to the fort. The cavalry were mounted but hidden behind their stone corrals, troops were placed with the Army families inside all residences, a detachment of soldiers was concealed in Grierson's front room. Everyone had

**GERONIMO** came to Sill in 1894 after exile in Florida, was officially carried on Army rolls as a scout but spent most of his time enjoying his retirement in sleeping, eating, tale telling, and sampling post liquors. He died in 1909, now rests with other members of his family in Apache cemetery at post. Satanta, who committed suicide in prison, was reburied here in 1964. Quannah Parker and his white mother, Cynthia Ann Parker, are buried in post cemetery.

SHERMAN HOUSE is now occupied traditionally by Fort Sill's commanding general even though more elaborate quarters are available for him. Front porch saw 1871 parlay with Indians. Behind windows soldiers hid, appearing suddenly when attempt was made to kill Sherman.

instructions what to do and where to go when a signal bugle sounded.

At first the meeting on Grierson's front porch seemed friendly. The Indians were patted good-naturedly on the back and everyone but Sherman took seats. The general paced up and down the porch and did all of the talking.

But when Satanta moved to walk down the steps, two soldiers blocked his way. An old Indian crouched on the ground when he saw the pointed rifles of the guard. They tickled him with their bayonets until he got on the porch.

Sherman demanded to know who had been present at the Jacksboro killings. Satana stepped forward, thumped his barrel-like chest and boasted scornfully, "I am the man."

He was informed that he would have to pay the train's owner 41 mules and that he, Satank, and Big Tree would be arrested and taken to Texas to stand trial. Satana flew into a rage and grabbed for a revolver under his blanket.

The shutters on the porch opened and Satana saw the soldiers. Their carbines were leveled at him.

Meanwhile, Big Tree had been spotted in the trader's store and was caught after a muddy chase through the gardens. Other Indians had wandered into a residence and tried to give the alarm by breaking a window when they found it filled with soldiers.

The bugle was sounded, the gates of the stables were opened, and the mounted cavalrymen took positions about the parade ground. Another chief rode up to the porch and defiantly handed two rifles and a pistol to the Indians. Sherman began to pace again and the bluffing resumed.

The Indians were grouped closely together talking to themselves when Chief Stumbling Bear drew his bow on Sherman. A chief grabbed his arm and the arrow went wild. General Grierson saw that Lone Wolf had leveled his carbine at Sherman and grappled with him.

Sherman cooly eyed the confused melee on the porch, told the soldiers to raise their rifles, and the tension relaxed. His bluff had won. The Indian trump card had been drawn unsuccessfully.

Satanta, Satank, and Big Tree were manacled and taken to the guardhouse. On June 4, General Mackenzie met with them at their cell and narrowly missed death. Satank lurched at him as if to shake hands, but the Indians knew Satank had a knife under his blanket and pulled him back.

CHAPEL DATES FROM 1870's, is still in use, especially by new lieutenants who believe good luck follows any marriage solemnized here. Fort Sill was considered temporary installation for first 20 years and only in late 1880's did signs of permanence appear. That was when roofs and floors were repaired and tin bathtubs installed in quarters and barracks. In 1890's real sign of permanence came; porcelain tubs were put in quarters of commanding officer and, of course, post supply officer.

STONE CORRAL was built to prevent Indians from stampeding herd, has loopholes in event of attack, although some oldtimers claim they really were windows for ventilation or so mules could have good view of landscape. Fort was scene of Indian scare in 1898 when rumors spread that Apaches under Geronimo were going to rebel because most of garrison had left for Spanish-American War. Geronimo denied this vehemently and rebellion was determined to be only imaginary.

They were loaded onto a wagon and started for Jacksboro. Satank began his death song while he slowly worked his thin wrists free from the manacles. The wagon was 1,500 yards from the flagpole when he jumped free, grabbed his guard's carbine and almost immediately went down in a hail of bullets from the escorting troops.

Satank was left dead beside the road, blood still gushing from his mouth. The Kiowas were notified they could have the body, but they were too busy fleeing to the west. Satank was buried in the Fort Sill cemetery, taking to the grave with him many of the hopes and outmoded way of life of his vanishing breed.

ENLISTED MEN and their families lived in rude quarters of this type in early years. This building stands near post chapel; despite rough exterior, its interior is modern and air-conditioning is sign of changing times and attitudes.

TO GET THERE: Fort Sill is three miles north of Lawton, Oklahoma on U.S. 277. Most of the buildings of the old post are in use today and the old quadrangle is virtually unchanged in exterior appearance. The former guardhouse and quartermaster and commissary storehouses house excellent museums. The stone corral is carefully maintained in its early appearance with examples of early Army transportation on open display. Visitors are welcome and cordially guided about the old post.

POST HEADQUARTERS shows only two signs of change: telephone wires and air-conditioning. Its administrative functions have moved to larger and more modern building, but this squat limestone structure still oversees old parade ground. Sill was home until his death in 1927 of Chief I-see-O, last surviving Indian scout, who was carried on active duty rolls until death as Army's "senior duty sergeant." He was credited with keeping Sill reservation peaceful during 1890 "Messiah" scare in Northwest.

# FORT MARCY AND POST SANTA FE, NEW MEXICO

It was on August 18, 1846 that United States forces first came to Santa Fe and announced that it now was part of the United States.

As he had at other towns along the way, General Stephen Kearny announced to the townspeople assembled in the shady plaza, "We come amongst you as friends—not as enemies; as protectors—not as conquerors," he said. "We come among you for your benefit—not for your injury."

Recalling the Mexican government's ineffective attempts to protect them, Kearney promised, "My government will correct this. It will keep off the Indians, protect you in your persons and property; and, I repeat again, will protect you in your religion."

As Lieutenant William H. Emory, a topographical engineer with Kearney wrote, "The citizens grinned, and exchanged looks of satisfaction, but seemed not to have the boldness to express what they evidently felt—that their burdens, if not relieved, were, at least, shifted to some ungalled parts of the body."

Kearney had marched his 1,600-man force from Fort Leavenworth, Kansas. Entering what is now New Mexico, he made his declaration of possession at towns along the way. Before him was the Mexican Army, but as he advanced it melted away and his entry into Santa Fe was unopposed.

He found it a collection of adobes, mud bricks as Emory termed them, with a population less than 4,000 of what Emory considered "the poorest people of any town in the province."

By sundown of the 18th he had been greeted at the Governor's Palace by toasts of wine and brandy and the Stars and Stripes were hoisted over the building. A 13-gun salute was fired from artillery emplaced on a hill overlooking the town, the site of what was to become Fort Marcy.

**ON BLUFF** overlooking Santa Fe, Fort Marcy was termed "an irregular hexagonal polygon." Its adobe walls were nine feet high and five thick and were surrounded by a ditch 270 by 80 feet. The two buildings inside were of logs, one served as a magazine. Thirteen cannon were mounted on the walls. Blockhouse was north of main fort. It was built of logs and was surrounded by a moat, the area shown outside of center area in this plat. Militiaman writing in 1862 said Fort Marcy was "an old field work" with a "dilapidated parapet . . . and is now used as a cemetery." (Redrawn from plat at National Archives.)

**GOVERNOR'S PALACE** served as headquarters of District of New Mexico. Post headquarters was near flagpole. Plaza was in front of this building. In 1862 it was described as "twelve to 15 rods square and a street running either way from each corner about the same distance, measures the business portion of the town which is closely built city fashion, presenting a dirty, miserable appearance. Traders, sports, and those connected with the government are the only white people residing here." (Redrawn from Division of Missouri Report, 1876.)

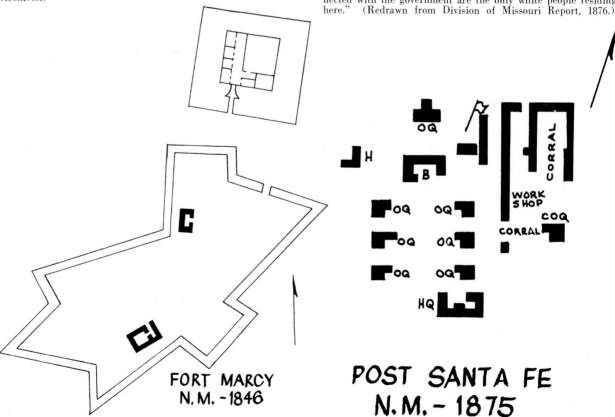

FORT MARCY
N.M. - 1846

POST SANTA FE
N.M. - 1875

QUARTERMASTER'S CORRAL is in foreground in this picture dating from 1870's. Quarters and barracks are in rear. Officer's wife in 1895 wrote, "Fort Marcy formed a part of the town itself. The quarters were cottages of gray adobe, surrounded by fields of alfalfa . . . Hospital and barracks were, of course, on the reservation; and the bandstand on the public plaza brought us pleasantly in touch with our neighbors of the town."

Marcy became a fort that was never finished, and from which no battle ever was fought. As with many a fort of the West, its very presence won its battles without the need for bloodshed.

Emery said it was "within 600 yards of the heart of the town and is from 60 to 100 feet above it. The contour of grounds is unfavorable for the trace of a regular work, but being the only point which commands the entire town, and which is itself commanded by no other, we did not hesitate to recommend it."

Within two weeks 120 Mexican laborers and stone-masons were hard at work building a fortress designed for 280 troops.

For the United States was here to stay. Santa Fe was essential to the control of New Mexico, and New Mexico was essential to American possession of the West. As Emory put it:

"As a military position, it is important and necessary. The mountain fastnesses have long been the retreating places of the warlike parties of Indians and robbers, who sally out to intercept our caravans moving over the different lines of travel to the Pacific."

The troops found that the poverty of the Santa Feans was balanced by their gaiety. The trail captains had been enthusiastic about their descriptions of the hospitality of this sun-baked place, and of the wild "fandangoes" that greeted the sunsets, the holy days, the arrivals of wagon trains, and just about any other occasion considered sufficient excuse.

The gaiety had its drawbacks. When Colonel Edwin V. Sumner became departmental commander in 1851 his "first step was to break up the post at Santa Fe, that sink of vice and extravagance."

A company of artillery was left in the town. A year later, Sumner realized the value of Santa Fe and re-garrisoned the city with upwards of 100 men.

Commanding though its location might be, the post of Fort Marcy did not house anything but cannon and powder. The troops lived in public buildings in the city. Offices, barracks, and other elements of the post were located around the Plaza. The Governor's Palace —today the oldest government building in the United States—became the headquarters for the district and the commanding officer's quarters and barracks were located near it. The fortress on the hill became a refuge from which the Army could withstand a siege but a siege never came.

Confederates threatened Santa Fe but were turned back at Glorieta Pass. From thenceforth, the tide of the Confederacy abated in New Mexico and Fort Marcy and Post Santa Fe became the king pin post of the New Mexico-Arizona area.

By 1867, the Fort Marcy name as such had been abandoned, as had most of the buildings that bore its name. Officers' quarters housed married soldiers or laundresses, barracks became offices and warehouses, and other officers' quarters were allotted to staff offices. A new adobe post took shape next to the Governor's Palace. The Fort Marcy name was reinstated in 1875.

TO GET THERE: Original fort is on bluff directly north of downtown Santa Fe. Remainder of post is north of Plaza, bounded by Federal, Washington, Palace, and Grant Streets.

HEADQUARTERS of New Mexico District was Santa Fe's Palace of Governors, now restored to its early appearance. When Colorado militia came to Santa Fe in 1862, post commander put them on 10 hours' fatigue duty and "kept back their usual allowance of fatigue whiskey," trooper later wrote. "As a token of their esteem, they marched to his quarters one day and gave him three groans." They were sent to guardhouse at Fort Union, but no one knew what to do with them. So, "they camped in the bottom and made themselves at home." As governor of New Mexico 1878-81, Lew Wallace lived in Palace and finished *Ben Hur* here.

# FORT UNION, NEW MEXICO

"The fort was located in a dreary, treeless and practically grassless plain," said a letter from a private at Fort Union in the Civil War. "Our life in garrison at Fort Union was monotonous and uninteresting. The fort, of adobe quarters for officers and men, faced a square which contained a star-shaped earthwork in the center, mounting a few cannon."

One hundred years later, the situation at Fort Union has changed but little. It still is the only thing in a vast plain across which ruts of the Santa Fe Trail are obvious. The adobe quarters have collapsed into eerie ruins. The star-shaped earthwork must be traced more with imagination than with actual ruins. But the legend of this outpost that helped win the West for the North lives on.

Fort Union came about so that troops could be centralized at a key location in northern New Mexico. The second reason was equally important. "Both economy and efficiency of the service would be promoted by removing the troops out of the towns," the Secretary of War determined, where they would be distant from the temptations of saloons and dancehalls.

Started in 1851 amidst an economy drive by the War Department, Fort Union went up piecemeal with soldier labor. Unseasoned, unbarked green wood was used in no particular style, some upright in the buildings, some horizontal. More than 30 buildings were scattered about, causing "the post to present more the appearance of a village than a military post," according to one description.

The start was not promising. A new barracks rotted so fast it had to be torn down to prevent "any untoward accidents that were liable at any moment to happen from the falling of the building." The hospital had a dirt roof that meant not a single room remained dry during the rainy season. The other buildings were so lice infested that the soldiers slept under the stars when the weather permitted.

The economy drive had caused the soldiers to build the fort and then was the same reason they had to perform other jobs usually handled by the civilians. As the major supply and troop depot for the Southwest, Union usually would have many civilian blacksmiths, teamsters, herders, and artisans. Instead, the soldiers had to do these jobs. The result was that the buildings, once up, had no maintenance and did not long stay up.

In 1862 work began in rebuilding the post and its regimental headquarters was moved temporarily to Albuquerque. The clouds of the Civil War hovered close, and urgent priority went to digging a massive earthen fortification. This so-called "star fort" was basically a square, topped by parapets at each corner, from which arrowhead-like angles jutted out 200 feet. Quarters, storehouses and magazines were inside—occupying the same green, warping construction as before.

Although some observers said the fort was so strong it could withstand all of Texas, one artilleryman pointed out that its interior could be raked by fire from the nearby mesa. What is more, guns mounted on the parapets could not reach the mesa where the Confederates undoubtedly would locate their cannon.

The soldiers' solution to the living situation was the same as before. Rather than live among bedbugs in damp half-underground dugouts, the troopers camped outside of the parapets.

A Colorado Volunteer wrote later, "The armament is poor, consisting mostly of howitzers, but the supply of ammunition is deemed sufficient for any emergency. It has bomb-proof quarters in and surrounding it forming part of the works, sufficiently large to accommodate 500 men besides the necessary room for stores."

The same Colorodan commented that upon arriving at Union in '62 "with drums beating and colors flying," the militiamen had to stand while the Post Commander and "the Governor welcomed us in rather unintelligible words . . . I thought they might as well have permitted the boys, hungry and tired, to go to

**FORT UNION
N.M.–1877**

RIVALRY between two major elements of Fort Union was continuous. Depot was at left, post at right, with ordnance depot—only a few buildings—offset from main part of Fort. Although bulk of fort was built of adobe, remains of most of these buildings are left today. National Park Service has stabilized ruins and they are identified. Parade ground is a gigantic 1,500 feet by 300. (Redrawn from NPS data.)

**STAR FORT** had deteriorated by 1866, but its parapets still were obvious. Entire garrison was removed to it in 1862, but soon found it uninhabitable and moved into tent camp nearby.

their camp near the fortification as to have perpetrated this farce."

After the Battle of Glorieta Pass decided the fate of the Confederates in New Mexico, Fort Union's status was secure. General James H. Carleton located the headquarters for the Department of New Mexico there. A building boom began that later was turned off only after considerable debate at the War Department.

Millions of dollars were spent in constructing a sprawling installation that combined three Army installations at Fort Union, the Post, the Quartermaster Depot, and the Ordnance Depot. After six years, the fort presented an elaborate sight that was a far cry from its predecessors.

The "territorial style" of boxlike architecture was employed throughout. Adobe buildings stood on rock foundations and were protected from the elements by plaster and brick exteriors.

Despite the impressive appearance, the fort buildings had defective roofing. Rain water eroded the walls and constant repairs were required.

At the same time it was having problems of building, Fort Union was kept busy almost continually on the military front. From its first days, the Fort Union garrison frequently was called upon to drop its hammers and saws, grab its rifles, and thunder off on an Indian-chasing patrol.

When two Fort Union patrols suffered at the hands of the Jicarilla Apaches in 1854, the 200 Dragoons and infantry of the post were sent into the mountains of Taos in pursuit. They routed the Apaches and then spent a month trying to pin them down. Another battle was fought in the mountains west of the fort before the Jicarilla threat was replaced with another one.

Two Colorado towns were ravaged by the Ute Indians and a few Jicarillas, prompting Union's commander to field every man he could gather. New Mexico Volunteers increased his force to 500 men and he pushed them into an intense screening of the area centered on Fort Massachusetts, Colorado.

On April 28, 1855, he surprised a 150-warrior Ute camp with a two-pronged night assault. Forty Utes were killed and their village burned. Peace came in July after a few minor skirmishes by holdouts.

No major field activities interrupted the regular escorting of Santa Fe Trail trains until the Kiowa-Comanche War of 1860-61. Six Mounted Riflemen companies joined with expeditions from Fort Riley, Kansas, and Fort Kearney, Nebraska, in a five-month

**STAR FORT** today still is southwest of main fort and mounds mark where troops intended to withstand Texans in '62. Fort Union proper surrounds flagpole in distance. Star fort was objectionable because, as artillery expert pointed out, "The work has a dip toward these hills which causes its whole interior to be revealed." The hills were the ones at west which overlook five-and-a-half-mile-wide valley.

SIDEWALKS of Fort Union were uncovered when National Park Service began restoration. This shows ruins of laundresses' quarters amidst stone ruin of prison cells. Remains of bakery are to rear of cellblock.

search for the hostiles. This ended in another surprise attack on a village, although the Kiowa-Comanche threat was to continue for many more years.

Carleton pursued the Civil War campaigns against the Indians with specific orders: "All Indian men . . . are to be killed whenever and wherever you can find them," he directed. "The women and children will not be harmed, but you will take them prisoners." With Militiaman Kit Carson leading the field troops, Carleton slashed vigorously throughout the Navajo country and spread his efforts to the unresolved Kiowa-Comanche threat.

The battle of Adobe Walls was a highlight of this latter campaign. Involving Carson's regiment at the ruins of one of William Bent's old trading posts, it added little luster to the Carson name. The Indians were close upon him, held back only by mountain how-

itzers until the troops could withdraw at night after burning the Kiowa village.

The postwar years were divided into expeditions against the Mescalero Apaches and the Kiowa-Comanche combination. Usually operating as the western arm of an expedition—as it did during Sheridan's Winter Campaign of '68—Union's troops were in the field regularly until 1874.

Five years later in 1879, the railroad reached Watrous, below Union. The post lasted another ten years, but each year its future became more and more uncertain. In 1869, Phil Sheridan had criticized the post and when it was abandoned, his 20-year-old words rang prophetically:

Fort Union, he said, "has grown into proportions which never at any time were warranted by the wants of the public service. Quartermasters and command-

HOSPITAL actually was three buildings with a single purpose. Each measured 81 feet long by 37 wide, separated by six-foot walkways. Six wards each contained ten beds under 12-foot-high ceilings. Wide hallway ran through the center of buildings, as can be seen by large door area in middle of facing wall.

MARKER was placed in 1867 and has survived much better than barracks row in rear. Surgeon report in 1870 criticized construction, commenting, "The barracks are one story high, with flat tin roofs, which in this climate, do not answer, for the reason that where artillery is used, the firing springs the nails and solder, and severs the attachments. The adobe settles and causes the tin also to loosen; the tin rusts; the high winds detach it; and, in every respect, it is more expensive and less serviceable than shingles." Commanding officer's wife commented that as plastering was finished, "the ceilings fell one by one." An estimated bushel of plaster landed in one bed, and another incident ruined dinner for 17 guests, "filling every dish with plaster to the top."

ing officers have gone on increasing and building up an unnecessary post, until it has become, by the waste of public money, an eyesore.

"I do not accord with the opinion of anyone as to its military bearings for protection of field operations, nor do I see any necessity for it as a Depot."

TO GET THERE: Fort Union is now a National Monument administered by the National Park Service. Take U.S. 85 north from Watrous, N.M., one-half mile to seven-mile-long State 477, a hard surface road that ends at the old post.

OFFICERS' ROW shows permanence of rock foundations and chimney-supported front and rear walls. Quarters were better than at most Western forts and one wife reported, they "had an unusually wide hall which was superb for dancing, and three rooms on each side. We had only to notify the quartermaster that a hop was to be given, when our barren hallway would immediately be transformed into a beautiful ballroom, with canvas stretched tightly over the floor, flags decorating the sides, and ceiling so charmingly draped as to make us feel doubly patriotic." As headquarters fort, post had regimental band which was employed on these occasions.

MARRIED ENLISTED men once occupied buildings in this area. Fireplace is now supported by restoration work. Officers' quarters can be seen across parade ground. Unmarried soldiers lived in barracks that contained 21 single bunks apiece, measured 72 by 26 feet and were 12 feet high.

(PHOTO BY LAURA GILPIN, COURTESY NATIONAL PARK SERVICE.)

**FORT UNION TODAY** shows depot at left, post at right.  Row of officers' quarters is in foreground.  Santa Fe Trail ruts parallel far side of fort; the deeper ruts running diagonally to horizon are of old road to timber reserve.  Fort had two tunnels at one time that connected it with water supply in event of siege.

**GUARDHOUSE** once was surrounded by a large adobe building.  Adobe had disappeared, leaving only stone cells, probably most solid remnants of once-elaborate installation.  Adobe at right is corner of barracks.

TROOPERS guaranteed safety of this Hays City stage in 1867, though it is unlikely they retained these positions throughout ride.

(KANSAS STATE HISTORICAL SOCIETY.)

# THE WAY WEST, YOUNG MAN

*"The coach was filled with arrows which they shot into it and which stuck to it. We kept up a steady fire from our revolvers at them, but I do not know how many, if any, we killed or wounded . . . The troops went out after the Indians, but never learned whether they got any of them or not."*
—Contemporary account of Butterfield Texas trip, 1859.

HORACE GREELEY pointed the way, but it took more than a newspaper editor to open the West and keep it safe for everyone who followed his advice.

That job fell to the Army, of course.

The Northwest had its water routes along the Missouri and the Columbia that cut deep slices into the unknown. Except for a short distance of the Rio Grande and the Colorado, the Southwest's navigation was confined to stages and dry land "ships of the desert."

Forts were established along the routes most frequently used by travelers and traders. Troopers also were stationed at mail stations and stage relay stops.

Despite the tales told today, most Western stages got through without disaster, something to the credit of the hardy passengers, the enterprising drivers, the protecting soldiers, and other factors as noted in this 1859 Denver advertisement:

"Special attention is given to the comfort of ladies traveling in the coaches . . . Our drivers are sober, discreet, and experienced men. The teams are the choice of 800 miles."

# FORT STOCKTON, TEXAS

For 100 years and 1,000 miles from the Arkansas to the Rio Grande, the first full moon in September brought a sense of terror to Texican and Mexican alike. This was the time of the "Comanche Moon," when the braves struck a swath of destruction deep into Mexico along the infamous Great Comanche War Trail.

When the Army was charged with protection of the settlers in the new state of Texas, this annual Comanche blood bath was a prime concern. As long as the Indians were free to move along their "Trail" on these excursions, the frontier would remain only a frontier.

Getting at the heart of the situation, a series of Army posts was established in 1858. One of them was set squarely in the path of the raids and right next to a main watering spot. The fort was Fort Stockton, the spring, the third largest one in Texas, Comanche Springs. Even today it pumps thirty million gallons of water a day except during irrigating seasons when the sources are diverted.

Stockton was host to the travelers of the Camino Real, the California Trail and the San Antonio-San Diego Stage Line. It brought a measure of security to the El Paso road that was so essential that the Confederates even used it for a period during the Civil War. Many patrols of the pre-war Army originated at or passed through Stockton, and the Camel Experiment based a detachment there for a short period.

Confederates burned most of it when they decided that the West Texas frontier no longer could be held. A returning Federal Army in 1867 began from nothing to build an adobe post on a new site near the original fort.

"Although the place is called a 'fort,' strictly speaking there is no fortification at the post," observed the post surgeon in 1870. He noted that Stockton was a collection of adobe buildings with stone foundations. The hospital was "an old building which was formerly used as an officers' quarters, but it does not deserve the name."

He noted that "a permanent hospital is in the process of completion" and a year later the surgeon had his hospital. It was also of adobe with stone foundations, included six rooms and a porch, and measured 101 by 30 feet.

The post-war activities of Stockton differed little from before but the Indians w e r e not as active. "Though they yet roam in thieving bands," the surgeon reported, "the road is comparatively safe, as they rarely attack the mail or a passing train."

The occasional attack included at least one incident in which a stage arrived at the fort, the driver dead of an arrow in the middle of his forehead.

In the 1870's, the post took on a permanent air. A traveler of the time passed through the town next to the fort, but because "it was the Fourth of July . . . the travelers felt that they should not take time to visit the military quarters. Viewed from a distance, the government buildings appeared to be large and roomy adobe structures, more uniformly arranged and more pleasing in appearance than those at Fort Concho."

FORT STOCKTON
TEXAS – 1875

**ONLY FOUR OF THESE** buildings remain today, three officers' quarters and guardhouse. Famed Comanche Springs are southeast of hospital. In 1870, post surgeon reported, "The kitchens have no special furniture; the cooking is done in camp kettles . . . and the men generally eat their meals out of doors, each man supplying his own knife and fork and seat." Departmental Medical Director condemned this as "unsuited to the needs of a permanent post . . . exceedingly objectionable . . . in violation of sanitary laws . . . subversive of good order." It is assumed mess rooms behind barracks were used soon after this report. (Redrawn from Division of Missouri report, 1876)

During this time, Stockton also commanded three sub-posts "with a view to making the mail route safe, and the settlements in its vicinity, by forcing the Indians out of that region and keeping them out of it," as explained in an official report.

These were Camps at Rainbow Cliffs, Frazier's Ranch, and Escondidos. In 1879, Frazier's Ranch established a record for the Department of Texas by fielding between April 2 and July 31 patrols that traveled 4,703 miles. Under Captain George A. Armes, the activity was "in search of Indians, or raiders, and to obtain information in regard to the country."

The results of Armes' energies spoke for the future of Fort Stockton: "No signs of Indians discovered and no depredations reported."

Although Fort Stockton was involved in the 1878-81 campaigns against Victorio and the Warm Springs Apaches, its days were numbered. The railroad had no need for springs and forts, and its route left Stockton 63 miles from the nearest station.

The Army made repeated attempts to abandon the fort. It looked like 1884 would be the date but barracks to receive the troops were not finished at Fort Davis. The Departmental Commander remarked in his annual message, "The proprietors of the site of Fort Stockton, and citizens in the vicinity, being so anxious to keep the peace there as to offer the site for another year at a mere nominal rental, it was thought best to allow the troops to remain another year."

Finally in 1886, the Army left. The original owners had a fort on their hands, because the government did not own land nor most other fort sites in Texas. The choice was obvious and today the town and site of Fort Stockton are a single entity, the latter merely being a small area on the south side of the former.

TO GET THERE: Fort Stockton, the town, is at the intersection of U.S. routes 290, 285, and 385 in West Texas. Site of the fort is three blocks south of U.S. 290 and 285 intersection on Spring Drive between Fifth and Second Streets.

**SOLID DOOR AND BARS** combined with its stone construction, made guardhouse almost escape proof. Legend tells of post-Army days when bandits locked jailer up in his own jail, then looted town—but legend does not say whether old fort or town jail was involved. Guardhouse had three rooms, one for jailer, one with leg irons for prisoners, and a dungeon for solitary confinement.

**"AS TO ITS FITNESS** for the purpose," wrote surgeon in 1870 about guardhouse, "it is very well fitted, since it combines security with punishment, but punishment which deprives a man of light, ventilation, and of fire in winter." The 18-by-4-inch slits were only means of ventilation and light and in 1875 surgeon said there was no heat "except by the exhaled air of its occupants."

**SEVEN OFFICERS' QUARTERS** faced Fort Stockton's 1,360-by-540-foot parade ground, but only three remain. Eighth residence shown on plat, at south end of row, probably was not built. Quarters have 14-foot ceilings and adobe walls are two feet thick. Trees are recent innovation; 1875 report says there was only one tree at entire fort, a cottonwood in post garden.

# FORT QUITMAN, TEXAS

Young Robert Grierson went searching for adventure in his summer vacation of 1880. He found it near the adobes of old Fort Quitman.

The teenage son of General Benjamin Grierson, commander of the Tenth Cavalry, Robert found his adventure while holed up at a fortified waterhole with his father and seven soldiers. Opposing them were 150 warriors led by Victorio, the Warm Springs Apache who had learned his brand of generalship under Mangas Coloradas, the best the Apache had to offer.

Victorio had combined two Apache bands and broken out of the reservations in 1878. He was not without provocation after the wavering Indian Bureau policies wore out his patience by shunting his tribes between three reservations in less than a year. He led his followers to the hills, and the Army moved in to calm things down.

By the time he met the Grierson duo in the shadow of Fort Quitman, Victorio had ambushed, plundered and raided on both sides of the Rio Grande. He slipped back and forth across the border at his own convenience until he had forces of both armies trailing him in close pursuit.

Grierson had gathered his regiment at Fort Davis and put sub-posts along the Rio Grande at Viejo Pass, Eagle Springs and Fort Quitman.

The last had been less than a soldier's dream when first it was built in September, 1858. Four hundred yards east of the Rio Grande, it was built of adobe on a rolling sandy plain whose only vegetation was stunted chaparrel, mesquite bushes and tall, wild cactus. The Quitman Mountains, with steep, rocky barren sides, looked down on it from the east. Mexico's Sierra del Huesco Mountains could be seen across the Rio Grande, backing several miles of destitute, rolling desert plains.

Quitman was not much of a post before the Civil War, although it did fight frequent engagements with Indians ambushing traffic on the San Antonio-El Paso road. This track passed from the east through Fort Davis then to the Quitman Mountains where it moved to the Rio Grande at Quitman Pass.

Here the fort had been built, named after a Texas militia general w h o led the now legendary U. S. Marine assault on Chapultepec, the famed "Halls of Montezuma" in the Mexican War.

It was abandoned during the Civil War, although occasionally outposted by a squad of Confederates. Federal troops raised the Stars and Stripes over it on August 22, 1862, but left the next day. When reoccupied in the spring of 1868 by three companies of cavalry and one of infantry, it was termed by the post surgeon "entirely unworthy of the name of fort, post, or station for United States troops."

He pointed out that during its inactive stage, "the rebels, Indians, and all travelers passing back and forth over the road made it their stopping place, and while resting here apparently made every endeavor to dismantle the houses, tearing away and burning doors, windows and all available wood in their reach."

Only the walls were left standing in many cases, he noted, and the barracks were so insecure "that every rain we have floods the rooms, and all bedding becomes wet and muddy. The doors and windows are only so many holes in the wall."

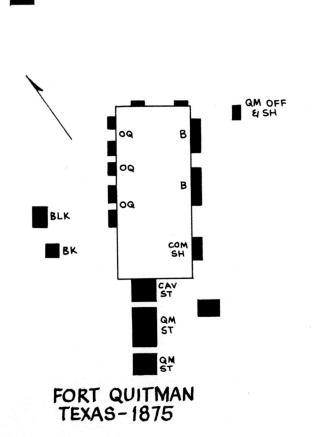

## FORT QUITMAN TEXAS—1875

ADOBES of Fort Quitman "when new were doubtless comfortable quarters," surgeon wrote in 1870, "but are now in a deplorable condition, entirely unfit for the accommodation of troops." Commanding officer in 1870 used both buildings at northeast edge of parade ground; unlabeled building offset from southern corner was guardhouse. (Redrawn from Division of Missouri report, 1876.)

This last condition had its advantages, he added, because "the dormitories of the barracks, having neither doors or windows, have an abundant ventilation."

Quitman had upwards of 200 men at this time of his report in 1869, but went out of business a year later. Periodically it was regarrisoned, and the Grierson's expedition of 1880 was one of these times.

Grierson's small party had left Fort Davis after receiving a message from the Mexican commander, General Valle. Valle had 400 soldiers across the Rio Grande and alerted Grierson that Victorio's band had bested him and was heading toward Quitman. Grierson arrived there on July 27, turned over food and forage to the destitute Mexican soldiers camped across the river, and set out with his tiny escort to check his lines.

Alerted that Victorio had fired on the patrols and was riding up Quitman canyon, Grierson fortified the waterhole in the canyon and sent word for reinforcements.

The request was garbled. Instead of reinforcements he received a 15-man detachment which was expecting to escort him to Camp Eagle Springs.

"As I had no thought of being escorted there, or anywhere else," the Civil War hero later wrote, "I immediately sent two of these men back with peremptory orders that all available cavalry be at once sent to my support."

He now had 21 men—and a boy—to defend the waterhole when Victorio headed up the canyon. Spotting the entrenched soldiers, Victorio tried to bypass the position, but Grierson sent out a 10-man patrol to engage the Indians.

After an hour of skirmishing, the troops were heartened by the arrival of the Eagle Springs troop. This turned to chagrin when the Eagle Spring soldiers opened fire on Grierson's detail, mistaking them for Indians. The 10-man detachment withdrew to the waterhole, hotly pursued by part of the Indians while the rest faced the other soldiers.

Another hour and the warriors began to melt away when the Fort Quitman detachment appeared in the distance. Cavalry cut off their retreat to the north and they "fled in great haste and confusion toward the Rio Grande."

Grierson and Victorio met again in August. But this time the fight was near Van Horn, Texas, and Grierson had left his son behind. The wily Indian once again had to flee toward the Rio Grande. Within two months, he died of a sharpshooter's bullet during a Mexican Army attack on his camp.

Quitman saw two further incidents when Victorio's followers tried to take up his traditions. In October, four soldiers were killed at a tiny outpost near Ojo Caliente, on the Rio Grande below Fort Quitman. The following January, another party attacked a stagecoach in Quitman canyon, killing the driver and a gambler passenger. Texas Rangers searched out these marauders and killed or routed all of them in the last Indian fight in Texas.

In 1881, Fort Quitman again was outposted. By this time the Indian troubles had ended, and their only occupation—aside from trying to keep the crumbling adobes from collapsing about them—was unglamorously preventing remnants of the Victorio band from crossing over into Texas.

TO GET THERE: Site of Fort Quitman is now only approximate as there are no surface remains. From El Paso, take U.S. 80 east 55 miles to McNary. Continue on highway for 10 more miles, turning right at "Lower Valley Road." Follow this south five and a half miles to Quitman Cemetery on right; Fort Quitman was four more miles south. Quitman Mountains are to left of road, Rio Grande parallels right side a half mile to a mile.

MORE THAN 100 graves are in Quitman Cemetery about four miles north of fort site. Except for one 1955 marker, no legible gravestones are more recent than 1940. Most wooden markers have bleached out and seasonal rains have scattered them around enclosed graveyard. Artificial flowers and rosaries on some graves indicate care at this isolated resting place.

QUITMAN MOUNTAINS, background, overlook general site of Fort Quitman although these adobe ruins probably are more recent than days of post. Soldiers at fort were able to buy fresh vegetables but complained that 75-mile ride over dusty, rough road did not improve their condition. Milk was five cents a gallon, butter, 70 cents to $1 a pound, eggs 50 cents a dozen, chickens $1 a pair.

# FORT SELDEN, NEW MEXICO

At least one thing about the Indians around Fort Selden was that they were a nervy lot.

The adobe fort was at a strategic location near a crossing of the Rio Grande in southern New Mexico. In addition to helping keep the peace for the stages, it seemed to serve as a beacon for Indian troubles.

Indians camped in the shadows of Selden almost from the day it was established in April, 1865. A fort in the area was not new to them. The Spaniards had a Presidio nearby 100 years before, and the U. S. had Camp Robledo on the Presidio site in 1853. In 1863, a garrison known as Post of Las Cruces was started at that town, but it became a sub-post of the new fort in 1865.

To show their attitude, the redmen never let the chance slip by to make off with whatever the soldiers did not have bolted down or guarded. The cattle herd was stolen on one occasion after the soldiers were decoyed by Indian harrassments farther south in the Mesilla Valley.

A rope ferry connected the fort with Mount Robledo, the 6,200-foot mountain on the opposite side of the Rio Grande. During the Indian troubles of the 1870's this was used for a heliograph station, flashing messages between Forts Bliss and Selden. The Indians did not quite figure out how it all worked, but they took one definite step. They cut the ferry line across the river. For good measure, they also stole one of the cows owned by a Selden lieutenant.

When a man was sent from the fort to work the coal pits, the Indians jumped him. Then when a wagon train got within sight of the post, the Indians openly attacked it.

Finally the patience of the Army was exhausted. With the subduing of Geronimo and the Apaches in neighboring Arizona, the frontier settled down and the Indians adopted a more docile attitude.

It was about this time that Fort Selden had one of its most famous occupants. As a four-year-old, Douglas MacArthur accompanied his parents to Fort Selden in 1884. His father was the captain of Company K, 13th Infantry, and his duty kept the MacArthurs at Selden for three years.

Remembering it in his reminiscences for "its low and dusty adobe buildings," General MacArthur wrote that "here I learned to ride and shoot, even before I could read and write."

He said that he and his brother "were frequent passengers on the water wagon which supplied the fort. And, toward twilight each evening, there was the stirring ceremony of retreat, when we stood at attention as the bugle sounded the lowering of the flag."

Diversions of the older occupants of Fort Selden included visits to Leesburg, one and a half miles south. In 1870 the only civilian inhabitants of the area lived here. The post surgeon described it as consisting "of a small store and grog shop and about 20 miserable huts. The residents are principally Mexicans of the lowest class, having no occupation except prostitution by the females."

**FORT SELDEN N.M. – 1869**

**ADOBE** plastered inside and out was the mainstay of Fort Selden. Barracks were 90 feet long, 24 wide. All buildings were single-storied with flat dirt roofs. After fort was abandoned in 1890, civilian was granted permission to keep wooden parts of buildings if he would transfer soldiers' bodies from fort cemetery to Fort Bliss. Last Army unit left in 1892; it was a detail to assist in removing doors and windows. Only crumbling adobe is left today after unsuccessful attempts by owner to donate it to government as a monument. (Redrawn from Surgeon General report, 1870.)

**FORT SELDEN** in early 1880's was overshadowed by Selden Mountains and Mount Robeldo. Soldiers are on parade ground with barracks in far rear, hospital at right rear. Hospital had two wards, each containing five beds, and surgeon considered health condition of post as good with "no prevailing diseases."

**FORT SELDEN** today is wasting away. Because of nearness to highway, fort is victim of vandalism and indiscriminate souvenir hunts. Police have been called out frequently to chase "hot rod" speeders who consider its parade ground test track. This view approximates that of 1880's. Brush hides parade ground, but near edge of hospital is at right, barracks are in rear.

**OFFICERS' QUARTERS** had flat earthen roofs and fireplaces in common with all other Selden buildings. Post stood on sandy prairie above cottonwood-covered river bottom and post surgeon in 1870 complained, "Wolves and skunks are annoyingly numerous about post."

CORRALS at Selden as seen across parade ground from officers' quarters. Troops from Selden fought in Apache wars in 1870's, but post was temporarily abandoned with coming of railroad in 1879. Post was re-manned for Mexican Border patrolling in 1881.

SUNSET at Fort Selden darkens remaining walls of barracks. Because of its compact design with all buildings facing inward to parade ground, fort resembled earlier stockaded posts.

The next point of diversion was Las Cruces, 18 miles south. Here the Amador Hotel beckoned. From the 1850's this place had been a rendezvous for the Army men in the area. The English translation of the Spanish name, Amador or Lover, apparently had significance. Even today there are 23 rooms in the place with a girl's name inscribed over each doorway: La Luz, Maria, Esperanza, Natalia, Dorotea, and company!

TO GET THERE: From Las Cruces, take Interstate 25 north about 17 miles. The Interstate meets U.S. 85 at Fort Selden and passes immediately next to its hollow adobes.

# FORT ELLIOTT, TEXAS

"The roughest and most inaccessible district of the country," is how General Nelson A. Miles described the panhandle of Texas. From the earliest days of the Southwest, this was the place in which the outcasts of both white and Indian society sought refuge, for here no man would follow them.

It was part of the fabled "Staked Plains" of the West, that area considered by early explorers to be beyond hope . . . no water, no grass, no potential, no future.

With the West opening up, the Staked Plains were found to be a vast area that belied the early dire predictions. All that was needed, it was found, would be control of the hostile human element there. The Army provided that control, and, almost after the fact, Fort Elliott retained it.

In 1874, Quannah Parker t o o k his Comanche braves in the opening of the end of the mysterious Staked Plains. Sixty miles northeast of Amarillo, he attacked 28 buffalo hunters who were holed up in a trading post, Adobe Walls. Although outnumbered 20 to one, the hunters patiently picked off the warriors. The methodical, unerring aim of the sharpshooters took heavy toll of any braves within a thousand yards.

Their leaders among the 30 dead, the Comanches withdrew. Three days later, troops arrived and the pursuit of the hostiles was on. Across the waterless, sunbaked plains Miles and Ranald Mackenzie pressed the Indian sign. Wagons were left behind. On August 30, nine troops of the 6th Cavalry, supported by gatling guns, fanned out at a gallop.

"Forward! If any man is killed, I will make him a corporal!" Adna R. Chaffee, l a t e r a general, is quoted as yelling to his charging cavalrymen.

The Indians were panicked by a double attack. They retreated in a 20-mile chase that never gave them a chance to stop and fight back. Only when the cavalry mounts could go no farther did it end.

The rout of the Comanches seemed complete, but they returned in sporadic attacks throughout the next months. In September a six-man courier team was ambushed by 115 hostiles. They fought them off from the sanctuary of a buffalo wallow until help came.

In November, the camp of Gray Beard's Cheyennes was attacked by troopers. Two white girls, Julia and Adelaide Germaine, were rescued and the soldiers were told that two older sisters still were Indian captives.

Miles pressed close to the Indians, not giving them a chance to make camp or rest their mounts. In January, he sent a message to the Indian main body near the New Mexico border, demanding their immediate and unconditional surrender. To the girls, he had a friendly Indian slip them a family photo of themselves, on the back of which he had inscribed the heartening words:

"Your little sisters are well and in the hands of friends. Do not be discouraged. Every effort is being made for your welfare."

His confident prediction came true. The Indians were tired, hungry, and cold. They realized that further resistance meant death. They gave up and permitted the troopers to march them 200 miles back to the reservation. The four sisters were reunited, the Indian ringleaders interned in Florida, and the Staked Plains made safe for settlement.

As a direct result of Miles' experiences, a temporary post, "Cantonment North Fork of the Red River," was established in February, 1875. In July it was moved 27 miles i n t o the Panhandle and near the waters of Sweetwater Creek, and named Fort Elliott.

No Indian fights occurred out of the new fort, but its presence provided security to the area. Settlers moved in and the refuge for lawbreakers and renegades was tamed.

On one occasion, an Elliott troop provided protection to a wealthy English landholder while he vis-

**FORT ELLIOTT
TEXAS - 1882**

**PARADE GROUND** measured 450 feet by 650. Although Fort Elliott was designed for six companies, buildings were of adobe and frame, none permanent enough to last after fort was abandoned. (Redrawn from plat in National Archives.)

**FORT ELLIOTT** in 1877 from southeast corner of parade. Barracks are at left, officers' quarters at right rear, commissary storehouse at right. Bat Masterson was at Fort Elliott on a scout in spring, 1876, and many other Western characters frequented out-of-way Panhandle area.

ited the area in the face of kidnapping threats. In 1890, Elliott forces assisted in enforcing the peaceful settlement of the Cherokee strip.

By then, the most desperate activity was the nearby town of Mobeetie. Originally called Sweetwater, that name was rejected by the post office because of the other Texas town of the same name. Mobeetie, Indian for "sweetwater," was the substitute.

"There was just one store," wrote one rancher about Mobeetie. "It was patronized by outlaws, thieves, cutthroats, and buffalo hunters, and a large per cent of prostitutes. Taken all in all, I think it was the hardest place I ever saw on the frontier except Cheyenne, Wyoming."

Today Fort Elliott, abandoned in 1890, has disappeared. It went out of style when the Panhandle blossomed forth as a farming and grazing center dotted with some of the country's most productive natural gas and oil fields.

**ONLY TANGIBLE** evidence of former Army use is this Texas State marker erected in 1936. Although marker states that post was abandoned in 1889, its last troops did not leave until October 20, 1890, according to War Department records. Report when fort was established in 1876 says there were no local Indians, but there were frequent visits by roving tribes.

TO GET THERE: From Mobeetie, Texas, take State 152 one mile west from Mobeetie Junction. Marker is next to road.

**FORT ELLIOTT TODAY** is farm area. It was at crossing of Sweetwater Creek, at bottom of hill (center of picture), and this entire area was part of fort. (Modern pictures are by George Grant, National Park Service.)

# FORT BISSELL, KANSAS

When Charlie Fredericks thundered into Phillipsburg, his frantic yelling arrived in town long before his horse did. It guaranteed a good crowd and most of the town turned out to hear him sputter a message between gasps for breath:

"Just came from Fort Hays," legend records his words, "and the soldiers say the Indians are heading this way. Want us to get our guns and get ready to fight."

No repeating of his warning was necessary. Weapons, ammunition, food, and other essentials were gathered up and Phillipsburg, Kansas, started to build itself a fort in that day of 1872.

No one bothered to ask Charlie for details. The tiny town had been living with Indian dangers since the Civil War and they had been expecting this day.

Not far away, seven years earlier the Army had built a 90-foot-square stockade called Fort Kirwin. This had been abandoned after a few months. Just the year before, in 1871, settlers in the town of Kirwin had erected a 50- by 90-foot stockade when the wandering Indians came too close.

And in 1867, 5,000 redmen had attacked a company of U.S. Cavalry only a couple of miles from Phillipsburg. In this two-day running fight, Captain George Armes led his men from sure defeat to victory in what became known as the Battle of Prairie Dog.

So when Charlie said "the Indians are coming," no one bothered to ask questions. Contemporary newspapers give flavored accounts of what happened.

The townspeople went to the Bissell ranch two miles west of town and threw up a log stockade. It was protected on three sides by Bissell Creek and inside they put lean-tos to cover their supplies and on which sentries could watch.

With many Civil War veterans in the 100-person population of the fort, the settlers were confident that any Indian attack could be turned.

Shortly after the stockade was up, their confidence was shaken. In the middle of the night the sentries heard fiendish yells and the thundering of hooves. For 30 minutes the fort's defenders rushed about, knocking over their only light, losing their weapons and ammunition, and waiting for the first shot.

As quiet finally descended, they learned the attack was merely the stampeding of their horse herd, apparently frightened by two obstreperous mules.

The next night, the settlers again turned out when a sentry fired at a "lurking Indian." A veteran drummer beat a long roll on a tinpan, the impromptu guard fell in, and a detail charged across Bissell Creek to find the carcass of a calf. As the sentry commented, "Didn't I hear him groan like a dying calf after I fired?"

Another morning a reconnoitering detail near the fort ran into what they thought were Indians.

"To Arms! To arms!! They come! They come!" the lead rider warned the stockade. "Ten thousand strong, 5,000 mounted hostiles and as many more on foot!"

There was a casualty in this affair, one man thrown by his mule into Bissell Creek. He had to have a few bones rearranged after being fished out.

The Indians in this case turned out to be buffalo hunters who were as frightened as the settlers. They thought they had seen Indians, too.

The next night, a Civil War veteran volunteered to stand guard where the calf had been killed, because this was considered the danger point. The fort was alerted at dawn when his rifle went off. He explained this was only to test it because time was getting monotonous and it did not seem that he would have any Indians to try it on.

Reprimanded for his false alarm, the sentry reminded his critics that he was only a citizen soldier and, further, he did not think there were any Indians within 500 miles. Besides that, he intended

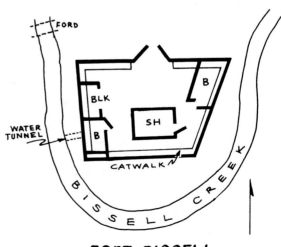

FORT BISSELL
KANSAS - 1873

MEMORIES of settlers provided basis of this ground plan and depressions next to Bissell Creek will back up its approximate size. Cattle and wagons were kept in open area in front of stockade. Catwalks for sentries ran along inside of log walls. (Redrawn from information gathered by Cecil Kingery, Phillipsburg.)

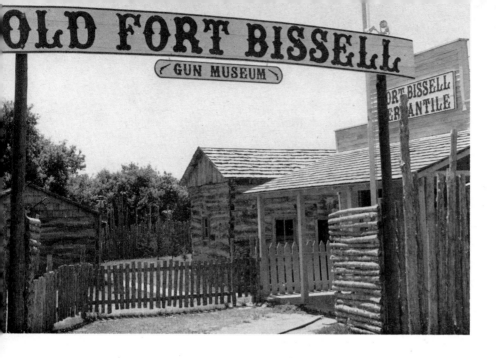

**REPLICA** of Fort Bissell does not profess to match original stockade, but two of its cabins are from 1870 period. Built by Phillipsburg Chamber of Commerce as a free museum, modern Fort Bissell has mementos of frontier days, including valuable collection of frontier firearms.

"to throw up the job and go home this morning before breakfast!"

The rest of the fort's occupants took the signal, decided a week at Fort Bissell was enough.

Until 1878 they would rush to the stockade at the first sign of Indian alarm. It always was kept well stocked for such emergencies.

Except for its ex-soldier defenders and occasional military patrols that passed nearby, Fort Bissell never was a military post. But it, and many others like it, gave security to an unsettled West even if the passage of years make its activities seem less than serious,

TO GET THERE: Reconstruction of Fort Bissell, a vague replica, is a half mile west of Phillipsburg, Kansas, on the south side of U.S. 36. The original site is on Davis Ranch. From center of town take Second Street (U.S. 183) north to dirt road at city limits immediately south of refinery. Turn left (west) to ranch, two miles on left side. Site is short walk behind ranch house on private property.

**SETTLER CABINS** were donated to fort replica. Building on left was built in 1872, on right 1873, and were brought to site by civic boosters. They fell apart in moving, were rebuilt to original appearance.

**ORIGINAL SITE OF** Fort Bissell was here. Depressions and mounds are believed to be traces of fort which was abandoned in 1878. Bissell Creek flows below brow of hill, trees marking its trace. This is north end of fort; covered water route was in bank at right.

MORNING AFTER in Hays City, Kansas, sometimes meant business for the undertaker and Boot Hill.

# THE WILD ONES

*"The soldiers drew their pay and slid off around the quarters to the sutler's store, or waited till nightfall and went in groups to the little collections of gin-shops usually just outside the confines of the reservation and invariably called a city, even if there were but six huts."*

—Elizabeth Custer, *Following the Guidon*, 1890.

THE LAWLESS West was no different from other new, raw, untamed frontier. The men who braved the perils of the unknown were of the bold and reckless natures essential to taming these hazards. They were the searchers for something new, or the outcasts of something old.

The fact that the West was there and possibly held their future was good enough reason for them to heed its call.

They were not the sort to take their leisure quietly. The cowboy, teamster, railroad worker, trooper, all had to blow off steam after months of keeping the lid on.

And blow off steam they did. Next to every Army post was the disreputabable "hog ranch," the purveyor of all that was illicit and unavailable on the post. Whiskey, cards, women followed the man who would support the trade. The forts, the frontier towns, the "end of track" tent sites could do so.

From the beginning, the Army and the reputable civilian elements—for they, too, came West— frowned on this unrestrained illegitimacy. And as the frontier disappeared, so did the wild breed and his habitat. Today they live only in the stories of oldtimers, as told to them by their fathers.

What follows are some of these stories and the places at which they occurred. Only a few appear, but they were representative of many in a Southwest of long ago.

139

# FORT HAYS, KANSAS

Wild Bill Hickok and the 7th Cavalry came to Hays City at just about the same time. Hickok was supposed to clean up the town; the Custer troopers were to clean up the Indian situation and protect the railroad workers.

When the cavalrymen decided they wanted to clean up Wild Bill in the process, Hickok is quoted as saying, "I can't fight the whole 7th Cavalry," and he lit out for Abilene and parts westward.

In its early days, Hays City was merely a couple of saloons and a general store under the hill on which Fort Hays stood. Later it had 20 more saloons and one more store.

The fort was founded in 1866 as Fort Fletcher 15 miles from its ultimate site, but was washed away by a flood in June, 1867. Several soldiers were killed. Mrs. Elizabeth Custer later wrote of trying to help

rescue drowning soldiers and using her bed as a raft.

The Army post was moved next to the railroad and thereby hangs the tale. At the time the railroad ended at Hays City and the fort found itself right beside an "end of track" town.

Mrs. Custer said that the town "was typical Western place . . . There was hardly a building worthy of the name, except the stationhouse. A considerable part of the place was built of rude frames covered with canvas; the shanties were made up of slabs, bits of driftwood and logs, and sometimes the roofs were covered with tin that had once been fruit or vegetable cans, now flattened out."

**HEADQUARTERS** of Fort Hays was this blockhouse, only real Indian protection available. Hexagonal shaped, it was built in 1867 and has lookout positions and rifle loopholes in second floor. Custer had his 7th Cavalry at Hays for several summers in late 1860's, but they did not occupy post buildings. Their camp was on Big Creek, several hundred yards away. Mrs. Custer wrote she seldom went to town because of its reputation; one trip was in closed buggy and peeking out she saw "the tables in the saloons with heaps of money, guarded by knives and revolvers."

**TWENTY-SEVEN** different types of buildings were at Fort Hays, including four frame barracks, 24 by 118 feet, which had kitchens and mess halls attached. Only stone buildings were blockhouse, used as post headquarters, and guardhouse and these are only buildings on original locations today. Post never underwent Indian attacks, but nearby stage stations periodically were burned by Indians. From here Sheridan initiated his winter campaign of 1868-69. Post was abandoned in 1889 and most of property turned over to state for educational purposes. (Redrawn from Division of Missouri report, 1876)

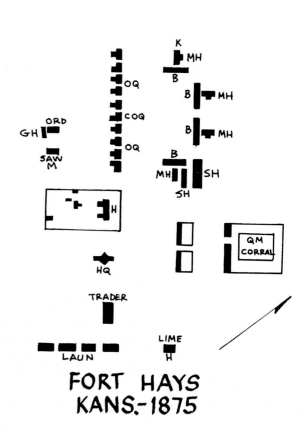

FORT HAYS
KANS.-1875

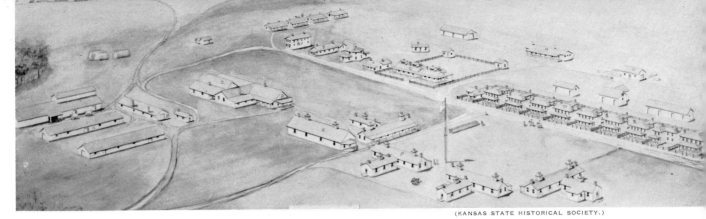

**BASED ON SURVEYS** and old photographs, this is probably how Hays looked in its heyday. Barracks are on three sides of parade ground behind flagpole, officers' quarters facing them. Hospital is to left of residences, with blockhouse next to it. Band quarters is next to blockhouse and double-storied building is post trader. Across from blockhouse are stables, shops, storehouse, with post chapel in wing at near end of large storehouse.

As if the appearance were not bad enough, General Custer's better half observed, "The carousing and lawlessness of Hays City were incessant. Pistol shots w e r e heard so often it seemed a perpetual Fourth of July, only without the harmlessness of that pyrotechnic holiday . . . As we sat under our fly in camp, where all was order and there where harmony reigned, the report of pistol shots came over the intervening plains to startle us."

The station house mentioned as being the only worthy building in town was once the place of refuge for Generals Custer and Nelson A. Miles during a Hays City shoot out. "The air was filled with flying bullets, and no one had any thought, seemingly, but of murder," Mrs. Custer recalled. "The two officers in the station could not attempt to quell this maddening crowd, and their only course was to remain quietly in the building."

Custer was not the one to let action go unobserved and Miles is quoted as having to warn him, "Lie low, Custer, lie low!"

When Wild Bill was brought to Hays City, it was General Custer who sponsored him for appointment as deputy U.S. Marshal. When he was not passing the time with what Western writers liked to call "the fair Cyprians," he was striving to bring some measure of peace to Hays. He is credited with killing

from three to seven men in the line of duty while there. The last two were his undoing.

General Custer was a teetotaler but his brother, Captain Tom, made up for him. Legends persist of Tom's frequent bouts with Hays City rotgut, especially of the occasion when he rode up and down Main Street shooting up the town.

Wild Bill packed him off to the fort, an inexcusable insult as far as the younger Custer was concerned. According to versions of which Mrs. Custer's account is not one, Tom mustered several troopers and led them into Tommy Drumm's saloon, Hickok's favorite watering place.

One soldier jumped Hickock from behind and tried to pin his arms. Hickock got his gun hand free and shot over his shoulder, killing his assailant. As he shot the man in front of him, bystanders moved in and stopped the action.

When he heard that Fort Hays soldiers were plotting revenge, Wild Bill decided discretion was the byword and departure was better than trying to face all of the 7th Cavalry.

TO GET THERE: Hays City is in west-central Kansas at the intersection of U.S. 40 and 183. The fort site is on a hill immediately south of the city where the old parade ground is now the city golf course. It is at the intersection of Main Street and U.S. 40 bypass.

**FORT HAYS** in 1875 appeared this way in barracks area. The four pine barracks faced officers' quarters (water barrel from easternmost residence is at left edge of picture). In 1870 surgeon commented that winds "thoroughly ventilate the buildings . . . by passing through the walls and roof . . . The beds are double-tier wooden bunks, two men sleeping together in each tier, four men in each bunk, the whole arrangement being very objectionable."

**GUARDHOUSE HAS** c h a n g e d little from early days, except for addition of bushes. In 1869, Indian survivors of Battle of Washita w e r e imprisoned in stockade next to guardhouse. When post commander tried to move three chiefs into guardhouse, misunderstanding arose and "upon the failure of the chiefs to comprehend what was required of them the soldiers attempted to push the chief from the stockade by force," Custer later wrote. "An attack was at once made upon the guard with knives which they carried beneath their blankets." Two Indians were killed, several soldiers and Indians wounded. Custer had to be called from his camp to explain the situation to the tribe before it settled down.

**INTERIOR OF GUARDHOUSE** probably h a s changed little. Three cells for prisoners are in general prison room behind barred door. Post surgeon in 1870 complained it was heated by a single stove in guard room, ventilated imperfectly by windows, and was "not well fitted for the purpose intended."

**PHIL SHERIDAN** might have lived here, and then he might not. Except for nine-room post commander's house, other seven officers' quarters looked exactly the same and Sheridan lived in one of them. Moved from original site in 1901 to 5th and Main Streets in Hays City, two-family residence was converted to single family use, kitchen wing at rear removed, and windows substituted for fireplaces. Mrs. Custer writes that walls in quarters were so thin that one family found it necessary to settle arguments by standing in center of parade ground, rather than disturb other half of duplex. House was donated in 1963 to Fort Hays Society by Ralph Engel and at time of photography it was planned to move it back to fort. This had been done by the time the site was revisited in 1964.

# FORT DODGE, KANSAS

Soldiering at Fort Dodge seems to have had two unruly objects of attention, the marauding Indians and the equally dangerous citizens of Dodge City, five miles from the post.

That five miles was the key to the problem, for that put the town just off of the post reservation and beyond the Army's control. The town grew from a single soddy built in 1871, almost six years after Fort Dodge was started officially. Apparently up until then, the soldiers were too busy trying to keep their dugouts habitable—for they lived in 70 of them hollowed out in the creek bank—and had little time for off-post entertainment.

Even more important than dugout housekeeping was Indian subduing. Early Fort Dodge had its full quota of this.

General Custer wrote that no sooner had he joined his 7th Cavalry command near Fort Dodge, than they were set upon by a band of Indians. They "dashed close up to our camp and fired upon us," he said. "This was getting into active service quite rapidly."

It was decided that the harassment was designed to lure the troops into a chase and subsequent ambush, and Custer did not bite, for once.

Before his men were aware that sightseeing in the countryside was unsafe, two of Custer's officers decided to take a swim in a nearby "beautiful clear stream of water." Thirty Indians surprised them when they were devoid of weapons, insignia of rank, and, in fact, of everything. With no pun intended, the lieutenants rode bareback at high speed to camp, the Indians at their heels.

"It was a long time before they ceased to hear allusions made by their comrades to the cut and style of their riding suit," Custer commented.

The general blamed the audacity of the Indians on the fort's failure to patrol aggressively into the countryside. So one night he sent four patrols into different directions determined to flush out the Indians and stop the agitation.

Three patrols returned with reports of seeing nothing. The fourth came back much later, their civilian scout tied to his horse. They could report having charged an Indian camp . . . but only because

the scout's whiskey imbibing had conjured up one for him. In the midst of his delirium tremens he had led the charging cavalrymen, until the patrol commander realized there was more fire water than firing Indians involved and sounded the "recall."

The Indian attacks had their less ridiculous moments. In September, 1868, four soldiers were killed and 17 wounded when Comanches and Kiowas attacked the fort. At about the same time, 16 members of a Mexican wagon train were killed and scalped by Cheyennes and Arapahoes near the fort.

Colonel Richard I. Dodge, the first commander and nephew of General Grenville M. Dodge, after whom the post was named, wrote of the Indian use of what today would be called psychological warfare. Camped near the post, his command was nearly routed one night when "suddenly a hugh ball of fire came rushing to the camp, accompanied by the most terrific yells that ever split the throats even of Indians."

The braves had tied grass and other inflammable materials to the back of a pony, set it afire, and aimed it in the direction of the Army horseherd. The idea was to panic the horses and soldiers and make off with the mounts in the confusion. Dodge added that it did not work.

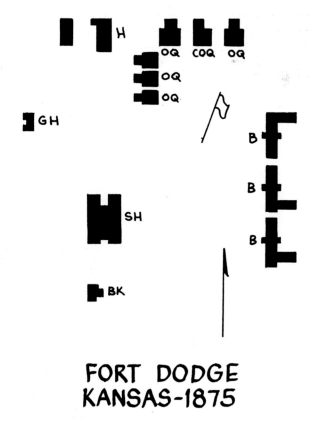

## FORT DODGE
## KANSAS-1875

**WHEN SHERIDAN** arrived at Fort Dodge for his 1868 campaign, a newspaper correspondent with him wrote that it would be difficult to defend because of bluffs which were immediately behind officers' quarters. "Shortly after our arrival," he pointed out, "four or five warriors rode directly through the fort, shooting one soldier, and making their exit in safety." Post was built of stone after several years in dugouts and shanties, was abandoned by Army in 1882. (Redrawn from Division of Missouri Report, 1876.)

FORT DODGE in the 1870's looked like this from the northeast. Rear of officers' quarters is at left; side of hospital at right. This is same side of hospital that appears in modern photograph. Commanding officers' quarters is the story-and-a-half building in center. At one time during this period, Fort Dodge was vacated while soldiers searched for escaping Cheyenne band under Chief Dull Knife. Townspeople erroneously thought Indians were approaching them, had governor rush 100 rifles to them for self-defense.

The single shanty of Dodge City quickly was followed by a few more for a final total of 19 whiskey emporiums. Then problems of Fort Dodge had to be shared between redmen and scarlet women—and the usual gambling and rotgut accomplices of the latter.

Military efforts to keep the soldiers pure had only small measures of success, despite a post order of 1878: "No heavy wagons or wagons containing prostitutes are allowed to be driven through the Fort Dodge garrison."

The railroad and the cattle drives brought all of the assorted and sordid riffraff of "end of track" to Dodge. "Beautiful Bibulous Babylon of the Frontier —with one saloon for every 50 residents," reads one contemporary description. "Her principal business is polygamy, her code of morals is the honor of thieves, and decency she knows not.

COMMANDING OFFICER'S quarters, supposedly occupied by Custer, Sheridan, and Nelson Miles on occasion, has nine rooms, was palatial compared to most other officers' quarters in 1870. Post surgeon reported then that "officers, ladies, children, and servants lived several families per house in a total of eight rooms, 18 by 18 feet each, 30 people to be sheltered from the weather; by dint of crowding into attics, closets and shanties, the difficult problem is solved; but, of course, health, comfort and convenience are not taken into consideration."

"Her virtue is prostitution and her beverage is whiskey. She is a merry town and the only visible support of a great many of her citizens is jocularity. The town is full of prostitutes and every other place a brothel."

When wagon trains passed Dodge, the less adventuresome groups steered a wide path clear. One team asked for Army protection while moving through the town. This was turned down, but an officer volunteered to guide them safely through.

Before entering the outskirts, the passengers left their bullet-scarred wagons—for they had undergone several Indian attacks—to pray, "Oh Lord, we have our greatest danger. Dodge City lies just ahead, and we must pass through it. Help us and save us, we beseech Thee." Then with canvas sides rolled down and eyes straight ahead, the pioneers steered a straight course past the roistering of Front Street, no one once looking left, right, or to the rear.

Well they might have feared the reputation of Dodge; it was based on fact. Its lawmen included Bat Masterson and Wyatt Earp, but these men contributed as much to the coffers of Front Street as they did to keep things at a low roar with everyone's aim at least straight.

Things got so bad that in 1873 a Vigilante committee was formed. Unfortunately, some of its members were the very desperadoes who were the reason for its existence.

Rumors came to town that the Fort Dodge soldiers "had orders from Washington to burn the town off the face of the earth." Supposedly this was to avenge the wanton murder of a soldier by several alcoholic townsmen.

A group of 40 armed vigilante types rode to the edge of the military reservation, leveled their rifles at the post commander and his three officers, and said they would be shot dead if the Army moved.

The governor of Kansas gave Major Dodge authority to take action "with great care and only in extreme cases." The next day, Dodge led his cavalrymen into town, had all of the streets blocked, and started to search for the killers of the soldier. One was found, but another hid inside a saloon icebox and got away that night.

Dodge left a seven-man provost guard in town with orders to prevent all soldiers from entering "any barroom, saloon or other disreputable place in town except under orders" and to "arrest every enlisted man found in Dodge City day or night without a written pass from the commanding officer."

Although the major's assumption of authority was contested as being contrary to Federal law, which it almost was, the Secretary of War upheld it.

The Vigilantes disbanded, but apparently the citizens of Dodge were too much for the town guard. "It having been reported to the commanding officer that the provost guard stationed at Dodge City has been behaving in a disorderly manner," a later order read, "the provost guard are hereby relieved from duty at that place and will return to this post without delay."

TO GET THERE: Dodge City is in southwestern Kansas at the intersection of U.S. routes 154, 56, and 283. The Boot Hill Museum and Front Street replica are southwest of the downtown area at 4th Avenue and Spruce Street. Fort Dodge is four miles west of the city on the south side of U.S. 154.

POST HOSPITAL building appears little changed from early photograph. Built in 1868, it was scene in 1872-73 when post surgeon performed 70 amputations on railroad workers and hunters. He reported that due to weather, more than 200 men lost hands or feet or part of them near the fort. Hospital and the three barracks were of similar construction; latter still are on eastern side of parade ground. Originally 130 by 30 feet, with 50- by 30-foot kitchen and messroom wings behind, each contained 22 double-tier bunks. Two of barracks remain, are now used by state soldier's home and have been connected together.

# FORT GRIFFIN, TEXAS

No one waited for dessert back in '76 at the Fort Griffin mess hall. That was when a drunken buffalo hunter staggered in and announced he planned to "run all them damyankees out!"

In fact, it is likely no one even bothered to excuse himself. The hunter started to fire in the air, and the troopers beat a hasty and strategic withdrawal out the back door.

It was not always like this at Fort Griffin, but things were lively enough on a regular basis so that it did not upset anyone too much. Except the targets of the hunter's shooting, that is.

The officer of the day dispatched the guard to the building. The sheriff of the town of Fort Griffin rushed up the hill and arrested the lively celebrant. He was put in a vacant shack in town to sleep off his drunk. But the cold night was too much for him. He tore up the floor to build a fire, and the sheriff dragged out the sputtering but sober man just as the shanty collapsed in flames.

Nothing came of the incident because rivalry between the fort and its civilian counterpart was a daily fact of life. The fort had come first, founded in 1867 where the town later was located. The low

ground next to the Clear Fork of the Brazos seemed too likely to be flooded, so the post was moved atop a 100-foot bluff to the south and named Camp Wilson.

The Wilson name gave way to Griffin. And about the same time the first site was occupied by what a contemporary newspaper termed "all the elements of man and woman kind. Sharp's rifle and Colt's six-shooter are the supreme law of the land. Among the roughs, thieves, and outlaws there is a class of good men here that are endeavoring to check the lawlessness."

Despite this last hint at lawful citizenry, the so-called "Flat" could claim only one each of the quiet businesses—drug store, hotel, restaurant, music hall, and wagon and blacksmith shop—but ten, c o u n t 'em, ten, saloons.

The "good" people at the Flat had gathered there partly for protection against Indian raiders. Earlier they had forted up at a stockaded "Fort" Davis nearby, but most moved to the shelter of the Army post when it was built.

Some of them also came because of the trade they could do with the soldiers and, even more, with the cowboys on the Texas trail herds and the buffalo hunters. In 1871, more than half a million head of cattle passed through the Fort Griffin country, and in 1877 the Buffalo market hit its peak with 200,000 hides freighted out of the Flat.

The lawless element that swarmed to this ready money center gave the Flat a reputation not uncommon to many other places, "The Wickedest Town of the West."

Contributing to this were records of 35 public killings in 12 years, eight to 10 killings that were considered less public only because the bodies were found after the murders, and 12 hangings. One account says that there "were 30 men killed around Fort Griffin in the month of April '77," but this seems unlikely.

In 1872, the post commander determined that the Flat was within his jurisdiction and he ordered the gamblers and "transient women" to leave. Although the reports say "the low whiskey shops and gambling halls were weeded out," they soon returned.

While Generals Mackenzie and Shafter were using

# FORT GRIFFIN
# TEXAS – 1867

FIRST VERSION OF FORT GRIFFIN was b u i l t rapidly for $22,000 but green wood was used and buildings soon let in more air than they kept out. Soldiers lived in four rows of small frame huts 13 by 8½ feet intended to accommodate six men each. Additional troops had to occupy tents. As ruins suggest, later construction improved this situation. (Redrawn from National Archives data.)

the Army post to chase Indians in a number of bloody exchanges, the Flat was going strong. By the late 1870's, its main street was a mile long and it boasted more than 1,000 people.

Many of these were like Mollie McCabe, the proprietor of the "Place of Beautiful Sin." Mollie and her fellow sinners followed illegal occupations, but had a license of sorts. Once a year each girl was haled into court and fined $100. As long as her transgressions did not change from that for which she was originally arrested, she was then free to stay in business another year. Mollie is listed as paying her $100 forfeit in 1880, for instance.

Another of the Flat's emporiums was the Beehive, but it was more of a saloon. Carl Coke Rister reports that the sign for this place showed a beehive surrounded by a swarm of bees and under which was written:

> In this hive we are all alive,
>   Good whiskey makes us funny:
> If you are dry, step in and try
>   The flavor of our honey.

In these Main street boozeries, the Army periodically fought among itself. Once a poker game between a lieutenant and a soldier ended when the lieutenant shot the soldier; another time a drinking bout between a captain and a soldier ended when the trooper was shot dead.

Attempts at law and order were tried, but success usually was short-lived.

Vigilantes posted notices that certain characters should leave town, and "Long Kate," "Big Billy," Minnie Gray and Sally Watson, prostitutes, and Pony Spencer and Tom Riley, rustlers, took the hint. Another man, a horse thief known as "Reddy," was held in the Army guardhouse, but enroute later to stand trial he wound up dangling from a tree three miles from the post.

Texas Rangers established themselves nearby at what they called Camp Sibley. This brought a measure of peace to the Flat. The biggest calmer was the abandonment of Fort Griffin in 1881. The businessmen tried to corral business by sending out agents to praise the town, but it was no go.

When the dives packed up and the saloons and 40-girl dancehalls formed wagon trains to follow the the hunters and the cattle drives, the Flat was out of business. The buffalo were no more and neither was the town of Fort Griffin, once a center of the buffalo hide trade.

TO GET THERE: From Albany, Texas, the town that outbid Fort Griffin for the railroad line, take U.S. 283 north about 15 miles. Fort Griffin State Park straddles highway; entrance to fort is through stone arch at left. Road winds up hill to fort site where building sites are indicated and 40-ton marker memorializes Army occupation. North of site and below hill is site of town, also approachable from U.S. 283. Thousand yards north of fort site entrance, on right side of road is headquarters for Fort Griffin State Park, a double-story building built in 1874. Camping facilities available. Watch for rattlesnakes.

**COMMANDING OFFICER** had a stone building after his wooden quarters warped beyond limits of habitability. After fort was started, one of its first patrols of 45 soldiers and 22 scouts made contact with hostiles and killed three, took one squaw prisoner, captured 22 horses and mules. They also came across remains of five men killed by Indians.

POST SUTLER had one of the more solid buildings at fort, supplied canned tomatoes, fruits, oysters, sperm candles, and something still on market today, Borden's Eagle Brand milk. At northwestern edge of fort, these ruins are some of most impressive of Fort Griffin.

ONE FALSE-FRONT ruin remains on the Flat, although some modern farmhouses are scattered over area. Army post was on hill in background. Flat can claim many Western characters, including Wyatt Earp and Pat Garrett. Here is where legendary episode supposedly took place when "Big Nose" Kate set fire to hotel to draw attention from Doc Holliday so he could escape.

# LOMA PARDA, NEW MEXICO

Loma Parda never was a fort, but sometimes it had more soldiers than many forts combined. It had a close relationship to the Army, even though that relationship bordered on the illicit.

It was the extralegal element of most western forts, the so-called "hog ranch." Here the trooper could find those three elements most conspicuous by their absence at the post: wine, women, and gambling.

Here, too, he could find a broken head, a flattened wallet, or a knife in the back.

Loma Parda was a half hour ride from Fort Union, New Mexico, far enough from the flagpole that it was not concerned with Army regulations. It predated Union by an estimated 20 years, having been started somewhere in the 1830's or '40's. This gave it an air of permanency uncommon to the average hog ranch.

Soldiers stationed at Fort Union have left varying accounts of Loma Parda. Terming it "the chief recreation center," Private Frank Olsmith said, "The population derived their subsistence largely f r o m catering to the desires of the troops for social entertainment, amusement, wine rooms and restaurants. Dancing pavilions, most of them with gambling places in connection, were plentiful and were for the most part well patronized from early eve to dewy morn."

He said that the main attractions of the town were dancing, music, and gambling. "Every night parties were formed with consent and often the participation of our commanding officers, where we danced, smoked and indulged in flirtations with the native damsels over glasses of white Mexican wine . . . With it all there was little drunkenness, the utmost of g o o d humor."

A member of the Colorado Volunteers had more critical comments. When militiamen considered the goods of the post sutler as lawful loot and broke into his place, the plunderers adjourned to Loma Parda. As the Coloradan remembered, the men were "burying plunder, drinking, fighting, and carousing with Mexican women at the Lome, a 'Sodom' five or six miles from Union.

"There were a dozen of us too drunk to know friends from foes, consequently most provokingly troublesome. Many came in during the night with rough usage painted on their faces in unmistakable colors."

As it did with other hog ranches, the Army tried to eliminate Loma Parda by stopping the soldier trade. Fort Union's General Order Number 11 of September 13, 1870, was a step in this direction:

"No enlisted men belonging to this garrison," it read, "will go to the town of Loma Parda without the express permission of the commanding officer. Ordinary leaves to be absent from the garrison will not be considered as consent to visit that town. This order will be published to the troops of this garrison at retreat roll call."

The punishment for violation was loss of a month's pay plus restriction to the post and a month's extra duties. One method of checking was to require all men to turn in their leave passes at the guardhouse upon return. Here they were checked for sobriety and cleanliness. Those who did not pass did not leave the guardhouse.

TO GET THERE: This is strictly a jeep or pickup truck route. From Watrous, New Mexico, and U.S. 85, go north on dirt road that starts midway between Mora and Sapello Rivers. Take right fork in 6 miles. Loma Parda is 8.1 miles total from Watrous on north bank of Mora River, and 2 miles north of the fork. Road runs right into what is now a collapsing but out-of-the-way ghost town.

BACA DANCEHALL was at north end of street and was nearest to Fort Union. Owner did so well legend says he lit his cigars with dollar bills. Fights between soldiers and civilians were regular features of Baca place, though most customers did not carry guns—only knives. One fight was settled when two employees used bow and arrows, hitting one soldier in the nose and two others in a more appropriate part of the body, considering the troopers had started to run.

SQUARE DANCES WERE called in this room in Baca place by owner's brother who used English, a violin, and a guitar. Band once played at location of overturned table, dancing was in far end. Apparently bar was in foreground, partitioned off from rest of room.

**STORE OF** McMartin brothers had everything for sale, legal and otherwise. Legal business, including whiskey sales, went on in this double-story ruin. Other activities were dancehall to rear, now a church, and row of cubicles that cut right in a long wing on other side of this building. Unlike adobe construction of most of town, McMartin's place was of stone. Remains of stockade wall can be seen to rear of tree at right.

**ROW OF TINY** rooms behind Baca Dancehall is where "ladies" of Loma Parda's nightlife did business. This is an enclosed yard with cribs facing center. Once a Loma Parda lawman killed a soldier from roof of building. Despite court's decision killing was justified, soldiers came to town and hanged policeman from a lone pine tree at edge of town. Next time lawman killed in self-defense, post commander locked him up in fort guardhouse until troopers' tempers quieted.

**LARGE STOCKADE** was behind McMartin store. Ruins in foreground are of brothel wing; church was adobe dancehall. Stockade of which stone ruins were part measures at least 70 by 50 yards with walls ranging from man-high to 11 feet; to its rear is a second stockade, apparently a corral, about 50 yards square. McMartins were leading businessmen of Loma Parda who employed taxi service for soldiers whenever a big dance or celebration was scheduled.

INDIAN CAPTIVES march into Camp Supply after Battle of Washita, as pictured in Elizabeth Custer's *Following the Guidon.*

INDIAN PRISONERS ON THE MARCH.

# CAMPAIGNING WITH PHIL SHERIDAN

*"Realizing that their thorough subjugation would be a difficult task, I made up my mind . . . when winter came to fall upon the savages relentlessly, for in that season their ponies would be thin, and weak from lack of food, and in the cold and snow, without strong ponies to transport their villages and plunder, their movements would be so much impeded that the troops could overtake them."*

—General Sheridan's plan for the Winter Campaign of 1868-69.

WHEN THE Indian problem reached the crisis stage after the Civil War, the man sent to solve the situation was the hero of Chattanooga, Yellow Tavern, the Shenandoah, and Appomattox . . . and, as most school children know, the "Sheridan's Ride" of poetry.

The man was Major General Phillip Henry Sheridan, a 36-year-old major general who was less than five and a half feet tall, had black hair and a square head. He used this square head to hit the crux of the Indian problem: catching them where they would be hurt rather than chasing them about the prairie like will-o'-the-wisps.

His 2,600 men—1,200 mounted and 1,400 infantry—plus a regiment of Kansas Volunteers swung into action in November, 1868. The main column of troops were Custer's 7th Cavalry and the Kansans at the new Camp Supply, Oklahoma. Another column, mostly cavalrymen of the 3rd Cavalry under Colonel A. S. Evans, came from Fort Bascom, New Mexico, while General Carr led the 5th Cavalry from Fort Lyon, Colorado.

Doggedly the troops pressed the Indians. Villages were raided and the winter "rest" interrupted. From Kansas and Oklahoma, across the Staked Plains, and into Colorado the pursuit continued. Finally in July, 1869, the last major resistance ended and temporarily the Army had the upper hand over the Indian.

Peace was not to last. The so-called "Peace Policy" was instituted and rights were granted Indians who did not know what they meant. They interpreted any conciliatory gesture from the whites as admission of defeat. Soon the prairie was aflame again and by 1874 Phil Sheridan had to be called back.

This was the Red River War when Sheridan fielded 46 companies of troops into a tightening of the noose that centered on the Staked Plains. Sheridan renewed his tactics of relentless pursuit, wearing down the foe, driving him until he was physically incapable of doing anything but surrender.

The statistics show this was one of the most successful campaigns. It had few casualties, relatively speaking, and it brought permanent peace to the plains of the Southwest.

# FORT SUPPLY, OKLAHOMA

Few western forts had a less promising beginning than Fort Supply. Born in the middle of a snowstorm and intended merely as a storehouse for the beans, bandages and bullets needed for Sheridan's Winter Campaign of '68, it was not even dignified with a high sounding name. For a utilitarian place, a utilitarian name was decided upon. It was not until 1878 that it was changed from simple Camp Supply to the greater dignity of Fort Supply.

Dignity ranked as just about the last item when Supply was founded. General Sully had been to this northwestern Oklahoma spot before, but when Sully and Custer arrived in November, 1868, they had to start from scratch. They had five companies of infantry, the 11 troops of the 7th Cavalry, and a 450 wagon supply train.

The troops were divided into details that chopped logs, cut logs, dragged logs, planted logs, each to its own place in the mass production scheme until a post began to take shape. Tents and dugouts made up the earliest days of Supply. These soon were replaced by a stockaded fort that was described by one visitor as "one of the most defensible works of its kind on the plains."

Defensible or not, Supply was not the most comfortable. The bride of a lieutenant wrote later that "our sleeping room has no canvas on the walls inside,

and much of the chunking has fallen out, leaving big holes, and I never have a light in that room after dark, fearing that Indians might shoot me through those holes. They are skulking about the post all of the time."

She wrote this in 1872, four years after Supply was started, and apparently lived in one of the original buildings. Despite the four-year time passage and the heavy attrition suffered by the Indians, their boldness seemed unchanged.

The post surgeon reported in 1870 that the mail was "comparatively regular, but liable to interruptions from snow, floods, thieves, and Indians." In 1872, the Army wife was able to report that 50 Indians rushed into the post, past the officers' quarters, and "out to the company gardens where they made their ponies trample and destroy every living thing."

An infantry company was sent after them, but was restricted from using anything but bayonets to push the ponies away. When the cavalry were sent, "none of the troops were allowed to fire on them, and that the Indians knew very well," the lieutenant's spouse recorded. "It might have brought on an uprising."

Despite the truce that seemed to have settled over the Camp Supply country by the seventies, the lady wrote that Indian bucks out for a frolic "seem to be watching the post every second of the day ready to pounce upon any unprotected thing that ventures forth, be it man or beast."

It was not like that when Supply first was founded. Custer at that time braved a snowstorm that Sheridan later said "hid surrounding objects and so covered the country as to alter the appearance of the prominent features, making the task of the guides doubly troublesome."

Custer said that it had started to snow the evening of November 22, 1868 "and continued all night, so that when the shrill notes of the bugle broke the stillness of the morning air at reveille on the 23rd we awoke at four o'clock to find the ground covered with snow to a depth of over one foot and the storm still raging full force."

His adjutant asked, "How will this do for a winter campaign?"

CAMP SUPPLY
OKLA - 1875

STOCKADE had given way to standard frontier fort by time this arrangement was completed. Barracks flanked 800- by 600-foot parade, with officers' quarters at one end. Redoubt was at site of first encampment, provided refuge in event of Indian attack. (Redrawn from Division of Missouri report, 1876.)

Opera House, Fort Supply, Oklahoma.

(OKLAHOMA HISTORICAL SOCIETY.)

**OPERA HOUSE** was built in late period at Supply. Fancy name for a recreation building may almost have been to make up for absence of fancy name for post. Post varied in strength from 100 to 600. When larger numbers were present, temporary sod dugouts had to be used. Supply never was considered permanent, but it was not abandoned by Army until 1893.

(THOMAS H. GILCREASE INSTITUTE.)

**HURRIEDLY ERECTED** stockaded fort was soon outgrown at Camp Supply in late 1860's. First outpost was constructed of heavy timber "loop-holed for musketry; the stockade is ten feet high, and the blockhouses are also ten feet in height, with a parapet of four feet."

"Just what we want," Custer retorted. And the results seem to bear him out. He took his 800 or so troopers over 70 miles of Oklahoma plains and in a dawn attack obliterated the village of Black Kettle. This was the same Cheyenne chief whose village was the subject of the Sand Creek Massacre four years earlier. Now it was the Battle of the Washita.

Custer had been able to sneak up on the village in a four-pronged movement. The surprise charge, to the tune of "Garryowen" played by the 7th Cavalry band, swept through the village, but a spirited fire fight continued. It was then that Custer learned he had only cut off the first village in a series of winter camps that stretched for ten miles.

After killing almost 800 ponies, rather than let them be recaptured by the Indians, and burning the village, Custer reformed his troops. Although one element under Major Joel H. Elliott was missing, Custer led the formation of cavalrymen and captured Indians directly toward the other Indian camps.

The Indians watching him from the surrounding hillsides rushed ahead of Custer. At 10 p.m. he about faced and headed back through Black Kettle's camp and away from the hostiles. The Battle of the Washita was over, but there were some afterthoughts.

Elliott's 19-man command was found later, dead and mutilated. This was to remain a black mark against the Custer legend which his detractors could

**FIRE STATION** at Supply still remains, fully equipped with somewhat obsolete fire engine. Modern hospital fortunately does not depend upon this picturesque equipment.

**"POWDER MONKEY HOUSE"** is term applied to this building at Fort Supply by present hospital staff members, though its origin is unknown. It was probably a married sergeant's quarters, but present occupant is hospital chaplain who prizes its "antique" appearance.

**GUARDHOUSE** from final days of Fort Supply still retains bars on windows, but present use is as storehouse.

refer to when appropriate. But when Custer neared Camp Supply, only good words were heard.

From his "Depot on the North Canadian,"—Supply—Sheridan sent congratulatory dispatches to the command, thanking them and Custer "for the efficient and gallant services rendered, which have characterized the opening of the campaign against hostile Indians south of the Arkansas,"

TO GET THERE: The town of Supply, Oklahoma, is at the entrance to the Panhandle where U.S. 183 intersects with U.S. 270. Site of the fort is now the Western State Hospital, about a mile east of the town on the north side of U.S. 270.

**SHERIDAN LIVED HERE,** according to tradition, but proof is lacking. General Nelson Miles probably lived here in 1874 when he led troops south from Supply to Antelope Hills for first battle of Red River War. His forces used Gatling guns against Indians, forcing them to withdraw to Staked Plains. Chase was so trying on soldiers that some opened their veins trying to stop their thirst.

# CIMARRON REDOUBT, KANSAS

"At the small window are turkey-red curtains that make very good shades when let down at night. There are warm Army blankets on the camp bed, and a folded red squaw blanket on the trunk. The stove is as bright and shiny as the strong arm of a soldier could make it, and on it is a little brass teakettle singing merrily."

The writer of these homey lines was the new bride of an Army lieutenant. The year was 1873, the place, a 50-foot-square earthwork midway between Fort Dodge and Camp Supply that was not big enough to be called anything but a "redoubt."

It was one of two such places along the mail line between Dodge and Supply. Both were similar in appearance, but it seems that Cimarron Redoubt was the only one at which an officer was accompanied by his wife.

Both redoubts were right smack in Indian country. Ambushes of small troop patrols were common, but most contacts at the redoubts were with so-called friendly Indians. In their first meeting with a chief, the bride, Mrs. Faye Roe and her husband, invited him and his wife to dinner. She wrote later that the chief did all of the eating, leaving the scraps for his squaw. But when the Roes gave him some brandy in answer to his dessert demand for "whisk," the brave barely touched it while his wife finished off the flask. This did not please the Roes, she said, but delighted the chief.

Mrs. Roe described her month-long home as a place that had one officer, a sergeant, and ten privates. It "is made of gunny sacks filled with sand, and is built on the principle of a permanent fortification in miniature, with bastions, flanks, curtains, and ditch, and has two pieces of artillery.

"The parapet is ten feet high, upon the top of which a sentry walks all the time . . . We have two rooms for our own use, and these are partitioned off with vertical logs in one corner of the fortification, and our only roof is of canvas."

This outpost apparently matched the other redoubt, known as the North Redoubt. Lieutenant Richard T. Jacobs superintended its construction by two companies, and described it as having loose dirt piled against the filled burlap bag walls "sloping down to a trench which was about 15 feet wide. The wall was about ten feet thick at the base . . . There was a stable for mules on the inside of the enclosure, built against the wall on the western side.

"On the eastern side was a living room and kitchen for the men. Both of these were of 'hackall' or stockade, the earthen bank forming one wall of each. The roofs were covered with earth, a foot or two lower than the walls planned for defense in attacks."

Despite the traditional fortress design, the mission of these redoubts was a little less than that taught in West Point classrooms.

As Mrs. Roe recorded, the redoubt's commander was "to inspect each sack as it is being carried past by the ox trains" because "it was discovered that whiskey was being smuggled to the Indians in sacks of oats."

TO GET THERE: From Main Street in Ashland, Kansas, go west for a half mile to gravel road. Turn left (south) and follow this road until it crosses Cimarron River, about 12 miles. Take next turn to left to Lewis George Ranch. Cimarron Redoubt is beyond ranch house on private property, and permission to visit should be obtained.

ONLY SLIGHT outline of Cimarron Redoubt's earthworks remain to mark site. Path crosses through center of redoubt. In 1876, two Benedictine clergy stayed at abandoned Cimarron Redoubt, found it large enough for a wagon to be turned around inside. Army wife living there three years before wrote that sentry always walked along top of wall, but during blizzard he was taken off. "I am positive that unless one goes on soon at night," she added, "I shall be wholly deaf, because I strain my ears the whole night thru—listening for Indians."

CIMARRON RIVER is hardly a trickle between sandy mud flats most of year, but roaring torrent in rainy season. It flows immediately north of Cimarron Redoubt, and trains sought refuge in outpost before attempting crossing. Cimarron Redoubt was immediately behind cluster of trees to right of center in picture.

# FORT WALLACE, KANSAS

When General Custer came to Fort Wallace in 1867, the situation was anything but promising. During a dry and torturous march that swung a wide loop through Kansas and Colorado, his 7th Cavalry had encountered the traces of massacres a n d had weathered several desertion attempts.

Custer's drastic measures during this march—which included "shoot to kill" orders to the patrol sent to recover the deserters—became subjects of his court-martial later in the year. Thoughts of this probably were far from his mind as he led his troops into Fort Wallace, however.

"Our arrival at Fort Wallace was most welcome as well as opportune," he wrote later. "The Indians had become so active and numerous that all travel over the Smoky Hill route had ceased. Stages had been taken off the route, and many of the stage stations had been abandoned by the employees . . . No dispatches or mail had been received at the fort for a considerable period, so that the occupants might well have been considered as undergoing a state of siege.

"Added to these embarrassments, which were partly unavoidable, an additional and, under the circumstances, a more frightful danger stared the troops in the face.

"We were over 200 miles from the terminus of the railroad over which our supplies were drawn, and a still greater distance from the main depot of supplies." It was found that the reserve of stores

at the post was well-nigh exhausted, and the commanding officer reported that he knew of no fresh supplies being on the way.

The conduct of this isolated fort set the stage for one of Custer's famous rides. These were ostensibly to perform a military function, but always seemed to lead him directly to the wife he had left behind.

He decided to lead 100 men to Fort Harker, 200 miles away, where supplies could be obtained. He was to continue farther east, to Fort Riley, where Elizabeth Custer was staying. Custer's memoirs do not recount the results of the trip. He was arrested and court-martialled on seven counts, and suspended from rank and duty for a year. His actions against the deserters and his departure from the Fort Wallace troops were the main complaints in the court-martial.

But he could not be kept down and a year later he was back on duty. General Sheridan reassured him by telegram that the Army wanted him back and asked, "Can you come at once? Eleven companies of your regiment will move about the first of October against the hostile Indians."

Custer returned and the Battle of the Washita soon followed, but that is a story told elsewhere.

Meanwhile, at Fort Wallace, the hostile situation had not improved. Just before Custer arrived, Indians had attacked the garrison twice in as many days. Most of the fighting was on a level plain near the fort. Indian and Army cavalry drove against each other, charging and countercharging, "the combatants of both sides becoming at times mingled with each other."

Custer recounted how a bugler boy was swooped up by a warrior and, "still maintaining the full speed of his pony, he was seen to retain the body of the bugler but a moment, then cast it to earth . . . The bugler had been scalped."

Fort Wallace's m o s t memorable Indian affair

## FORT WALLACE
## KANSAS - 1875

ALTHOUGH NOTHING remains at Fort Wallace site of these many buildings, stone from them was used throughout county when post was abandoned in 1882. Caretaker was stationed there, but he winked at the stealing because building material was scarce in area. Wallace's pinkish stone is common ingredient in buildings that date from that period. In 1880 departmental commander said, "One important and well-located point in Western Kansas only is necessary for protection of that frontier, and accomplishes far better and more economically the object for which the four posts of Lyon, Wallace, Hays, and Larned were established. That point is Fort Wallace, which commands all the routes traveled by Indians to and from the Indian Territory in the south and the Indian reservations north of the Platte. A glance at the position of this post and the trails leading near it will show this fact." Despite his desire in 1880 to increase Wallace from a two-company post to one of six companies, in two years the place was abandoned. (Redrawn from Division of Missouri report, 1876.)

FORT WALLACE in 1879, as depicted by modern painter, had officers' quarters grouped around northern end of parade ground. Flagpole is at southern end of parade ground, although some versions place it in front of center of officers' row. Guardhouse is left of flag, magazine at right. Painting shows hospital which replaced one that burned in early 1870's.
(KANSAS STATE HISTORICAL SOCIETY.)

started on September 10, 1868, when Major George A. Forsyth led 50 white scouts from the post in search of Cheyenne marauders. It ended on September 30 when Forsyth, wounded four times, and 44 of his men returned to the post. Half of the men were wounded. The six missing were buried on a sandy island in the Arikaree River, across the state line in Colorado.

Forsyth's detachment had been under siege by upwards of 1,000 Indians. In their first day, his command had suffered 45 per cent casualties. Only through careful firing discipline and the courage and skill of Forsyth, his second in command, Lieutenant Fred Beecher, and the scouts, was survival possible. Famed "Sharp" Grover was one of the scouts, and to a great extent he ran the defense when the officers were shot.

After repeated attacks, the Indian onslaughts finally were broken when Roman Nose, a near legendary warrior with reputed invincible powers, was killed. This happened on the second day. After several half-hearted charges on the third, the Indians stopped their attacks. They disappeared after the sixth day.

Despite the absence of an enemy, Forsyth's situation was desperate. All of the horses were dead, and the men were forced to eat the putrifying flesh.

GUARDHOUSE stood here at one time, though only hole remains. Post surgeon criticized guardhouse in 1870 because it was inadequate whenever Fort Wallace housed more than two companies. Building was of stone, 34 feet wide by 31 deep with 8-foot veranda in front. There were five cells, five by eight and a half feet each, and a 29 by 13 foot prisoners' room, plus a guardroom and room for guardhouse sergeant.

CUSTER'S MEN erected this marker in 1867 in memory of 10 members of 7th Cavalry and 3rd Infantry killed in Indian skirmishes. In 1956 Fort Wallace Memorial Association restored marker and placed plaque at its base, and Veterans of Foreign Wars provide flags and flowers on continuous basis. This is in fort cemetery, from which soldiers' bodies have been moved to National cemetery but civilian graves remain.

Half were wounded, and maggots, despair, and the cold were serious threats.

Two pairs of men had been sent through the Indian lines earlier. One duo, their feet bound in rags, limped into Fort Wallace, 125 miles away. A courier was rushed to a 10th Cavalry unit to the west and it sped to Forsyth's aid. Arriving on the ninth day, it found Forsyth feigning indifference to his dire situation: he was pretending to read a copy of *Oliver Twist* as he lay amidst rotting horses and desperate men.

TO GET THERE: Wallace, Kansas, is on U.S. 40 in far western Kansas. From once lively but now largely abandoned town, take U.S. 40 east one-half mile, turn on dirt road to the south. Fort cemetery is on north side of road, two miles, fort site is south of road between it and Smoky River. Museum and restored Pond Creek stage station are at eastern edge of Wallace town.

SIXTY-FIVE WOODEN markers have been restored on civilian graves in old fort cemetery. Town of Wallace once was 1,500-person shipping center described by a pioneer: "The buffalo hunters, bone pickers, and cowboys who made up a considerable part of the population of Wallace were a care-free, fun loving bunch of fellows with little respect for human life. Killings were common and practically all went unpunished, as the friends of the killers would testify that it was in self-defense." Businesses in Wallace included first Fred Harvey restaurant, in 1870's, and Peter Robidoux Store, once largest between Kansas City and Denver. Robidoux closed shop suddenly in 1895 in accordance with his vow that it would be shuttered the first day he failed to make at least one sale. When inventoried years later, store was found to have $20,000 worth of rotting bustles, buggies, beans and expensive 19th century items.

# FORT HARKER, KANSAS

"The unfortunate women were brought in to Fort Harker, their arrival being the first intimation to the military that hostilities had actually begun," so wrote General Sheridan in his *Memoirs* of the Indian war of 1867.

It was this incident, and others like it, that triggered Sheridan's campaigns to settle the Indian situation once and for all in the plains states.

This affair found Fort Harker right in the middle. After General Sully had been hoodwinked by the Indians and agreed to issue them arms "for hunting," some tribesmen took off to hunt. They were more interested in hunting settlers than buffalo, apparently.

"Traveling northward," Sheridan wrote, "they skirted around Fort Harker and made their first appearance among the settlers of the Saline Valley, about 30 miles north of that post."

There were more than 200 Cheyennes with a few Arapahoes and Sioux. They were able to beg supplies from the settlers who also offered them well-sugared coffee, something the Indians usually considered a luxury.

"Pretending to be indignant because it was served them in tin cups," Sheridan described, "they threw the hot contents into the women's faces, and then, first making prisoners of the men, they, one after another, ravished the women till the victims became insensible."

The farmers were uninjured, and as soon as the Indians left, they brought their wives to the fort. Captain Benteen—later of Custer's Little Big Horn fame—took a cavalry troop and caught the raiders surrounding another farmhouse.

Sheridan saw from the Indian tactics at that incident that only a full-scale campaign would end the depredations. He described the situation: "Hearing the firing, the troopers rode toward the sound at a gallop, but when they appeared in view, coming over the hills, the Indians fled in all directions, escaping punishment through their usual tactics of scattering over the plains, so as to leave no distinctive trail."

Sheridan fielded troops from his Kansas forts. It was on this expedition that General Custer stopped at Fort Harker to collect two troops of cavalry and to replenish his supplies. This was in the spring of 1867. The following fall he again passed through Harker enroute to meet his wife, the affair which resulted in his court-martial and year's suspension from duty.

Harker was a point of rendezvous for many troops and their commanders because of its central location. It was next to the Smoky Hill River, near the old Santa Fe Trail, and within a few hundred yards of the Kansas Pacific railroad.

Both the quartermaster and commissary warehouses were close to a side track of the railroad, according to an 1870 surgeon's report, "so that cars can be unloaded into them, and both are admirably adopted for the purpose of storing large amounts of supplies."

This proximity to the rails meant that Harker received mail twice a day, from the east in the morning and the west in the evening, and it took only 36 hours for mail to reach department headquarters at Leavenworth. When General Nelson Miles moved from Hays to Harker, he found it "more agreeable and more within the confines of civilization."

The brand of civilization still was fairly basic. Harker was about five miles from Ellsworth, Kansas, another bearer of the "wickedest town in the west" tags. Originally, under the name Fort Ellsworth in 1864, Harker had been built a mile nearer to the town by Iowa Volunteers, but was moved after three years to the permanent site.

The town took its name from the first post and the movement of the fort had no effect on its activities. Cattle trade and railroad business kept it lively in the early '70's, and new businesses were opening regularly.

**WHEN TROOPS** moved from Fort Ellsworth site to new post many of these buildings were a while in being built. Some officers lived in quarters at the old post and commuted daily until new quarters could be finished. Fort and area were site in late '60's of cholera epidemic that was first noted among men supplying beef to post. Before it had run its course, more than 200 persons had died.

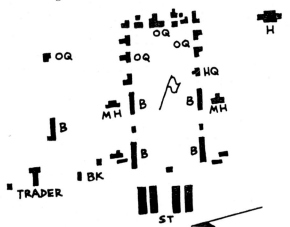

## FORT HARKER
## KANSAS-1875

FORT HARKER in 1867 shows garrison apparently ready for an expedition. Cavalry, cannons, infantry and supply wagons all are lined up near the 252-by-125-yard parade ground. One Harker expedition was conducted by 5th Cavalry in 1869 under Major E. A. Carr, in which troopers pursued Indians for six days, fighting them regularly but with both sides apparently calling a truce for night camps.

On one occasion, the night before a new store was open a man was killed by "several cowboys, having an unusual amount of liquor under their belts," according to a contemporary account. Not knowing what to do with their late comrade, the cowboys carried him to the store and propped him against the front door.

The next morning, the new storekeeper noted with pleasure that someone was anxious to do business. Muttering, "Ah yes, we are ready to do business," and reportedly stepping lightly to the door, he opened it with eager anticipation. His first customer fell into his arms, stiff and dead.

The businessman is said to have walked from Ellsworth to Fort Harker w h e r e he boarded the first train headed east. He did not wait for any explanations.

Ellsworth had good reason for its unsavory reputation. One description of it noted, "Strangers came and went, or came and left their bones behind . . . One had the right to kill, or stand up and be killed . . . If he shot a man, he was expected to treat the crowd. If he was the victim of a bullet, he was expected to die promptly, and remain quiet in his shallow grave.

"In one saloon it was the custom to shoot a man in the back; in another to kill him as he drank with you at the bar; in a third to stand in the front door and fire. Customs varied, but the law was always the same—shoot your man before he shoots you."

To confine its lawlessness, much of Ellsworth's disorderly elements was restricted to "Nauchville," a district on the river bottom a half a mile from the center of town. Saloons, gambling joints, a race track all supplemented the usual entertainments of the red-light district. In computing lawbreaking and killings for Ellsworth, Nauchville was never counted; that was an "anything goes" area where anyone who went there knew what to expect.

In Ellsworth proper, or improper, 13 saloons dispensed liquor at an annual tax of $535 per bar. The town fathers figured if they could not control the places, at least the city could profit by them. The Topeka Commonwealth in 1873 noted that Ellsworth

THESE ARE TWO officers' quarters shown in northeastern corner of parade ground. Each had four rooms and a kitchen, sometimes had to be shared by more than one family when post was crowded. Only stone quarters remain. Wooden buildings, including 117-by-22-foot barracks, provided materials for other construction after settlers took over. State had asked that post be contributed by federal government for educational purposes, but this was turned down and it was opened to settlers in 1880.

"realizes $300 per month from prostitution fines alone . . . The city authorities consider that as long as mankind is depraved and Texas cattle herders exist, there will be a demand and necessity for prostitutes, and that as long as prostitutes are bound to dwell in Ellsworth it is better for the respectable portion of society to hold prostitutes under restraint of law."

Or, as the *Ellsworth Reporter* pointed out, "If it can't be rooted out, the vicious vocation should be made to contribute to the expense of maintaining law and order."

Policing Ellsworth was a problem and at times the police were accused of being as bad as the lawbreaking visitors. Once during a visit by Ben and Billy Thompson, the notorious gunmen, the mayor found it necessary to fire the whole force. It has been claimed by some that at this time a 25-year-old Wyatt Earp was then named marshal and he talked Ben Thompson into holstering his guns.

Other sources, including contemporary newspapers, credit the mayor with settling things by calling a general truce. Although Earp later claimed his fame began at Ellsworth, it appears this is based more on hindsight than on facts.

**COMMANDING OFFICER'S** house at Harker is now a home with air-conditioning and new siding. Original stone, with closed window area, is obvious on first floor area. This was largest officers' quarters, contained eight rooms and a kitchen. Most of fort building were taken over by settlers after post was abandoned in 1873. Until that time it was important supply point for forts in Kansas, Oklahoma, Texas, and New Mexico.

TO GET THERE: Fort Harker is now the location of Kanopolis, Kansas. From Ellsworth in central Kansas, take U.S. 40 six miles east to intersection with State 111. Turn south, two miles. From center of Kanopolis, fort site is two blocks west.

**GUARDHOUSE** is a vivid reminder of early fort. Now in use as town museum, it still has barred windows. First floor had three rooms for the guard, second floor included two rooms and six 7-by-3-foot cells. Post surgeon in 1870 commented, "The ventilation of the cells is defective, and it is difficult to remedy this in the present building without giving many of the more daring prisoners chances to escape." Soldiers had opportunities to let off steam at nearby Ellsworth and at so-called Halfway House, roadhouse midway between fort and town. Its reputation was so notorious that one night a group of men took its owner to one of a few trees in area and lynched him.

# FORT COBB, OKLAHOMA

Fort Cobb's role in Sheridan's Winter Campaign outshadowed anything else in its history, but by that time it was more a general location than a military fort.

"The name of the post was more in remembrance of what it had been, than what it was at the time of our visit," wrote De B. Randolph Keim, the newspaper correspondent who accompanied General Sheridan.

"The site had been selected some years before as a cavalry station from which to watch the movements of the southern wild bands," he said. "It was, however, soon after abandoned, and the few mud huts, which had been constructed, were destroyed by the savages. The position, in a defensible point of view, amounted to literally nothing, and were it not for the fine water, abundance of timber, and winter grass, it might, quite naturally, be concluded that the person who selected the site never visited this spot."

These words harkened back to 1859 when Cobb was begun on a site selected by the Indian Agent headquartered at Fort Smith. Although military officers favored a spot at Medicine Bluff, to the south, the agent decreed that this location next to Pond Creek was better.

A log and mud fort was built in the traditional fashion of the early eastern forts, rather than the open layouts of the western frontier. Barracks and other buildings were crudely put together with cottonwood poles set upright in trenches. Other poles were laid across these walls, covered by sod, then covered again by poles. One building was built of adobe—though Oklahoma rains did not favor this material—and one was of sandstone.

Pre-Civil War days at Fort Cobb were busy protecting the Indians from each other, and all of them from the settlers. The post and its adjacent Indian agency had been established to receive Indians forced from Texas reservations, and some Texans felt that even this place was too close for comfort. Frequent brushes with soldier patrols highlighted Cobb's records until the Civil War.

Cobb's four companies were marched away in 1861 over what later became the Chisholm Trail. Two days later, Texas state troopers occupied the abandoned place, but even they did not stay long. Although Indians were sworn in to protect the agency, this was less than satisfactory. The Confederates negotiated a treaty of sorts with the tribes, a needless step in the eyes of many Texans who considered any feeding of them was a needless expense.

A company of Texas troops was stationed at the post in 1862. Other than gathering 60,000 pounds of flour and other supplies, they accomplished little and left by August. Finally, the Indians sacked the agency, burned the buildings, and the agent was forced to flee in his night clothes. The camp of the Tonkawas also was burned and its population massacred because they refused to join with the rebellious savages.

When Sheridan began his 1868 campaign, all Indians desiring peace were told to gather around Fort Cobb. This post had been regarrisoned in 1865 by two companies. After the Battle of the Washita, many more tribes rushed to Cobb's security, and the ones already there began to fear this was just another white man's attempt to gather them together for a massacre.

The fort at this time was in ruins. The one stone building was covered with thatch and used as a commissary warehouse, and some of the other buildings

FORT COBB in 1859, as envisioned by Vinson Lackey after studying descriptions of post and inteviewing descendants of persons who visited it. When new, fort was considered comfortable and defensible, but its rough construction was not made to last. When Sheridan was here in 1868, a stockade was built on the hill where earlier days had seen a lookout station and guardhouse.
(THOMAS H. GILCREASE INSTITUTE.)

were covered and used as quarters. "The men, anticipating some stay in that locality," wrote Keim, "began to exercise their ingenuity in contriving such additions to the limited space allowed by their 'dog' tents as would not only increase their accommodations, but materially improve their personal comfort."

Dugouts topped by tents or log shanties were made, and fireplaces added, and "in the course of a week, the camp had the appearance of a regular winter cantonment."

A private in the command commented later that these dugouts dotted the entire hillside. He said that the occupants amused "themselves by poking their heads out and barking at the occupants of the adjacent huts in imitation of the prairie-dog, whose comfortable nests had probably suggested the idea of dugouts."

When Sheridan and Custer arrived—the latter camping his troops on the site of the present-day town of Fort Cobb—it took considerable talking to convince the Indians they were not going to be slaughtered. Equal talking had to be done to convince the soldiers of the same thing.

Satanta and Long Wolf, Kiowa chiefs, were confined by Sheridan when their insulting attitude threatened trouble. Soon afterward, it was learned that their tribe had disappeared, despite a promise to come into Cobb.

Sheridan informed them that unless their tribes returned by the next day, they would be hanged. "Both chiefs were completely unnerved by this exhibition of decision," Keim wrote. They sent an old chief to tell the tribe to return and as he left they motioned him "to hasten, acocmpanying their gestures with the words, 'hudeldy, hudeldy.' "

The Kiowas returned, the chiefs were not hanged. Sheridan later lamented, "I shall always regret that I did not hang these Indians; they have deserved it many times."

Weather was the final breaking point at F o r t Cobb. It shifted from freezing to snow in December '68, and the dugouts became untenable.

Finally Sheridan called General Grierson, one of the proponents of the earlier Medicine Bluff site, "This is a hell of a place, Grierson, how about that camp of yours at Medicine Bluff?"

After a freezing reconnaissance, Grierson reported Medicine Bluff would be more satisfactory. On January 6, 1869, Sheridan led his troopers away from their dugouts at Fort Cobb and headed for what is today Fort Sill.

TO GET THERE: The town of Fort Cobb is 30 miles north of Lawton, Oklahoma, on State 9, seven miles west of its intersection with U.S. 281. After entering town, turn right on gravel road (Ponjo Avenue), cross creek. Fort site is 200 yards farther east on hillside to north.

**ONLY KNOWN** representation of Fort Cobb appears on marker at entrance to town. Actual fort site is about half a mile northeast of this spot. Major events in Cobb's career are recorded on this Oklahoma State marker.

**FORT COBB TODAY** has been obliterated by time and spring plowing. Slight traces remain of fort, primarily of stockade on hill, but these can be found only by conscientious searchers. Here in 1868 Sheridan's troopers held a review for the generals and Indian chiefs. A private's diary of period noted,"Our guns have been polished, also buckles on straps and belts. We have to have clean clothes and boots to look as well as we can make them without polish . . . every man to look as clean as soap and water can make him. I have spent most of the day cleaning and polishing, even going over my saddle and bridle with a greasy woolen cloth."

# FORT RENO, OKLAHOMA

When things at the Agency got so bad that the employees took to carrying guns, the time was ripe to call for the Army.

That was the case back in '74 at the Darlington Agency in Oklahoma. The Cheyenne Uprising of that year caused loyal Indians to warn the Agent that his life was in danger, so he headed for Wichita, Kansas, for help. Troops sent from Fort Sill ran into such a battle at the Wichita Agency 30 miles south that another call had to go out. Four cavalry troops and an infantry company responded from Fort Leavenworth.

Order was restored, and with that encampment a new Army fort was located. While General Sheridan pressured the War Department for funds, the troopers began leveling the ground, digging wells, and, with a sawmill borrowed from the Agency, put up a few buildings. "Post at Cheyenne Agency" was authorized on April 7, 1875, with an initial appropriation of $20,000, upped another $9,000 by the end of the year. The following February it became Fort Reno, after the abandoned Wyoming fort of the '60's.

The first buildings were the usual rough log structures common to the frontier. One of these still remains. In common with the Washington-Grant-Lee-Custer Was Here tradition of early America, this one bears the claim "Sheridan's Headquarters," although there is little evidence to back it up. But it appears the building is authentic and, therefore, has value as probably the earliest Reno building extant.

Soldiers divided their time between fort building and Indian controlling until the last Cheyenne dissidents gave up in mid-'75. After the leaders were shipped to Fort Marion, Florida, Reno activities slowed a bit, but were highlighted by at least two displays of uncommon personal bravery.

After Custer's Little Big Horn defeat, the Indian roundups sent 937 Cheyennes to Reno. The job of guarding, moving, and feeding these latter-day warriors was handled by Lieutenant Henry Lawton, 17 troopers, and 20 white mule skinners.

Although Lawton kept his charges in line on the difficult march, a year after they arrived at Reno a large band broke loose and ravaged through Oklahoma and Kansas. Another Army post, known simply as "Cantonment," was established midway to Fort Supply to provide security at this time. It never received a more complete name although it lasted until 1882.

In 1880 the Reno Cheyennes became surly because of a cut in the meat ration, venting their anger by slashing at the Agent with a riding crop. Into the midst of 1,500 agitated Comanches, Captain George M. Randall led a squad of troopers, and faced the Indian leaders down. He told them to go home, or await the wrath of reinforcing troops supposedly on the way from Kansas.

The Indian guns were lowered and they went back to their camps. They did not know the reinforcements were merely a bluff. Nor did they know cannon from Fort Reno were trained on them with orders to fire if Randall was attacked.

Five years later the Indians again indicated less than friendly feelings about the Agent. This time they hinted that a big bonfire was in the offing, the Agency buildings providing the fuel.

General Sheridan personally rushed to Fort Reno to quell this one. Perhaps he stayed a night or two in the log hut with the "headquarters" claim—the

**FORT RENO OKLA.-1891**

**MANY BUILDINGS** on this ground plan remain today. Large building behind flagpole is most imposing, once was used as guardhouse and storehouse by both commissary and quartermaster. Barracks flanking it have disappeared. Stables to its rear saw considerable use in later years when Fort became Army Remount Station. During World War II it was also prisoner of war camp. Department of Agriculture took it over in 1948. (Redrawn from plat in National Archives.)

164

**TROOPS AND INDIAN** police in formation in front of warehouse in the 1880's. Reno's forces were called upon frequently to quell troubles between various Indian tribes. In 1892, a company spent a month at Choctaw capital in Tuskahoma settling tribal election disputes after several politicians had been assassinated. A year later they rushed to Antlers, Oklahoma, and restored order between same factions who had been reinforced by tribal "militia." Again in 1900 a cavalry troop had to be sent to back authority of legitimate tribal chief.

fort's officers' quarters having burned the previous year.

Fort Reno's affairs involved more than just the traditional Indian fighting. Located in what was then termed "Indian Territory," it was charged with keeping it inviolate from white incursions. Every time ex-Army Captain David Payne (once stationed with Sheridan at Fort Cobb) led his "Boomers" into the territory, Reno's troopers headed him off. Several times he was locked up in the Reno guardhouse, but always won his freedom by paying a token fine.

When the territory finally was opened to settlement, Reno soldiers guarded the b o r d e r against "Sooners." They were spread in a thin blue line along the Unassigned Lands boundary. Patrols had searched the area to assure that no one got across early—though many did.

Shortly before noon on April 22, 1889, a captain

**SOLDIER DEAD** from many wars and many forts rest in Fort Reno National cemetery. Marker in foreground is for corporal killed by Northern Cheyennes at Turkey Springs in 1878. Behind low wall in background are 35 grave markers for German prisoners of war who died here in World War II.

**MAGAZINE** still has interior fittings of former use, though later years apparently saw it converted to latrine purposes. This is same building appearing next to storehouse in old photograph. Brick and stone construction of many buildings dates from 1881 though bricks at the time drew Army inspector's criticism because being "made at this post by the troops" they were "of a poor quality and badly burnt."

**ALTHOUGH HIDDEN** by trees, this is same spot as early picture. Commissary is now used as grain storehouse and some windows and doors have been closed off. Small magazine building, obvious in old photograph, can be seen in center background. Flagpole dates from turn of century, is caked with rust because Agriculture Department uses smaller pole in front of their offices, shown on plat as post headquarters.

of the 5th Cavalry raised his arm aloft. Thousands of eyes watched him. Exactly at n o o n, the arm dropped and Fort Reno buglers started to b l o w "reveille."

Its strains were drowned out by the thundering crash of wagons, horses, trains, and carriages racing forward to the accompaniment of hoarse yells

and exuberant pistol firing. The great land rush was on and the frontier was no more.

TO GET THERE: From El Reno, Oklahoma, take U.S. 66 west four miles to Fort Reno Livestock Research Station. At end of about half-mile drive is old parade ground around which many former Army buildings still are used by Department of Agriculture.

**SHERIDAN STAYED** here in 1876, according to claim of El Reno Chamber of Commerce that can neither be proved nor disproved. Two-room building has been restored and moved from fort to edge of town where it is on north side of U.S. 66. Furnishings inside fit it out as office, in front, and bedroom in back.

**FORT RENO'S** late construction is evidenced by this elaborate storehouse, front of which appears behind troops in old photograph. It shows signs of age now, cracks edging down walls, sills broken off, and windows and doors closed off. Twentieth century incident at Fort Reno occurred in 1906 when battalion of troops from Fort Brown, Texas, were brought here to be mustered out by presidential order after saloon killing in Brownsville, Texas.

TWELVE YEARS of fighting separated these two views of Ranald S. Mackenzie. Early one was taken in 1864, later in 1876.
(NATIONAL ARCHIVES.)

# MACKENZIE'S RAIDERS

*"You are to go ahead on your own plan of action, and your authority and backing shall be General Grant and myself. With us behind you in whatever you do to clean up this situation, you can rest assured of the fullest support. You must assume the risk. We will assume the final responsibility should any result."*

—Sheridan to Mackenzie, April, 1873, triggering the raid into Mexico.

HE WAS number one in the West Point class of '62, was brevetted all of the way to major general during the Civil War, was wounded a total of five times, and was instrumental in bringing peace to the plains.

Ranald Slidell Mackenzie was born in 1840, became the Army's youngest colonel, and was described by U. S. Grant "as the most promising young officer in the Army." Grant noted that Mackenzie was a corps commander when the war ended and "this he did upon his own merit and without influence."

When the campaigns in the Southwest resumed, Mackenzie operated on direct orders from Grant, Sherman, and Sheridan. His service took him to Forts Ringgold, Clark, McKavett, Concho, Richardson, Robinson, and Garland, plus visits to many others. He fought across the Staked Plains, at Palo Duro Canyon, and in Wyoming. His secrets to success: an inflexible but understanding discipline, everlasting training and imagination, and a quartermaster system that anticipated his moves and kept him supplied anywhere in the wilds.

But the main expedition on which his fame rests was his raid across the Rio Grande to the Indian village of Rey Molina, 50 miles deep into Mexico. Secret orders from Grant and Sheridan backed him up, but he knew that failure on his part would be his own responsibility.

Mackenzie and his raiders—to paraphrase a modern television version of his exploits—brought a measure of peace to the Southwest. But to Mackenzie, the man, peace was unattainable. His wounds bothered him, his temperamental irritability set him apart. When in his early forties his childhood sweetheart consented to marry this longtime bachelor, this seemed to tip the scales.

He was 49 years old when he died in a Staten Island mental hospital in 1889. By that date both he and the Southwest had found peace.

# FORT RICHARDSON, TEXAS

"I have not seen a trace of an Indian thus far and only hear the stories of people, which indicates that whatever Indians there be, only come to Texas to steal horses."

The speaker was General William T. Sherman, the date May, 1871, the location, near Fort Richardson, Texas. Sherman was on a tour of the West to see for himself the Indian problem. By the time he got to Richardson, he did not think much of it.

Look again, General, the Texans could have advised. And while he was looking, he would have seen a sight to change his opinion. It was the infamous "Jacksboro Incident."

This was the massacre of a Fort Richardson contractor's wagon train only 20 miles from the fort. The 12 corn-filled wagons were stolen, seven teamsters killed. Five survivors crawled that night into Fort Richardson to report the massacre. Sherman had passed the spot o n l y a few hours before the ambush.

He immediately dispatched General Mackenzie and 150 cavalrymen to hunt down the hostiles. The next day he reassured a crowd of 200 to 300 Jacksboro citizens the same thing he wrote one of his commanders, "It is all important that this case be followed up with extreme vigor," especially to determining if any so-called reservation Indians were involved.

The story of the confession and capture of Satanta, Satank, and Big Tree belongs to Fort Sill, and is told there. But the c l i m a x took place at Fort Richardson.

Despite his proud boasts at Fort Sill that he was

the leader of the Jacksboro killers, Satanta had a different line at the trial at Fort Richardson. This was a test of legal justice against the redmen and Satanta made the best of it.

"If I ever get back to my people, I will never make war upon you," he proclaimed to the jury. "I did not kill the Tehannas. I came down the Pease River to make medicine for wounded braves. I am suffering for the crimes of bad Indians . . . If you will let me go, I will kill them with my bare hands. There shall be peace."

The prosecutor had a different story about Satanta. He called the Indian an arch-fiend of murder, a coward, and a hypocrite. Big Tree was described as "a tiger demon who had tasted blood and loves it as his food."

Big Tree refused to comment, suggesting that this was the day for "white man's talk." Satanta, the self-proclaimed orator of the plains, did all of the talking. It did little good; the jury sentenced both to hang.

"I feel assured that a civil court in Texas will do them full justice and that on Texas soil they will find an early grave," predicted an Army officer before the trial. His prediction did not come true. A year later they were free to continue their depredations.

The release of the Indians was vastly unpopular in the Fort Richardson area where, as the 1870 surgeon's report stated, "There is scarcely a family . . . that has not suffered in property or the lives of its members within the past five years."

He pointed out, "The whole of the frontier line of counties . . . has been for the past four years subject to the inroads of Indians during the summer and fall of each year . . . The boldness of these predatory Indians is increasing from year to year, the scouting parties sent in pursuit of them failing to overtake or meet them, except in rare instances."

A disheartening matter to the soldiers was voiced by the surgeon. "It was noticed that this band of Indians was armed with breech-loading firearms, in

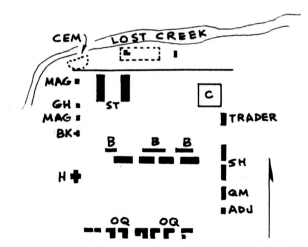

## FORT RICHARDSON TEXAS - 1869

**ADJUTANT** at Fort Richardson described the officers' quarters as five of frame, five of picket. "The former were one and a half story cottages with broad porches in front and rear ceiled and plastered, each containing four rooms. The picket quarters contained but one room; were set on the ground; had no porches; were unceiled, with rough 'parabolic' floors, and large stone fireplaces, where one might freeze his back and toast his face during a Norther." He said that when dried chinking dropped from wall partitions, "an arm could be readily thrust through into the neighboring officer's room, and any noise above a whisper was easily heard in the adjoining quarters." Fort was a parallelogram 1,400 by 1,300 feet long. Three left barracks were 85 feet long, 20 wide; right barracks was 100 feet long. (Redrawn from Surgeon General report, 1870.)

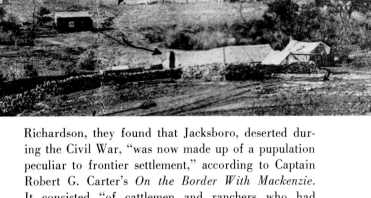

**FORT RICHARDSON** in its heyday, according to picture contributed to National Archives by Captain R. G. Carter, who made the ink marks on its face. As Adjutant, Carter's office was at far left. Officers' quarters were along rear, men's picket quarters in foreground across Lost Creek, hospital centered in grouping at right edge.

(NATIONAL ARCHIVES.)

some instances of a superior description to those of the soldiers." He referred to an 1869 fight between 50 cavalrymen and 200 Indians 60 miles from the post. It took an Army toll of two soldiers killed and 11 wounded.

This was in the early days of Fort Richardson. It had succeeded the Post at Jacksboro, the town next to the fort, and actually was a replacement for waterless Fort Belknap. Founded in 1867, Richardson's first duties involved both protection and cleaning up.

"In addition to the large amount of fatigue duty incident to building barracks and officers' quarters and removing rock and rubbish from the parade ground and other parts of the fort," the surgeon reported, the early years "were rendered more arduous on account of the incessant escort duty required by the civil authorities, in quelling disturbances . . . and in preserving the peace during the process of reconstructing the State."

Even with the readmission of Texas to the Union, the countryside did not quiet down. "Large scouting parties are almost constantly in the field endeavoring to check the depredations of, and to punish hostile Indians."

When Mackenzie and his 4th Cavalry arrived at Richardson, they found that Jacksboro, deserted during the Civil War, "was now made up of a pupulation peculiar to frontier settlement," according to Captain Robert G. Carter's *On the Border With Mackenzie.* It consisted "of cattlemen and ranchers who had fled in from their ranches to the protection of the Post, and a miscellaneous collection of Mexicans, Negroes, discharged soldiers, gamblers, and saloon-keepers—occasionally increased by a roaring, rollicking gang of cowboys on a spree."

These latter were described as spending most of their time "riding up and down 'Jacks' only street—screeching and yelling like a lot of wild Indians and firing their six-shooters at saloon windows and many other imaginary enemies."

Carter added t h a t the celebrants usually were "cooled off by a night's reflection in the guardhouse." This must have been effective, he said, because "when we first arrived these orgies had been of almost nightly occurrence, but after Mackenzie had sent over one or two warnings and then proceeded to apply force by bagging them and confining the worse ones . . . there was little to complain of."

TO GET THERE: From the Jacksboro square, go south a half mile on U.S. 281. Restored buildings are under the care of a custodian and former hospital is a museum.

**EDGE OF PARADE GROUND** shows hospital, left, with bakery and magazine recognizable in background. Bridge over Lost Creek is in center of background. Writing later of Fort Richardson, Captain Carter remembered "when savage Indians lurked about the Post, hostile bullets sung over the picket hut, and arrows hurtled about the heads of this devoted band of officers' and soldiers' families posted there for the advancement and expansion of the civilization of our country."

**HOSPITAL** was built of sandstone, was 128 feet long, matched specifications prescribed by Washington closer than most frontier hospitals. After fort was abandoned in 1878, it answered various uses. National Guard used it in 1930's, but 1955 newspaper article said, "Now it is vacant and windows are gone and doors are sprung open. Behind the hospital is the dead house, piled with machinery and with one of the old original doors nailed to a window." Jacksboro Historical Society now owns building and has restored it as a museum.

**FIELD GRADE** officer's family lived in this frame house, but usually it was shared by two families. Some quarters of similar size accommodated four families, the captains occupying two rooms, the lieutenants' families one. Lieutenants usually increased space by adding a canvas wing to rear of their rooms. This building has been restored by Jacksboro Historical Society. It is near right edge of officers' row in plat.

**STOREHOUSE** now is abandoned ruin separated from restored fort by railroad tracks. There were two storehouses, both of sandstone, 86 feet long, 29 wide, and 19 high. Original plans were for area between the two to have an archway which would be main entrance to fort, but wooden structure was built in space instead. Richardson troops carried on running feud with Jacksboro citizens, once had to be marched into town by Mackenzie to convince civilians they did not plan to burn it down. Incident was caused by killing of soldier in town "red-light" district.

# FORT CLARK, TEXAS

Tension ran high at Fort Clark. Something was up, the troopers knew, but no one was saying what. In fact, no one seemed to know, not even the officers. What was more, not even the most reliable source of information, the wives' gossiping, could come up with anything concrete.

For weeks the men of the 4th Cavalry had been training in intricate cavalry maneuvers. Targets were set up and rifle practice was held, something uncommon considering the traditionally parsimonious ammunition budget. Even saber sharpening was required until razor edges were produced.

Whenever the regimental quartermaster placed requisitions, department headquarters filled them with unexplained and unsurpassed speed. The quantity of items told him that something was coming up, but he could not guess what. General Mackenzie wrote out the supply list himself and passed it without explanation to the quartermaster.

A few at a time, horses were sent to forage areas away from Fort Clark. The explanation was that they had to be rested and fattened up, but it seemed that this could have been done as well at the fort. Then, troopers were sent to camps away from the fort.

Only two men at Fort Clark knew the plan, Ranald Mackenzie and his acting adjutant, Captain Robert G. Carter. The latter had been sworn to secrecy by Mackenzie when the mission was revealed:

"He then, in strictest confidence," wrote Carter in *On the Border With Mackenzie,* "informed me that through some renegade Mexicans and half-breeds he was possessed of certain knowledge with reference to the Indians who had . . . committed the massacre at Howard's Wells in which an officer of the 9th Cavalry had been killed.

"He had ascertained their exact locality . . . across the Rio Grande, and he should immediately commence preparations for an expedition against them. He proposed to punish them for the past, and check their raids in the future. . . . Relying upon Gen. Sheridan's declaration of absolute support, Mackenzie said he should not hesitate to take the risk. It 'was make or break!'"

Carter found that the 4th Cavalry had been sent especially to Fort Clark for this raid. "In naming the 4th for the Rio Grande," General Sherman had explained in his orders, "the President is doubtless influenced by the fact that Colonel Mackenzie is young and enterprising, and that he will impart to his regiment his own active character."

The 4th had arrived at Clark in April, 1873. "The column rode into a spacious live oak grove at the base of the hill where Fort Clark was located," remembered Carter. "The ground was dry, baked and intolerably dusty and dirty by having been used for a camp for a number of years." After cleaning the area, "it proved to be a most delightful camp in spite of all the dirt."

The regiment was waiting for the 9th Cavalry to leave its quarters in Fort Clark before moving in. While still in camp, it learned that the Secretary of War and General Sheridan were coming to consult with Mackenzie and the 9th's Wesley Merritt. It was obvious that the focus of attention in the Indian campaigns was being centered on Fort Clark.

The fort had been a kingpin in the Texas defense line from its earliest days. Founded in 1852, it was to protect that portion of the frontier and the San Antonio road from Indian and Mexican depredations. "Fort Clark was a pleasant post," wrote an officer's wife of an 1855 stay. She said, "It was very agreeable to us all, the garrison being a large one with a number of officers and ladies."

She did not seemed fazed by her quarters, "a funny little house . . . built of green logs with the bark left on them, and they were set up on end, not like the usual log-cabin . . . All being green at first, they dried during the intensely hot summer, and very soon the floor and walls were far apart, so that the rats and mice came and went without ceremony."

LAS MORAS Creek winds around Fort Clark and its spring, near northern corner of parade, is main reason for location of fort. Legend is that anyone crossing Moras Creek has his sins washed away. Present headquarters for Fort Clark Guest Ranch is at location of quartermaster storehouse, northern corner of parade. Hospital indicated nearby was the old hospital in 1875; its function had been taken over by large, double-story hospital to left of barracks. (Redrawn from Division of Missouri report, 1876.)

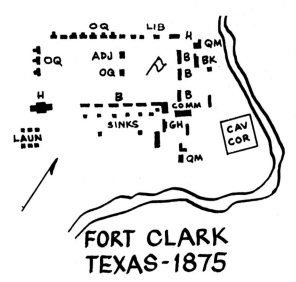

FORT CLARK
TEXAS - 1875

This vertical log construction was common at Army posts of the 1850's, but not all Clark buildings adopted it. Many dating from that period were of stone, including the hospital, a storehouse, and at least one officers' quarters.

Activity was fast paced at Clark. On one 1857 occasion, a 5th Cavalry patrol had three engagements with Indians in the same day. In 1858, a 600-mile expedition chased redmen until they crossed the Rio Grande into the safety of Mexico. Although the soldiers set up an ambush to catch any returning warriors, no one came. Later in the year, a Clark patrol so thoroughly routed the Indians that the braves put 90 miles between themselves and the Army before stopping to make camp.

The Confederates garrisoned Fort Clark for a short time, but had to abandon it when they ran out of men. When the Federals returned in 1866, they began an extensive remodeling, adding new stone

OFFICERS' QUARTERS occupied by General Jonathan Wainwright when he commanded Fort Clark date to its early years. It is one of several accommodations at guest ranch. In 1892, wife of surgeon described her arrival at post: "The bugle was just sounding Retreat and the tempered sunset light lent a rosy charm to the rather severe and rectangular stone quarters. The vine-covered verandas, tiny lawns, and trim rows of China trees bespoke careful homemaking: for the trees were planted in trenches blasted out of the solid rock and silled with soil; the grass was a layer of sod placed over the outcropping limestone."

barracks, officers' quarters, a headquarters, and a wooden stables 200 feet long. But in 1873, Carter commented that it "had not been rebuilt, and the dilapidated and limited quarters, many of them rude log huts, proved anything but inviting to the troopers of the 4th Cavalry."

The post's proximity to Mexico was a reason for its existence. This escape route for marauding Indians was recognized. The post surgeon pointed this out in his 1870 report:

". . . The Indians operating in this region have been the Lipan and Kickapoo tribes, whose homes are in Mexico. The military operations have been, therefore, comparatively futile, as but little injury can be done to Indians unless their homes are reached."

Sage comments from the surgeon, because three years later that was exactly what Fort Clark's troopers did. The word to "pack up" came to the cavalrymen around 3 a.m. on May 17, 1873. From their various camps, the troops converged, skirting towns so that spies could not pass the word ahead.

Shortly before dark, the command reached the Rio Grande. Here Mackenzie briefed his officers on the campaign, not mentioning "the fact that he was acting without orders or authority from our government," Carter said, "or that he was taking the precious lives over the Rio Grande with merely the implied permission which General Sheridan had given or suggested to him at their conference in April at Fort Clark."

The night was clear and moonlit. "We r o d e rapidly, going where—we knew not—led by the half-breed guides on their fox-gaited beasts. They knew the importance of reaching the villages at daybreak, as planned, in order to surprise the enemy; also had measured the distance, and spared not their horses."

The mule loads proved too cumbersome and slowed the column. The packs were dropped, each man stuffing bread and ammunition into his blouse, and the saddle-less mules were able to keep up. The trot-

**FORT CLARK** in 1903 retained early appearance. Fort was used until 1949 and in modern years "Fort Clark, although isolated from any large city, is considered by cavalrymen as a desirable station," according to 1935 description. "It is famous for its wonderful springs of drinking water, its beautiful bridle paths, its shady groves of forest monarchs many centuries old." This view is from new hospital, looking down barracks row; these were smaller and older barracks than double-storied barracks in background.

ting column moved over the countryside to a point about 50 miles into the interior.

"This was the Rey Molina," recorded Carter. "We were now close to our objective—our mission of death . . . At the foot of the slope we could now clearly see the huts stringing out in a long distance, and the general outline of an Indian abiding place."

Firing and yelling, the troops charged the village, platoon by platoon. As each platoon delivered its first volley, it wheeled and fell into the rear of the other platoons, reloading as it went. The units worked their way down the length of three villages, scattering deadly volleys as they went.

"The sudden charge proved a complete surprise," commented Carter. "The warriors were yelling and flying in every direction, many half naked, from their huts."

The villages were put to the torch and prisoners rounded up. Many warriors escaped, but some were captured along with the women and children. One brave raised a rifle to fire on an officer. A shot by Carter, with a simultaneous one by a trooper, spun the man around like a top before he dropped dead.

Success in the village was one thing, but the question of returning to the Rio Grande was something far different. Scouts reported signs of Mexican and Indian groups approaching, and Mackenzie mounted up, heading home. A gruelling m a r c h followed. Carter said "this was the third night that many of us had been absolutely without sleep or rest . . . Everywhere the men drowsed and swayed in their saddles . . . We felt the entire command had expended about every ounce of energy and strength . . . and made the strain on the officers almost intolerable."

**QUARTERMASTER STOREHOUSE** can be recognized in background at right edge of old picture. It is one of most picturesque at present site because most other buildings have been removed.

Five days after leaving Clark, the command was back. It had gone 160 miles in 32 marching hours, averaging seven miles an hour enroute to Rey Molina, 4 3/5 on the way back. It had been tailed by hostiles and, while camped on the Rio Grande, had expected an attack any minute.

The guard was doubled at Fort Clark, a central building designated into which the women and children were to take refuge, and pickets were put out around the post. A revenge raid was expected. Other than a false alarm a week later, nothing came of it.

The Mexican government condemned the raid. The Texas legislature officially lauded it. And President U. S. Grant upheld Mackenzie, although the political repercussions rubbed off on Mackenzie's name in some Washington circles.

The raid had the desired effect. The Mexican government agreed to a reciprocal treaty, permitting the military of both countries to cross the border on the so-called "hot trail" of bandits, horse and cattle thieves, and other desperadoes.

TO GET THERE: Bracketville is on U.S. 90 about 30 miles east of Del Rio and 40 miles northwest of Uvalde. Fort Clark, now the Fort Clark Guest Ranch owned by the Texas Railway Equipment Company, is opposite Bracketville on south side of highway.

# FORT McKAVETT, TEXAS

Ranald Mackenzie hit a dilapidated Fort McKavett in March, 1869, but it did not stay that way very long. As far as he was concerned, the fact that the post was 17 years old and had been abandoned for most of the Civil War—well, this had no bearing on the subject at all. It was an Army post, and it should look like one.

Here is the story as recounted by the post surgeon in his 1870 report:

"Fort McKavett was built originally of stone, the roofing, flooring, etc., of wood. During the time of its abandonment, all the buildings went to ruin . . . When the post was reoccupied in April, 1868, one house alone was habitable, and that had been kept in repair by the owner of the post . . .

"Until March, 1869, very little work had been done, owing mainly to the lack of mechanics and the extreme slowness with which material was supplied." Upon the arrival of Mackenzie, "almost immediately the work of rebuilding the post commenced; ample and substantial corrals for the cavalry horses were built at once; the barracks for the men were put in complete repair, and company kitchens, guardhouse, sinks, and all outbuildings thoroughly renovated. Officers' quarters have also been enlarged, and in fact almost rebuilt, with new floors, roofing, windows, doors, etc."

The surgeon blamed much of the deterioration of the buildings on faulty construction of the stone walls.

In the 1853 Army inspection of the post, it was noted that most of the work was done by soldiers and "the buildings are put up of stone which is found immediately at hand in great abundance and of quality easily dressed."

Use of soldier labor was objected to, primarily for health reasons. The 1853 report commented, "as the men are doing the duty of laborers they should be allowed the same privileges, and I would recommend that the period of fatigue should in no case exceed eight hours out of 24, and be so proportioned as to allow the men shelter from the sun for a period of at least three hours during the intense heat of the day."

Despite this unpromising background, Fort McKavett underwent vast and rapid changes under Mackenzie. When the 4th Cavalry moved from Fort Concho to Fort Clark in 1873, Captain Robert G. Carter described Mackenzie's old command as "that beautiful little post on the San Saba."

The 4th Cavalry stayed several days at McKavett. Carter remembered later that General A. McD. McCook, the commander, gave a hop for the officers and their wives. "It was a revelation how the ladies managed to secure so much finery in such a short time," Carter commented, "but we always suspected that most of it was borrowed from the generous hostesses of the Fort McKavett garrison."

Apparently General McCook was the life of the party. He appeared at the ball wearing "a great white Mexican sombrero, presented to him by the citizens of Metamoras, with his name heavily embroidered with gold and silver bullion on the brim."

It appears that the bulk of Mackenzie's energies

**FORT McKAVETT**
**TEXAS—1874**

SUBSTANTIAL stone buildings made up most of Fort McKavett by 1874, courtesy of Mackenzie's rebuilding program. His quarters as post commander were the solitary officers' residence offset from left edge of bottom officers' row. Although post originally was contained within 100-yard-square parade ground, additional buildings were placed outside. (Redrawn from Division of Missouri report, 1876.)

FORT McKAVETT commanding officer's residence appeared in 1917 probably much like early years. It was considered "comfortably large . . . commodious, and in every way pleasant." It was destroyed by fire in 1942. (COLLECTION OF DONALD N. WILKINSON, MENARD.)

while commanding McKavett were directed in building rather than fighting. After he left the post, he called upon McKavett troopers frequently to augment his forces on expeditions, and in this role they fought in the Red River Indian War of 1874-75. Later, they were active in the Victorio War from 1878-81.

His attention to housekeeping was as strict and detailed as was his attention to military tactics. "I have served at no post . . . where more attention is paid to cleanliness of quarters," reported the surgeon in 1870, "and where all sanitary and hygienic rules are more thoroughly enforced, and where more deference is paid to the suggestions of the medical officer in regard to such rules."

In a statement uncommon to most medical reports, the surgeon announced without reservation, "there is no more healthy post on the Texas frontier than Fort McKavett."

The fate of Fort McKavett was similar to many others, but with a certain difference. After it was abandoned in 1883, it reverted to its private owners. Unlike other forts, it suffered little from the ravages of time and humanity.

Today the town of Fort McKavett is also the old fort, the various buildings still being occupied as residences. As buildings collapse or burn, it seems that families move into others. The fort has not been absorbed by the town, because very little post-

COMMANDING OFFICER'S residence is grotesque shell next to road today. As only two-story building at Fort McKavett, it was county landmark after fort was abandoned.

HEADQUARTERS, as seen from ruins of an officers' quarters, no longer hears the stomp of first sergeants' boots as they give morning reports and transact other company business. Building is now occupied as a private residence.

Army construction is evident. The fort is the town.

Apparently the relatively isolated location—distant from the major highways—and Mackenzie's solid, immovable construction have contributed to leave Fort McKavett a very real shadow of its former self.

TO GET THERE: Take State 29 from Menard, Texas, for 16 miles. Turn left (south) on Farm Road 864. In six miles this runs right into Fort McKavett.

NOT MANY years are left in these barracks, although stone walls still are solid. Soldiers considered that they offered "ample room." Each man was "furnished with an iron bedstead, and the quarters are kept strictly clean," surgeon said. He did not mention McKavett's "hog ranch," so-called Scabtown across creek where a half dozen illicit houses of business held forth. Records of fort do not indicate Scabtown put much of a dent in post's good health boast.

BARRACKS is now used for apartments. This was the barracks at the eastern edge of parade ground. During Mackenzie's tenure, post surgeon commented, "Unusual pains have been taken both as regards the cleanliness of the camp, carefulness in cooking, variety in diet, and personal cleanliness of the men."

# FORT CONCHO, TEXAS

Too many cooks almost spoiled the broth at Fort Concho, except that the cooks were self-styled architects and the broth was the matter of constructing the post. It was 22 years in the building and it was abandoned before it was finished.

The need for this West Texas installation had been recognized before the Civil War. A short-lived Camp Joseph E. Johnston was established somewhere near the later location of Concho in March, 1852, but was closed in November.

In 1867 the Army decided to protect the heartland of the area between the two chains of forts, and a post was established at the forks of the North and South Concho Rivers. It was a strategic location. The Butterfield, Goodnight, Comanche, Chihuahua, and California Trails all passed in the vicinity. For their protection, a detachment of 50 men and an officer was sent from Fort Chadbourne.

Confusion marked the first days. The first problems was in settling on an exact site. More than $28,000 was spent in preparing one area before it was rejected in favor of the final choice. Then despite a total of 16 officers, 372 enlisted men, and 137 civilian builders in December, 1867, progress was slow.

The buildings were to be constructed of pecan wood, but this proved too hard for normal use. Only a building of poles was completed within the first month, and this was for the post sutler. Everyone else lived and worked under canvas.

A succession of commanding officers caused the course of construction to shift as often as the prairie breezes. General William R. Shafter found the post "in a very bad condition in every respect" when he took over in 1870, and he ordered a reassignment of living spaces. The officers' quarters were reduced, a measure received so favorably by some that Shafter had to place two under arrest.

When Major John P. Hatch became commander, he soon earned himself the nickname of "Dobe." As far as he was concerned, adobe was the best building material around. Inexpert soldier adobe makers tried with little success to master the Mexican art. This experiment literally went down the drain in August when heavy rains disposed of the a d o b e brick stockpile.

Someone suggested the use of "pise work," the rubble-mixture of a concrete quality that had been used at Camp Verde. But finally wiser heads prevailed and the nearby sandstone quarries were tapped. With the decision to build the fort of this, work finally went ahead in earnest. This was four years after Fort Concho had been founded.

There was another hitch: the civilian builders' contracts and the source of materials usually were so ill-timed that when the employees were available, there were no supplies with which they could work. By the time the material arrived, the workers had been discharged and sent home.

**OFFICERS' QUARTERS** is now owned by museum and will be restored in future. In original plan, two 15-foot-square rooms were in front, separated by broad hall, with kitchen in wing to rear. When first built, some quarters had temporary summer kitchens added to back. Officer's wife who visited fort in 1869 had poor memories of it. "It was built on the prairie and struck me as gloomy in the extreme," she wrote. "The water at the fort was bad and the heat in summer almost insupportable."

**MOST OF THESE** buildings, or their sites, are recognizable today. Buildings were of stone, most of them with stone floors, and woodwork was of pecan. In 1875 surgeon said pecan was "a particularly intractable variety of our northern hickory, which by its twisting, curling, and shrinking hardly promises a permanence of symmetry." Hospital, largest building on post, burned in 1910. (Redrawn from Surgeon-General report, 1875, and data from J. N. Gregory.)

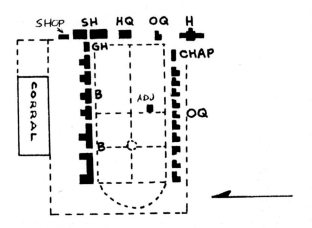

# FORT CONCHO
# TEXAS - 1878

(NATIONAL ARCHIVES.)

**FORT CONCHO** in 1886 was as finished as it was going to be. This view is from northwest. Barracks are in foreground, officers' quarters across parade ground. Double-storied hospital can be seen in far row, right center. North Concho river is in foreground. Periodically Army had to clear it of riffraff doing business in shanties along its banks. In 1881, flood was reported to have "swept several drinking saloons and miserable lodging places of outside camp-followers" from this area.

By 1875, when the fort was almost in its final state and while its Indian activities were at high level, General Sheridan suggested, "the usefulness of Fort Concho as a post will cease before long . . . and I must decline to spend any more money upon that post." With this he rejected a proposal for several new buildings, and a requisition for certain materials.

He was especially disenchanted by the justifications set forth in the requisition. He did not consider specific enough explanations of "putty for puttying, paint for painting."

Construction problems notwithstanding, Fort Concho's garrison had a busy time. Although no organized campaigns were undertaken in the first four years from Concho, in 1869 the troopers met Indians in two fights on the Salt Fork of the Brazos river. The first

ended a tie, but the second was a decided victory for the Army. Its major effect was to cheer up the Texas citizens who were undergoing the pangs of Reconstruction and the Indian depredations that seemed to go hand-in-hand with it.

Ranald Mackenzie took Concho troops into the field in 1871. It was a man-breaking, horse-killing expedition across the gypsum-alkali country of the Panhandle, but it resulted in the destruction of a Comanche village. A sudden weather break interrupted the attack when a sleet storm almost froze the lightly clad troops.

During the pursuit that followed, Mackenzie was wounded in the leg and ultimately had to return to his supply camp. The surgeon threatened to amputate the leg if Mackenzie did not submit to treatment,

**HEADQUARTERS** of Fort Concho also was commanding officers' residence. Court-martial room was small wing in rear. Disciplinary record of fort varied; in 1871 eight prisoners escaped from guardhouse by tunnelling through floor. Main troublemaker was town of "Saint Angela," early San Angelo, once hog ranch for Army post. Traveler in 1879 wrote, "Some of the most desperate sporting characters and card sharks in Texas frequented this town."

**MAGAZINE** stands today behind barracks, approximately three blocks from its original location. During restoration days, civic group had it moved and rebuilt stone by stone. It was important building in fort's active years. Post underwent frequent Indian visits. Surgeon in 1870 reported, "Horses have been repeatedly stolen within the post lines, and . . . a citizen has been killed and scalped within a mile of the adjutant's office."

mied before they had a chance to succeed—and eliminate the source of profit.

In September, 1872, Mackenzie jumped a large Comanche camp, killing a counted 23 Indians and capturing 127 women and children. The village was burned and 3,000 horses taken in tow. The horses were stampeded later. This taught Mackenzie a lesson he followed in the future: kill all captured stock rather than run the risk of its being recaptured by the Indians.

Captive women and children from the expedition were kept at Concho over the winter. To their surprise, and the rejoicing of their families, they were released in the spring to rejoin the tribe that had moved into the reservation at Fort Sill.

Mackenzie headquartered his 4th Cavalry at Fort Concho for a short time after this. Then after a tour at Fort Richardson, he moved the troopers back through Concho, gathered reinforcements there, and went on to Fort Clark. His famous raid into Mexico followed.

A year later, in 1874, Mackenzie took his troopers from Concho again. Other commands were to flush the Indians from their hunting grounds and Mac-

a recommendation ungracefully received by the Indian-fighter—but which he observed.

The following spring Mackenzie and the Concho troops were in the saddle again. In league with troops under Shafter, Mackenzie followed a "Comanchero" track with the unhappy assistance of a captive Comanchero. This man had been captured earlier by a Concho sergeant. After a primitive third degree, he admitted to being one of the renegade Mexican and American traders who made their living from running guns, ammunition, whiskey, and other illicit items to the Indians.

Connections also were hinted with the mysterious "Indian Ring" high up in Washington political circles. This group had been rumored to be in league with the Comancheros, sharing their profits, and occasionally influencing policy so that Army plans were sty-

**SUNDIAL** in front of headquarters building dates from early years of fort—a year too early, in fact. Fort Concho was not founded until 1867, but 1866 date appears on it. Closed fence had to be built around it to protect it from ravages of souvenir hunters.

kenzie was to be ready to hit them as they were driven South.

While General Miles met the Indians in the Panhandle area later to be occupied by Fort Elliott, Mackenzie in the south was attacked the night of September 25. The Army held off the Indians and prevented a stampede by the horses. Two days later, Mackenzie's scouts led him to Palo Duro Canyon just as dawn was breaking.

Below, Mackenzie could see hundreds of tepees. Not a soul was stirring. His surprise attack was tipped off when some early risers spotted the soldiers. But Mackenzie was able to rout the camp and destroy the villages. This time, he disposed of the 1,400 captured livestock. The carcasses of more than 1,000 slaughtered animals made a gruesome landmark, "The Bone Pile," until settlers hauled them away for fertilizer years later.

By Christmas, the campaign was over. The Indians had been harassed into surrendering. The Army had ground to a near-halt, bogged down in impassable mud and worn down by severe weather and difficult resupply conditions.

Other campaigns were fielded from Concho, but never of the magnitude of that of 1874. The engagements were small and, except for the chase of Victorio in 1880, did not involve many troops. For all intents and purposes, Mackenzie's "raiders" had brought peace to the plains.

Along with its sister forts of the frontier, it became

CHAPEL also served as schoolhouse, though schoolmaster was hard to obtain. On one occasion, he was ordered into field for expedition and children had unscheduled vacation. It is owned by Fort Concho Museum and has been restored.

increasingly obvious that the need had passed for Concho. In 1889 it was abandoned and the Army marched away. A crowd of prosperous and secure citizens watched as the flag came down for the last time, the band struck up "The Girl I Left Behind Me," and the troops swung into column and marched away.

TO GET THERE: From downtown San Angelo, take Oakes Avenue south across North Concho River about five blocks to East Avenue C. Turn left. Street runs beside parade ground; headquarters building (museum) is at dead end, three blocks. Fort buildings are maintained by civic group and can be toured for a small fee.

BARRACKS have been reconstructed from original stones, now house museum and collection of pioneer relics. Four of them originally were 100 by 27 feet, two larger ones were 180 feet long.

# ACKNOWLEDGMENTS

Hundreds of contacts went into accomplishing OLD FORTS OF THE SOUTHWEST and it would be unfortunate if these were allowed to pass without acknowledgment. Without the enthusiastic help of these kind folks, this book would not have come about, and any credit must be shared with them. (But the errors, if any, are purely the author's.)

First and foremost in giving everything from advice and file copies, to forwarding mail for wandering photographers, are historians and their associates of the National Park Service. These included Robert M. Utley and Robert Brown, Santa Fe; Ray Mattison, Omaha; Charles Snell and Robert Hussey, San Francisco; Roger Rogers, Charles S. Marshall, and Elbert Cox, Richmond; Thomas F. Norris, Ft. Smith; Michael J. Becker and Erwin Thompson, Ft. Davis; Homer Hastings and Mr. and Mrs. Dale Giese, Ft. Union; Jack McDermott, Ft. Laramie; Aubrey L. Haines, Yellowstone; and Roy E. Appleman, Charles W. Porter III, and John Porter Bloom at the Service's headquarters, Washington, D.C.

Staff members from these institutions or libraries deserve thanks: *National Archives:* Milton K. Chamberlain, Mrs. Sara D. Jackson, Elmer O. Parker (Old Army Branch); Josephine Motelywski and May E. Fawcett (Visual Aids); Charlotte Ashby and A. P. Muntz (Cartographic). *Smithsonian Institution:* Frank H. H. Roberts, Jr. (Bureau of American Ethnology) and George Howell (Military History). *Bureau of Indian Affairs:* Merrill Tozier. *Gilcrease Collection:* Paul Rossi. *McNay Art Institute:* Mrs. Lois Burkhalter.

*College of William and Mary Library:* James Servies. *Research Library, Marine Corps Education Center:* Mrs. Evelyn Daniels and George Mahoney. *Northwestern University Deering Library:* Florence Stewart. *West Point Museum:* Frederick P. Todd. *Virginia Beach, Va., Library:* Mrs. Maestas, Margaret Capps, Jeane Kaplan. *Denver Public Library Western History Department:* Alys Freeze.

The staffs of the Library of Congress, Army War College, Yale University Library, Newberry Library, Bancroft Library, Chicago Historical Society, Confederate Museum.

Folks who have researched this subject and offered advice and the loan of materials included Lee Myers, Carlsbad, N.M.; Barbara Neal Ledbetter, Newcastle, Tex., Margaret Bierschwale, Mason, Tex.; Marvin King, Arenas Valley, N.M.; William Covington, Placerville, Calif.; Aurora Hunt, Pacific Palisades, Calif.; Nell Murbarger, Costa Mesa, Calif.; James D. Horan, Newark, N.J.; Albert P. Salisbury, Seattle; and Colonels Fred Rogers, San Francisco, and George Ruhlen, San Diego, Calif.

Don Sharp's Roundup Book Company, San Francisco, and Kenneth Nebenzal, Chicago, were book dealers who took special pains to help although there was little or no financial gain possible.

In the final patching together of the book, thanks are inadequate to J. W. (Red) Richardson and his wife, Rosemarie, Imperial Beach, Calif., who processed all photography; Paul Hartle, who drew the plats; John J. Connolly and William Diederich, helpful advisors; the author's wife, Teresa, who was assisted in typing and proofing by Donna Schmidt and Giles Hagood; and to the author's three children, Bridget, Erin, and Bret—without whom the book would have been finished in half the time.

By states, here are the helpful folks who never rejected a cry for aid:

*Arizona:* Mrs. India S. Moore (Arizona Pioneers Historical Society), Rudolph Zweifel, John J. Bajart, C. S. Damon, Brother Raymond, O.F.M. *Arkansas:* Mrs. Helen M. Johnson. *California:* Allan R. Ottley (State Library), James de T. Abajian (Historical Society), Jack R. Dyson (Beaches and Parks); Louis Wakefield (Ft. Tejon), 1st Lt. Tom Grewis (Benicia), Postmaster Michael J. Fitzgerald.

*Colorado:* Mrs. Alice Wallace, Enid Thompson, and Kathleen Pierson (Historical Society), Rev. Leroy J. N. Boyd, C. W. Hurd, John G. Bolita, Bill Hoagland, Kent Riddle. *Kansas:* Nyle Miller and Robert W. Richmond (Historical Society), Robert Galvin (Civil War Centennial Commission), Clela Wilmoth, Captain D. D. Wingfield (Ft. Riley), Mrs. Al Deckert, Mrs. H. C. Campbell, L. H. Johnson, George Henrichs (Boot Hill Museum), Carl A. and Ralph Engel, James DeMarco, Grover Helm, Dale W. Harmon, Dorothy Scott, Grace and Kent Collier, Mrs. Jesse Clair Harper, Cecil Kingery, Warren W. White, Rose Truhlar, Rep. George Jelinek, Lt. Col. John J. Killian (Ft. Leavenworth), Mrs. Ruth Jackson, Frank Madigan, Dudley C. Chads. *Nebraska:* Johnny Hopp.

*Nevada:* Mrs. Clara S. Beatty (Historical Society), Fritz Buckingham, Rev. Albert Muller, O.P. *New Mexico:* Bill Slevin and Ben Bowen (Department of Development), George Fitzpatrick (New Mexico Magazine), Herman H. (Corny) Moncus, Jimmy Otero, Edward and Billy Sweet, Dr. Herbert Dick, George Bryant, Col. Laurence W. Varner, Mr. and Mrs. J. Paul Taylor, William Taylor, Helen P. Caffey (Thomas Branigan Library).

*Oklahoma:* Elmer L. Fraker, Mrs. C. E. Cook (Historical Society), Mrs. Le Schumaker (State Library), Gillett Griswold, Lt. Col. Gordon Cubbison, and 1st Sgt. Champion (Ft. Sill), Mrs. Lucille H. Terrell, R.N., Robert H. Weidemaier, Mrs. Mary Badgett, Mr. and Mrs. Jack Johnson, Jr., Dwight H. Stephens, Lyndsay W. Phillips.

*Texas:* Carolyn Berg (Historical Society), Madge Grba (West Texas Historical Society), Tom H. Taylor (Highway Department), James M. Thomas (Park Board), Vena E. Dickerson, Mr. and Mrs. Ray P. Lewis, Jim S. Hardy, Mrs. E. H. Chandler, W. H. Baker, Rev. G. C. Baker, Ben E. Pingenot, Harvey Seymour, Senator Ralph Yarborough, Barry Scobee, Fred Rowsey, Billy King, J. N. Gregory, Mrs. Nellie Cox, Maj. William Barrett USMC, C. O. Richards, Conda H. Wilie, Mr. and Mrs. J. Carrol Putman, A. W. Whiteley, D. W. Young, Mrs. J. W. Bullock, Carrie J. Crouch, O. M. Longnecker, Jr., W. C. Sanders, Mrs. E. E. Johnston, Robert Nail, Cal Newton, Justice H. A. Holmes, Mrs. G. F. Kilman, Mrs. Ralph R. Weiershausen, Jerald G. Follis, Mrs. Grover McDougall, Mrs. C. H. Hightower, Donald N. Wilkinson, Robert S. Weddle, Mrs. W. F. Hargrove, Jr., Hilton A. Crane, Florence J. Scott, G. R. Boyle, Mrs. Jacqueline Espy, George C. Lambkin (Fort Sam Houston).

*Utah:* John James (Historical Society), Ward Roylance (Tourist & Publicity Council), Andrew Terry. *Wisconsin:* Margaret Gleason (Historical Society).

# DIRECTORY OF MILITARY FORTS
# OF THE SOUTHWEST

Every available source was drawn upon to provide what is believed to be the most complete published listing in existence of nineteenth century Army posts. From the National Archives, Library of Congress, state historical societies, and the works listed in the bibliography, an attempt has been made to compile a complete directory of these military posts, something which can be drawn from no other single source. The bibliography will be included in volume III of the FORTS OF THE OLD WEST series.

This listing attempts to include all installations at which troops were stationed, ranging from the temporary camps and detachments to the more permanent forts. The term "fort" seemed to include many things; a fort could be a major, permanent installation, or it could be a temporary overnight affair. A camp could have been either, but more often the latter. This term sometimes was applied interchangeably, depending upon Army policy or the Congressional budget.

A "cantonment" was a semi-permanent camp before the Civil War, but usually a temporary place after the war. Detachments and stations usually were details of men under a sergeant or lieutenant located to protect a mail station, telegraph or heliograph post, or a stage line. Redoubts and batteries were protected small fort-like dugouts, the latter from which to fire cannon.

This list includes many non-Army places, some because of a contact with state militias or a short-term soldier occupancy, others for the sake of completeness. An asterisk indicates forts that were used by settlers, traders, rangers, and by the Armies of other nations. This part of the list does not claim to be all-inclusive.

Because of the sketchy records available, calculated guesses had to be employed in locating some posts and in determining their periods of activity. Old maps and records were empolyed to insure accuracy, but some forts still could not be located positively. These are so indicated by the blank under location or the "n.d." (for no date) under the date column. When old records gave an unidentifiable location, this is included in the hope that someone versed in local terms may have better luck. Approximate dates are included in the absence of positive dates.

Confederate forts are included, but not with the presumption that their listing is complete.

Forts changed names frequently, and this list carries each site by its most common name. Other names by which it was known are included. The abbreviations used are the same as those explained on the endsheet map. The locations sometimes are in terms of modern towns which did not exist at the same time as the fort.

A conscientious effort has been made to insure accuracy. The author would appreciate it if errors can be brought to his attention, by writing him care of the publisher.

## ARIZONA

| | | |
|---|---|---|
| Apache, Ft. (Cp. Ord, Cp. Mogollon, Cp. Thomas) | Near Fort Apache | 1870-1922 |
| Badger, Ft. | Junction Verde & Salado R. | c. 1866 |
| Barrett, Ft. | 100 mi. W. Ft. Breckenridge | 1862 |
| Beale's Spring, Cp. | 40 mi. NE. Ft. Mojave | 1871-74 |
| Bowie, Ft. | S. Bowie | 1862-1894 |
| Buchanan, Ft. (Cp. Moore) | Near Sonoita | 1856-61 |
| Cameron, Cp. | #1 at Calabasas #2 15 m. NE. Tubac | 1866-67 |
| Canby, Ft. | 28 mi. SW. Ft. Defiance | 1863-64 |
| Canon de Chelly, Ft. | 2 mi. NW. mouth of canyon | 1849 |
| Colorado, Cp. | 40 mi. N. LaPaz | 1868-71 |
| Crawford, Cp. | Cochise Co. | 1886 |
| Crittenden, Cp. | Near Ft. Buchanan site | 1868-73 |
| Date Creek, Cp. #1 | 3 mi. NE. Date Creek | 1867 |
| Date Creek, Cp. #2 | At Date Creek (4 sites) | 1867-73 |
| Defiance, Ft. | At Fort Defiance | 1851-61 |
| Ehrenberg, Det. at | At Ehrenberg | c. 1875 |
| El Dorado, Cp | El Dorado canyon | 1867 |
| Florilla, Cp. | Near Fort Canby | 1864 |
| Gaston, "Old Ft." | Colorado R. above Gila R. | c. 1867 |
| Goodwin, Cp. | N. of Geronimo | 1864 |
| Goodwin, Ft. | W. of Geronimo | 1864-71 |
| Grant, Ft. #1 (Ft. Arivaypa, Ft. Breckenridge, Ft. Stanford) | Mouth San Pedro R.; then vicinity Sand Pedro & Arivaypa R. | 1860-61; 1862 1865-72 |
| Grant, Ft. #2 (New Camp Grant) | Near Mt. Graham | 1872-1907 |
| Huachuca, Ft. | At Fort Huachuca | 1877- |
| Hualpai, Cp. (Cp. Devin, Cp. Toll Gate) | 40 mi. NW. Prescott | 1869-73; 1881 |
| Ilges, Cp. | 3 mi. S. Ft. McDowell | 1867 |
| John A. Rucker, Cp. #1 (Camp Supply) | San Bernardino Ranch | 1878 |
| John A. Rucker, Cp. #2 | 6 mi. to White R. | 1878-80 |
| La Paz, Cp. | N. of Ehrenberg | 1874-75 |
| Lake Carleton, Cp. on | Vic. Mormon Lake | c. 1866 |
| Lewis, Cp. | Near head Verde R. | c. 1865-70 |
| Lincoln, Cp. | Near La Paz | 1864 |
| Lowell, New Ft. | 7 mi. from Tucson | 1873-91 |
| Lowell, Old Ft. (Post of Tuscon, Cp Tucson) | At Tuscon | 1860-61; 1862; 1862-64; 1865-73 |
| Mansfield, Cp. | 7 mi. S. Ft. Defiance | 1863 |
| Maricopa Wells, Pt. at | Maricopa Wells | c. 1867 |
| Mason, Ft. (Ft. McKeen) | E. of Ruby | 1865-66 |
| McCleave, Cp. | 24 mi. S. Ft. Goodwin | 1864 |
| *McDonald, Ft. | E. of Payson | 1882 |
| McDowell, Ft. (Campo Verde) | N. of Phoenix | 1865-90 |
| *Milligan, Ft. | 1 mi. W. Eagar | n.d. |
| Mojave, Ft. (Cp. Colorado) | 15 mi. N. Needles, Cal. | 1859-61; 1863-90 |
| *Morini, Ft. (Ft. Rickerson, Ft. Valley) | 6 mi. N. Flagstaff | 1882 |
| Nogales, Cp. near | Nogales | 1882-88 |
| O'Connell, Cp. | Tonto Valley | 1868 |
| Ojo De Les Lemilas, Pt. | 100 mi. NW. Ft. Defiance | c. 1860 |
| Pickett Post, Cp. | Now Pinal | c. 1871 |
| Pinal, Cp. (Infantry Camp, Pinal Mountains) | 6 mi. W. Miami | 1870-71 |
| Price, Cp. | N. of Hilltop | 1881-83 |
| Rawlins, Cp. | 27 mi. NW. Prescott | 1870-71 |
| Reno, Cp. | Tonto Basin | 1867-70 |
| Rigg, Cp. | N. of Safford | c. 1864-70 |
| Rio Gila, Cp. on (HQ, Dept. of Ariz., Gila Depot) | Sacaton | c. 1867 |
| Rio San Pedro, Cp. | Vicinity Redington | 1859 |
| Rock Spring, Ft. | N. of Truxton | c. 1866 |
| San Carlos, Pt. at | San Carlos Reservation | 1871-1900 |
| San Pedro, Presidio of (Picket on the San Pedros) | Near Cp. Wallen site | c. 1878 |
| Skull Valley, Cp. (New Cp. Date Creek) | 25 mi. N. Date Creek #1 | 1867 |
| Sunset, Cp. | 6 mi. E. Winslow | c. 1858- c. 1882 |

| | | |
|---|---|---|
| Supply, Cp. | 2 mi. E. Holbrook | 1863 |
| Thomas, Ft. (New Post on the Gila) | N. of Fort Thomas | 1876-92 |
| Tonto, Cp. | | 1864 |
| Tubac, Cp. | At Tubac | 1862-65; 1867-68 |
| *Utah, Ft. | Near Lehi | 1877 |
| Verde, Ft. #1 (Cp. Lincoln) | 1 mi. N. Fort Verde | 1864-71 |
| Verde, Ft. #2 (New Cp Verde) | At Fort Verde | 1871-90 |
| Wallen, Cp. (New Pt. at Babocomari Ranch, New Post on Upper San Pedro) | 10-15 mi. W. Tombstone | 1866-69 |
| Whipple, Ft. #1 (Cp. Pomeroy, Cp. Clark) | 24 mi. NE. Prescott | 1863-64 |
| Whipple, Ft. #2 (Prescott Bks, Whipple Bks, Whipple Depot) | East of Prescott | 1864-98; 1902-13 |
| Wickenburg, Pt. at | Wickenburg | c. 1866 |
| Willow Grove, Cp. | Near Wikieup | 1867-69 |
| Wright, Cp. | Ft. Breckenridge site | 1865 |
| Yuma, Ft. (Cp. Calhoun, Cp. Independence) | At Yuma, Calif./Ariz. | 1849-51; 1852-85 |
| Yuma, Pt. at | Yuma | 1885; 1911-13; 15-22 |
| Yuma Depot | Yuma | 1864-85 |

## CALIFORNIA

| | | |
|---|---|---|
| Alcatraz, Cp. at | Alcatraz Island | 1859-95 |
| Alcatraz Prison Pt. | Alcatraz Island | 1895-1934 |
| Alert, Cp. | San Francisco | 1861-62 |
| Anderson, Ft. | NE. of Arcata | 1862-66 |
| Babbit, Cp. | Near Visalia | 1862-66 |
| Baker, Ft. (Fortification at Lime Point) | N. side S. F. Bay entrance | 1897- |
| Baker, Ft. | NE. of Bridgeville | 1862-63; 1864-66 |
| Banning, Cp. | At Banning | 1859 |
| Banks, Cp. | Near Detroit | n.d. |
| Barry, Ft. (Sub-post of Ft. Winfield Scott) | Part of Ft. Baker | 1904- |
| Benicia, Posts at (Barracks, Quartermaster Depot, Arsenal, Subsistence Depot) | Benicia | 1851-1964 |
| Bidwell, Ft. | Fort Bidwell | 1865-93 |
| Bitter Spring, Cp. | In Mojave Desert | c. 1860 |
| Bragg, Ft. | Fort Bragg | 1857-64 |
| Burton, Cp. | Near San Diego | 1855 |
| Butte Creek, Cp. near | | 1856 |
| Cady, Cp. | Harvard Stn., Mojave Desert | 1865-71 |
| Cajon, Cp. | 15 mi. from Cajon Pass | 1857-58 |
| Calhoun, Cp. | Near Yuma | c. 1849 |
| Calicienga Rancheria, Cp. at | | 1856 |
| Callahan's Ranche, Cp. near | | 1855 |
| Canoe Creek, Cp. on | | 1855 |
| Cap-Ell, Ft. | Above Ft. Terwaw | 1856 |
| Carleton, Cp. | Near San Bernardino | 1861 |
| Cass, Cp. | Near Red Bluffs | 1858-59 |
| Chouchille, Cp. on | | 1856 |
| Coco Mungo, Cp. | At Cucamunga | n.d. |
| Cook, Cp. | | n.d. |
| Coster, Cp. | Near Cp. Independence | c. 1867 |
| Crane, Cp. | In Sierra Nevada Mts. | 1852 |
| Crescent City, Cp. at | Crescent City | 1856 |
| Crook, Ft. | At Glenburn | 1857-69 |

| | | |
|---|---|---|
| Curtis, Cp. | N. of Arcata | 1862-65 |
| Defiance, Ft. | 4 mi. S. Ft. Yuma | c. 1850 |
| Downey, Cp. | Near San Antonio | 1861 |
| Dragoon Bridge, Cp. at | Honey Lake Valley | 1860-63 |
| Drum Barracks (Cp. Drum) | At Wilmington | 1862-71 |
| Elk Camp, Cp. at | 15 mi. NE. Ft. Anderson | c. 1862 |
| Far West, Cp. | Near Wheatland | 1849-52 |
| Fitzgerald, Cp. | Near Los Angeles | 1861 |
| Fitzgerald, Cp. | 20 mi. SSW. Ft. Yuma | 1855 |
| Frederica, Cp. | 150 mi. E. Monterey | 1850 |
| Fremont, Ft. (Ft. Jurupa, Ft. Rancho de Jurupa) | Near Riverside | 1852-54 |
| Gaston, Ft. | At Hoopa | 1858-92 |
| Gilmore, Cp. | At Trinidad | 1863 |
| Grant, Cp. | Near Scotia | 1863-65 |
| Guejarros, Ft. (Ft. Castillo Guijarros, Ft. Pio Pico) | N. side S. D. Bay | c. 1779- c. 1849 |
| Hill, Ft. | At Monterey | c. 1849 |
| Humboldt, Ft. | At Eureka | 1853-66 |
| Iaqua, Cp. | At Blue Lake | 1863-66 |
| Independence, Cp. | Near Independence | 1862-77 |
| Jones, Ft. | At Fort Jones | 1852-58 |
| J. W. Anderson, Ft. | 4 mi. S. Sacramento | 1849 |
| Latham, Cp. | Near Los Angeles | 1861-62 |
| Leonard, Cp. | 15 mi. N. Keysville | n.d. |
| Lime Point, Ft. at | Lime Point, S. F. Bay | c. 1867 |
| Lincoln, Old Cp. | Near Crescent City | 1862 |
| Lincoln, New Cp. (Lincoln's Ft., Ft. Lincoln, Cp. Long, Long's Ft.) | 6 mi. N. Crescent City | 1862-69 |
| Lippitt, Ft. | Near Ft. Humboldt | 1862 |
| Liscombe's Hill, Cp. at | Near Ft. Lyon | c. 1862 |
| Los Angeles, Post at | Los Angeles | 1847-49 |
| Low, Cp. | At San Juan | n.d. |
| Lyon, Ft. | 20 mi. E. Arcata | 1862 |
| Marl Springs, Cp. at | Mojave Desert S. Baker | c. 1866 |
| Mason, Ft. (Ft. Point San Jose, Ft. Black Point) | San Francisco | 1863- |
| McClear, Ft. | Ferguo R. | c. 1851 |
| McDowell, Ft. (Cp. Reynolds, Post of Angel Is.) | Angel Island, S. F. Bay | 1863-1946 |
| Miley, Ft. | Lobo Pt., S. F. Bay | 1900- |
| Miller, Cp. | Presidio, S. F. Bay | 1898 |
| Miller, Ft. (Cp. Barbour) | Millerton | 1851-64 |
| Monterey Posts: (Ft. Mervine, Post of Monterey, Ord Bks., Ft. Savannah, Ft. Cape of Pines, Ft. Stockton) | At Monterey | |
| Presidio | | c. 1770 |
| Monterey Redoubt | | 1847-52 |
| Ordnance Depot | | 1852-56 |
| Barracks | | 1865-66 |
| Montgomery, Ft. | San Francisco | c. 1850 |
| Moore, Ft. | Los Angeles | 1847-63 |
| Morris, Cp. | San Bernardino Co. | 1863 |
| Mulgrave, Ft. | | c. 1848 |
| Nome Lackee, Cp. | Next to Lake Tahoe | 1855-58 |
| Onion Valley, Cp. in | 84 mi. from Marysville | 1860 |
| Pardee's Ranche, Cp. at | On "Old Trinity Trail" | c. 1858 |

| Piute, Ft. | 20 mi. SW. Searchlight, Nev. | c. 1867-68 |
| (Ft. Beale, Ft. Piute Hill) | | |
| Point, Ft. | San Francisco Bay | 1853-1914 |
| (Ft. Blanco, Castillo de San Joaquin, Old Ft. Scott) | | |
| Pool's Fort | Fresno Co. | n.d. |
| Prentiss, Cp. | Near San Bernardino | 1859 |
| Rancho del Chino, Pt. at | 30 mi. SE. Los Angeles | 1850-52 |
| Reading, Ft. | At Redding | 1852-67 |
| Riley, Cp. | 12 mi. S. San Diego | 1849 |
| Rock Springs, Cp. | Mojave Desert | 1867-68 |
| *Ross, "Ft." | 30 mi. N. Bodega Bay | 1812-41 |
| San Bernardino, Cp. | At San Bernardino | 1855 |
| San Bernardino, Pt. at | On Dead Man's Is., Wilmington Harbor | 1858 |
| San Diego Posts: | San Diego | |
| (Ft. Stockton, Presidio of San Diego, Ft. San Diego, Garrison at San Diego) | | |
| San Diego, Pt. at | At Old San Diego | 1849-52 |
| Post Mission San Diego | At Mission San Diego | 1852-58 |
| New San Diego Barracks (San Diego Barracks) | At San Diego | 1858-66; 69-1903 |
| Rosecrans, Ft. | At Ballast Point | 1899-1950 |
| San Felipe, Cp. at | At San Felipe | 1855 |
| San Francisco, Presidio of Cp. | San Francisco | 1776 (Spanish) 1847-51; 1851- |
| San Jose, Cp. | San Jose | 1848 |
| San Luis Rey, Old Cp. | 35 mi. NW. San Diego, 2 mi. inland | 1847-49 |
| New Cp. | 40 mi. N. San Diego, 5 mi. inland | 1850-52 |
| San Miguel, Cp. | Tulare Valley | 1849 |
| San Pedro, Cp. near | San Pedro | 1892 |
| Santa Barbara, Cp. | Santa Barbara | 1847-48; 1864 |
| Santa Catalina Is., | On Santa Catalina Is. | 1864 |
| Santa Isabel, Cp. | Near Lake Henshaw | 1851 |
| Seward, Ft. | At Fort Seward | 1862-63 |
| Soda Springs, Ft. | Mojave Desert S. of Baker | c. 1867-68 |
| Sonoma, Cp. | At Sonoma | 1847-48; 1848; 1850-51; 1851 |
| Stanislaus, Cp. | 20 mi. from Stockton | c. 1848 |
| Steele, Cp. | Merced R. | 1852 |
| Sugar Loaf, Cp. | On Mojave R. | 1858 |
| Sutter's Ft., Cp. at (Redoubts at Sacramento) | At Sacramento | 1847; 1849-50 |
| Taylor, Cp. | 8 mi. SE. Ft. Crook | 1859 |
| Tejon, Ft. | N. of Lebec | 1854-61; 63-64 |
| Temecula, Cp. near | Near Temecula | n.d. |
| Terwaw, Ft. | E. Crescent City | 1857-62 |
| Tulare, Cp. | Tulare Ind. Res. | 1871 |
| Union, Cp. #1 | Across R. from Sacramento | 1861 |
| Union, Cp. #2 | Near Suttersville | 1861-66 |
| Waite, Cp. | Colusa Co. | c. 1863 |
| Weller, Ft. | SE. Willits | 1859 |
| Whitney Mt., Signal Station on | Mt. Whitney | 1883 |
| Whistler, Cp. | | 1858 |
| Wool, Ft. (Cp. Strowbridge) | 140 mi. above mo. Klamath R. | 1855 |
| Worth, Cp. | 5 mi. from Lighthouse Pt. | c. 1863 |
| Wright, Cp. | 203 mi. N. San Francisco | 1861-66; 69-75; 1887 |
| Wright, Cp. | Warner's Ranch Oak Grove | 1861-66 |
| Yerba Buena Is., Pt. on | In San Francisco Bay | c. 1868 |
| Yuma, Ft. | Across from Yuma, Ariz. | 1849-51; 52-85 |

## COLORADO

| *Bent's Old Fort (Ft. William) | 7 mi. E. LaJunta | 1832-52 |
| Brent, Ft. | | c. 1847 |
| Cedar Point, Ft. | 75 mi. E. Denver | 1867-68 |
| Chambers, Ft. | Boulder Valley | c. 1864 |
| Collins, Cp. | Near LaPorte | 1862-64 |
| Collins, Ft. (New Cp. Collins) | At Ft. Collins | 1864-67 |
| Crawford, Ft. (Cantonment on the Umcompahgre) | Near Montrose | 1880-90 |
| *Davy Crockett, Ft. (Ft. Misery) | 8 mi. N. Ladore | 1837 |
| Denver Depot | Denver | c. 1863 |
| *El Puebla, Ft. | Bent Co. | c. 1839 |
| *El Pueblo, Ft. | At Pueblo | 1842-54 |
| Evans, Cp. | 2.5 mi. NE. Denver | c. 1864 |
| Fillmore, Cp. | 2 mi. W. Boone | c. 1865 |
| Flagler, Ft. | Animas City | 1879 |
| Garland, Ft. | At Fort Garland | 1858-83 |
| Gilpin, Cp. | Central City | 1861 |
| Gray's Ranch, Stn. at | | 1864 |
| Las Pinos, Cp. near | Near Cathedral | 1880 |
| Latham, Ft. | 6 mi. S. Kersey | c. 1864 |
| Lewis, Ft. #1 (Cantonment Pagosa Springs) | Pagosa Springs | 1878-80 |
| Lewis, Ft. #2 (Cantonment on Rio de la Plata) | S. of Durango | 1880-91 |
| Lincoln, Ft. | Huntsville | c. 1864 |
| Livingston, Cp. | Near Julesburg | c. 1835 |
| Logan, Ft. (Ft. Sherman, Cp. near Denver, Post near Denver) | Denver | 1889-1946 |
| Lupton, Ft. (Ft. Lancaster) | N. Fort Lupton | c. 1864 |
| Lyon, New Ft. | At Fort Lyon | 1867-89 |
| Mackall, Cp. | In Round Valley | 1857-58 |
| Massachusetts, Ft. | 6 mi. N. Ft. Garland | 1852-58 |
| Monument Dell, Cp. | Monument | 1869-70 |
| Morgan, Ft. (Cp. Tyler, Pt. of Junction Station, Pt. of Junction, Ft. Wardwell) | At Fort Morgan | 1864-68 |
| *Old Stone Fort | Near Monument | c. 1865-68 |
| Pike's Peak, Stn. on | On Pike's Peak | c. 1873 |
| Pike's Stockade | 5 mi. from Stanford | 1807 |
| Pueblo, Pt. of | N. of Pueblo | 1867 |
| Reed's Springs, Pt. | | 1867 |
| Reynolds, Ft. (Marcy's Camp) | E. of Pueblo | 1867-72 |
| Rio Mancos, Ct. on | Vic. Ft. Lewis #2 | 1880 |
| San Felipe, Cp. | San Felipe | 1855 |
| Sedgwick, Ft. (Cp. Rankin, Pt. at Julesburg Stn.) | Near Julesburg | 1864-71 |
| Soda Spring, Cp. | | 1838 |
| *St. Vrain, Ft. | 6 mi. NW. Platteville | c. 1837-45 |
| Stevens, Ft. | Headwaters of Arkansas R. | 1866 |
| Trinidad, Pt. at | Trinidad | 1868 |
| Union, Cp. | | n.d. |
| *Vasquez, Ft. | 1.5 mi. S. Platteville | c. 1860 |
| Weld, Cp. (Cp. Elbert) | Denver | 1861-65 |
| Wheeler, Cp. | Denver's Lincoln Pk. | c. 1864 |
| White River, Cp. on | Meeker | 1879-83 |
| Wight, Cp. | Round River Valley | n.d. |

| Name | Location | Dates |
|---|---|---|
| Wise, Ft. (Old Ft. Lyon, Ft. Fauntleroy Bent's New Fort) | 20 mi. E. Ft. Lyon | 1860-67 |

## KANSAS

| Name | Location | Dates |
|---|---|---|
| Atkinson, Ft. (Cp. Mackay, Ft. Sod, Ft. Sodom Cp. #57) | W. of Dodge City | 1850-53; 1854 |
| Aubrey, Ft. (Cp. Wynkoop) | E. of Syracuse | 1865-66 |
| *Bain, Ft. | Bourbon Co. | 1857-58 |
| Bateman, Cp. | Sub-post of Ft. Leavenworth | 1857-58 |
| Baxter, Ft. | Baxter Springs | 1863 |
| Beecher, Cp. (Cp. Wichita, Cp. Davidson, Cp. Butterfield) | 1 mi. from Wichita | 1868-69 |
| Belmont, Ft. | 2 mi. W. Buffalo | c. 1860 |
| Big Creek, Stn. at | On Butterfield route | c. 1865 |
| *Bissell, Ft. | Near Phillipsburg | 1872-78 |
| Blair, Ft. | Ft. Scott blockhouse | c. 1861 |
| Blair, Ft. | Near Baxter's Springs | c. 1863 |
| Brooks, Ft. | Cloud Co. | 1864 |
| Caldwell, Cp. | Caldwell | 1884-85 |
| Carlysle Stage Stn., Det. at | 35 mi. SE. Grinnell | c. 1865 |
| Castle Rock Creek Stage Stn., Det. at | 1 mi. E. Castle Rock | c. 1865 |
| Chalk Bluffs Stage Stn., Det. at | S. of Gove | c. 1865 |
| Cimarron Redoubt | 12 mi. S. Ashland | 1873 |
| Clark, Ft. (Ft. Point, Ft. Osage, Ft. Sibley) | 40 mi. below mo. Kansas R. | 1808-27 |
| Crossing of the Arkansas, Stn. at | | 1864 |
| Dodge, Ft. | SE. Dodge City | 1864-82 |
| Downer, Ft. (Pt. at Downer's Stn.) | S. Wakeeney | 1863; 66-68 |
| Grinnell Sp. Stage Stn., Det. at | Gove Co. | c. 1865 |
| Harker, Ft. #1 (Ft. Ellsworth) | 4 mi. SE. Ellsworth | 1864-66 |
| Harker, Ft. #2 | 1 mi. NE. Ft. #1 | 1867-73 |
| Hays, Ft. #1 (Ft. Fletcher) | 14 mi. SE. Hays City | 1866-67 |
| Hays, Ft. #2 | 3/4 mi. S. Hays City | 1867-89 |
| Henning, Cp. | Ft. Scott blockhouse | c. 1861 |
| Henshaw's Stage Stn., Det. at | Near McAllaster | c. 1865 |
| Hoffman, Cp. | | 1867-68 |
| Humboldt, Ft. | | n.d. |
| Insley, Ft. | Ft. Scott blockhouse | 1861 |
| Jewell, Ft. | Jewell City | 1870 |
| Kickapoo, Cp. at | | 1858 |
| Kirwin, Ft. (Cp. Kirwan) | 1.5 mi. SW. Kirwin | 1865 |
| Lane, Ft. | W. Lawrence | 1856-57 |
| Larned, Ft. (Cp. Alert, Cp. on Pawnee Fork) | W. of Larned | 1859-78 |
| Leavenworth, Ft. (Cantonment Leavenworth) | N. Ft. Leavenworth | 1827- |
| Leedy, Cp. | Topeka | c. 1898 |
| Lincoln, Ft. | 12 mi. S. Fort Scott | 1863-64 |
| Lookout, Ft. (Lookout Station) | 15 mi. W. Ft. Hays | 1866-68 |
| Lower Cimarron Sp., Det. at | | 1864 |
| Magruder, Cp. | Near Ft. Leavenworth | 1860 |
| Mann, Ft. | Near Ft. Atkinson site | 1847-48 |

| Name | Location | Dates |
|---|---|---|
| Martin, Ct. (Ft. Kanses, Cp. Croghan) | Cow Is. in Mo. R. | 1818-20; 1826; 1861 |
| Marysville, Cp. | At Marysville | 1857 |
| Miami Valley, Det. in | Miami Valley | c. 1861 |
| Montgomery, Ft. | Eureka | c. 1862-67 |
| Monument, Ft. (Ft. Pyramid, Pt. Monument Stn., Det. at Monument Stn.) | Near Monument | 1865-68 |
| North Redoubt | Vic. Ashland | 1873 |
| Ogallah, Cp. | 1 mi. W. Wakeeney | c. 1867 |
| Prairie Dog Creek, Cp. on | | 1859 |
| Riley, Ft. (Cp. Center) | Near Junction City | 1853- |
| Roach, Ft. | S. Border Neosha Co. | n.d. |
| Russell Sp. Stage Stn., Det. at | Near Russell Springs | c. 1865 |
| *Saunders, Ft. | 12 mi. SW. Lawrence | c. 1856 |
| Scott, Ft. (Pt. of Southeastern Kansas) | At Fort Scott | 1842-55; 62-65; 70-73 |
| Shawnee Mission, Cp. at | Shawnee Mission | 1857 |
| Simple, Ft. | Topeka | 1863-66 |
| Solomon, Ft. | At Solomon | 1864-65 |
| Smokey Hill Stage Stn., Det. at | 20 mi. SW. Oakley | c. 1865 |
| Sully, Cp. | Redoubt at Ft. Leavenworth | 1864 |
| Thompson, Cp. | Near Ft. Leavenworth | 1858 |
| Titus, Ft. | 2 mi. S. Lecompton | 1856 |
| Topeka, Pt. at | Topeka | 1857; 1883 |
| Upper Cimarron Springs, Stn. at | | 1864 |
| Wakarusa, Ft. | 5 mi. SE. Lawrence | c. 1857 |
| Wallace, Ft. #1 (Cp. on Pond Creek) | S. of S. Fork, Smokey Hill R. | 1865-66 |
| Wallace, Ft. #2 | Near Pond City | 1866 |
| Wallace, Ft. #3 | 2 mi. below Wallace Stn. | 1866-82 |
| Zarah, Ft. | Near Great Bend | 1864-69 |

## NEVADA

| Name | Location | Dates |
|---|---|---|
| Baker, "Ft." | Las Vegas | c. 1864 |
| Big Antelope Creek, Cp. | Vicinity Eureka? | c. 1863 |
| Carson City, Cp. Near | Carson City | 1860 |
| Churchill, Ft. | S. of Silver Springs | 1860-69 |
| Deep Hole, Cp. | | c. 1862 |
| Dun Glen, Cp. | 20 mi. SW. Winnemucca | 1865-66 |
| Fish Lake Valley, Cp. in | SW. of Goldfield | 1866 |
| Halleck, Ft. | S. of Halleck | 1867-86 |
| McDermit, Ft. | Near McDermit | 1865-89 |
| McGarry, Cp. (Cp. at Summit Lake) | Near Summit Lake | 1865-68 |
| McKee, Cp. | NW. of Gerlach | 1866 |
| Overend, Cp. | | 1865 |
| Ruby, Cp. | Ruby Valley | 1862-69 |
| Schell Creek Stn., Det. at (Ft. Schellbourne) | 45 mi. N. Ely | 1860-65 |
| Smoke Creek, Cp. | W. of Empire | 1865-66 |
| Winfield Scott, Cp. | E. of Paradise Valley | 1866-71 |

## NEW MEXICO

| Name | Location | Dates |
|---|---|---|
| Alamo Vejo, Cp. | Alamo Vejo | 1885 |
| Abiquiu, Stn. at | Abiquiu | 1849; 1850-51 |
| Albuquerque, (Presidio at Albuquerque) | Albuquerque | 1847-67 |
| *Barclay's Fort | Near Watrous | c. 1850 |

| | | |
|---|---|---|
| Bascom, Ft. | N. Tucumcari | 1863-70 |
| Bayard, Ft. | Bayard | 1866-1900 |
| Bear Spring, Cp. | Near Gallup | 1858 |
| Blake, Cp. | 3 mi. N. Ft. Thorn | 1856 |
| Burbank, Cp. | | 1855 |
| Burgwin, Ct. | S. of Taos | 1852-60 |
| Burro Mts., Cp. at | Near Tyrone | 1859 |
| Butler, Ft. | N. of Tucumcari | c. 1860 |
| Canon Largo, Cp. in | Canon Largo | c. 1860 |
| Cariso, Cp. near | Cariso | 1858 |
| Carizallillo Sp., Cp. | Carizallillo Spring | 1885 |
| Casa Colorado, Cp. near | 5 mi. SE. Belen | 1855 |
| Chusco Valley, Cp. in | Near Tohatchi | 1858 |
| Cibolleta, Pt. at | N. of Laguna | 1850-51 |
| Cogswell, Cp. | 20 mi. NW. Ft. Stanton | 1860 |
| Comfort, Cp. | SW. Alamagordo | 1858-59 |
| Connelly, Cp. | At Polvadero? | n.d. |
| Conrad, Ft. | 10 mi. S. Socorro | 1851-54 |
| Cottonwood, Cp. | Halfway between Dona Ana & El Paso | c. 1854 |
| Craig, Ft. | S. of Ft. Conrad | 1854-84 |
| Cubero, Pt. at | 5 mi. SE. Domingo | c. 1862 |
| Cummings, Ft. (Cp. at Ft. Cummings) | N. of Deming | 1862-70; 82-85 |
| Datil, Cp. | Datil | 1885 |
| Dona Ana, Cp. | Dona Ana | 1855-56 |
| Eight, Cp. No. | On Rio Grande | 1860 |
| Eighty-three, Cp. No. | Near Ft. Craig | 1860 |
| Fernanda de Taos, Cp. at | | 1860 |
| Fillmore, Ft. | S. of La Mesilla | 1851-61 |
| Galisteo, Pt. at | Near Rowe | 1851-58 |
| Gallina, Cp. (Cp. Sierra) | W. of Corona | 1858 |
| Gila Depot (Cp. on Rio Gila; Rio Gila Depot) | On Rio Gila | 1855-57 |
| Guadalupe Mts., Cp. near | SW. Carlsbad | 1855 |
| Hatch's Ranch, Cp. at | 25 mi. SE. Las Vegas | c. 1861 |
| Johnson, Cp. | | 1862-65 |
| La Hoya, Cp. | | n.d. |
| La Mesilla, Pt. of | La Mesilla | c. 1863-65 |
| Laguna, Pt. | Laguna | 1851-52 |
| Las Animas, Cp. at | Near Dona Ana | 1854 |
| Las Cruces, Stn. at | 5 mi. S. Dona Ana | 1863-65 |
| Las Lunas, Pt. of | Las Lunas | 1852; 59-60; 1862 |
| Las Vegas, Pt. | Las Vegas | 1848-51 |
| Lazuma, Pt. at | Lazuma | 1851 |
| Loring, Cp. | Near Red River | 1858 |
| Los Pinos, Stn. (Cp. at Peralto) | 18 mi. S. Albuquerque | 1862-66 |
| Los Poros, Cp. | Los Poros | 1860 |
| Lowell, Ft. (Cp. Plummer) | On Chama R. | 1866-69 |
| Lyon, Ft. (Ft. Fauntleroy, Old Ft. Wingate) | SE. Ft. Wingate | 1860-61 |
| Magoffin, Cp. | Near Alto | 1864 |
| Marcy, Ft. (Pt. at Santa Fe) | Santa Fe | 1846-62; 62-67; 75-94 |
| Mason, Ct. | | 1855 |
| McLane, Ft. (Cp. Webster, Ft. Floyd) | S. Silver City | 1860-61 |
| McRae, Ft. | Elephant Butte Lake | 1863-82 |
| Mimbres, Cp. | W. Deming | c. 1864 |
| Mule Spring, Cp. | | 1856 |
| Niggerhead Sp., Cp. | | 1855 |
| Ojo Caliente, Pt. of | Ojo Caliente Ind. Reservation | 1859; 1874-82 |

| | | |
|---|---|---|
| Pleasant Springs, Cp. | | 1855 |
| Pope, Cp. | | c. 1868 |
| Rayoda, Pt. | Rayado | 1850-51; 1854 |
| Robbero, Cp. | Near Ft. Thorn | 1857 |
| Robledo, Cp. | Near Mt. Robledo | 1853 |
| Saguna, Pt. | 35 mi. W. Albuquerque | 1851 |
| Sangre de Christo, Pt. | | n.d. |
| San Simon, Cp. | San Simon | 1856 |
| Santa Tomas de Iturbide, Pt. | | 1854-55 |
| Schroeder, Cp. | N. Las Cruces | 1865-79; 80-92 |
| Selden, Ft. | | c. 1867 |
| Shoeneman, Cp. | | n.d. |
| Socorro, Pt. of | Socorro | 1849-51; 77-81 |
| Stanton, Ft. (Cp. Garland) | Fort Stanton | 1855-61; 1861; 62-96 |
| Stevens, Ft. | | 1866 |
| Sumner, Ft. | Fort Sumner | 1862-69 |
| Taos, Pt. | Taos | 1847-52; c. 1865 |
| Thorn, Ft. | Vic. Hatch | 1853-59 |
| Tulerosa, Ft. | S. of Reserve | 1872-74 |
| Tuni-Cha, Cp. | Near Newcomb | 1858 |
| Union, Ft. | Near Watrous | 1851-91 |
| Valverde, Pt. | 25 mi. above Socorro | 1851 |
| Vigilance, Cp. | Near Albuquerque | 1852 |
| Webster, Ft. #1 (Pt. at Gila Copper Mines) | At Gila Copper Mines | 1852 |
| Webster, Ft. #2 | 12 mi. E. #1 | 1852-53 |
| West, Ft. (Cp. Vincent) | Near Clint | 1863-64 |
| Winfield Scott, Cp. | W. of Corona | 1860 |
| Wingate, Ft. #1 (Ft. Fauntleroy, Ft. Lyon) | Grant | 1862-68 |
| Wingate, Ft. #2 | Near Fort Wingate | 1868-1911; 1914 |

## OKLAHOMA

| | | |
|---|---|---|
| Arbuckle, Cp. | Near Ft. Gibson | 1832-33 |
| Arbuckle, Ft. | 3 mi. E. Keystone | 1834 |
| Arbuckle, New Ft. | Near Davis | 1851-61; 61-61; 67-70 |
| Arbuckle, Old Ft. | Near Byars | 1850-51 |
| Armstrong Academy, Cp & Hospital | 3 mi. NE. Bokchito | 1862-65 |
| Augur, Cp. | 5 mi. SW. Grandfield | c. 1870 |
| Boggy Depot, Cp. at (Cp. near Muddy Boggy Ridge) | Atoka Co. | c. 1863-64 |
| Blunt, Ft. | Near Ft. Gibson | 1863-65 |
| Cantonment (Ct. on North Fork Canadian River) | 5 mi. NW. Canton | 1879-82 |
| Chickasaw Agency, Pt. at | Chickasaw Agency | 1834 |
| Chilacco Creek, Cp. | S. of Arkansas City, Kans. | 1885 |
| Choteau's Creek, Cp. on | Near Cherokee | 1838 |
| Cobb, Ft. | E. of Fort Cobb | 1859-61; c. 62; 65; 68-72 |
| Coffee, Ft. | N. of Spiro | 1834-38; 62-63 |
| Comanche, Cp. | 12 mi. N. Lawton | 1834 |
| Cross Timbers, Cp. | | n.d. |
| Davis, Ct. | Near Muskogee | 1861-62 |
| Edwards, Ft. (Ft. Holmes) | Near mo. Little R. | c. 1834 |
| Gibson, Ft. | At Fort Gibson | 1824-57; 63-90; 97; 1901 |
| Guthrie, Cp. | At Guthrie | 1889-91 |
| Jumper, Cp. | Near Eufala | c. 1862 |
| Leavenworth, Cp. | 2 mi. S. Kingston | 1834 |
| Mason, Cp. (Ft. Holmes, Mason's Ft.) | Near Purcell | 1835-40 |
| McCulloch, Ft. | 3 mi. SW. Kenefick | 1862-65 |

| | | |
|---|---|---|
| McIntosh, Cp. | 5 mi. E. Anadarko | 1861-65 |
| Nichols, Cp. | W. of Boise City | 1865 |
| Oklahoma, Cp. | | 1889-92 |
| Perryville Depot | Near Savanna | c. 1862 |
| Radziminski, Cp. #1 (Cp. Otter Creek, Otter Creek Stn.) | NE. Tipton | 1858 |
| Radziminski, Cp. #2 | 5 mi. NW. Mountain Park | 1858-59 |
| Reno, Ft. (Pt. at Cheyenne Agency, Cp. near Cheyenne Agency) | W. of El Reno | 1874-1948 |
| Robinson, Cp. | Otter Cr. at old Radziminski crossing | 1871 |
| Ross' Landing, Pt. at | | c. 1836 |
| Russell, Cp. | 7 mi. NE. Guthrie | 1883-85 |
| Schofield, Cp. | 3 mi. E. Chilocco | 1889 |
| Sheridan's Roost | Near Orion | c. 1870 |
| Sill, Ft. (Cp. at Medicine Bluff Cr., Ft. Elliott, Cp. Starvation, Cp. Wichita) | N. of Lawton | 1869- |
| Smith, Ft. | SW. Ft. Smith, Arkansas | 1817-24; 1833 |
| (Smith, Ft., Arkansas) | (At Fort Smith, Arkansas) | (1838-61; 61-62; 62-71) |
| Supply, Ft. (Depot on the North Canadian) | Fort Supply | 1868-93 |
| Towson, Ft. (Cp. Phoenix, Ct. Towson) | 1 mi. NE. Fort Towson | 1824-29; 30-54; c. 1863-65 |
| Washita, Ft. | NW. Durant | 1842-61; 61-65 |
| Wayne, Ft. #1 | E. Watts | 1839 |
| Wayne, Ft. #2 | Near Spavinaw | 1839-52: c. 1861 |

### TEXAS

| | | |
|---|---|---|
| *Anahuac, Ft. | Anahuac | 1830-32 |
| *Arkokisa, Pt. | Liberty | 1805-06 |
| Austin, Cp. (Cp. Sanders) | Austin | 1845-54; 65-75 |
| Barranca, Cp. | NW. Corpus Christi | 1860 |
| Barrell Springs, Cp. | NE. Ft. Davis | 1860 |
| Belknap, Ft. | 2.5 mi. S. Newcastle | 1851-61; 65-67 |
| Big Witchita, Cp. on | Near Ft. Chadbourne? | 1855 |
| Blake, Cp. | On San Pedro & Devil's R. | 1846 |
| Blake, Cp. | Near head, Rio Padro | 1854 |
| Bliss, Ft. (Cp. at Franklin, Military Pt. of El Paso, Cp. Concordia, Pt. at Smith's Ranche, Pt. opposite El Paso, New Mexico, Military Pt. opposite El Paso, Texas. | El Paso | 1848-51; 54-61; 61-62; 65-76; 77- |
| Bolivar Point, Ft. at | Bolivar Point | c. 1819 |
| Brazos Agency, Pt. at | Brazos Agency | 1859 |
| Brazos Is. Depot | Brazos Is. | 1846 |
| Brazos Santiago, Pt. at | Brazos Santiago | 1849-61; 67 |
| Brazos Santiago Is., Pt. | Brazos Santiago Is. | c. 1849 |
| Brenham, Pt. at | Brenham | 1869-70 |

| | | |
|---|---|---|
| Brown, Ft. (Ft. Taylor) | Brownsville | 1846-61; 61-63; 63-65; 65-1946 |
| Brownsville, Pt. of | Brownsville | c. 1867 |
| Bryan, Pt. of | Bryan | c. 1869 |
| Buchanan, Cp. | Near San Antonio | 1855 |
| Buffalo, Pt. | 200 mi. NE. Austin | n.d. |
| Buffalo Springs, Cp. | Buffalo Springs | 1866-67 |
| Bull Springs, (Cp. at Pine Springs) | Vicinity Littlefield | c. 1878-79 |
| Burwell, Cp. | Eagle Pass | 1855 |
| Byron, Cp. at | Byron | c. 1869 |
| California Sp., Cp. near | On El Paso Rd. | 1854 |
| Calvert, Pt. of | Calvert | 1869-70 |
| Cameron, Ft. | Cameron | 1870 |
| Canton, Pt. of | Canton | 1868-69 |
| Cantonment | Near Miami | c. 1874 |
| Casa Blanca, Cp. | NW. Corpus Christi | 1849 |
| Cass, Cp. (Cp. at Eagle Springs) | Near Ft. Quitman | 1854 |
| Castroville, Military Stn. | Castroville | 1849 |
| Centerville, Pt. at | Centerville | c. 1867 |
| Central Stn., Picket Post at | Near Ft. Concho | 1869 |
| Chadbourne, Ft. | 32 mi. SW. Abilene | 1852-61; 61-64; 67; 70 |
| Charlotte, Cp. | 42 mi. W. Ft. Concho | 1868; 1879-80 |
| Cibolo Creek, Cp. near | | 1850 |
| Cibolo, Ft; Relay Stn. at | Near Shafter | n.d. |
| Clark, Ft. (Ft. Riley) | Bracketville | 1852-61; 62; 66-1944 |
| Colorado, Cp. #1 | Colo. R., 5 mi. above Howe Cr. | 1855-57 |
| Colorado, Cp. #2 | 9 mi. NE. Coleman | 1857-61; 1869 |
| Columbus, Pt. at | Columbus | c. 1869 |
| Conception, Cp. | Near San Antonio | n.d. |
| Concho, Ft. (Cp. Kelly, Cp. Hatch, Ft. Griffin) | San Angelo | 1867-89 |
| Connor's Stn., Det. at | Richland Cr., E. of Brazos R. | 1848; 1860 |
| Cooper, Cp. | Near Ft. Griffin | 1856-61; 1871 |
| Corpus Christi, | Corpus Christi | 1845-52; 52-62; 62-65; 65-1918 |
| Corsicana, Pt. of Pt., Depot & Cp. | Corsicana | 1872 |
| Crockett, Ft. (Cp. Hawley) | Galveston | 1897 |
| Crogan, Ft. | 1 mi. SW. Burnett | 1849-55 |
| Davant, Cp. | Near Bandera Pass | n.d. |
| Davis, Ft. (Painted Camp on the Limpia) | Fort Davis | 1853-61; 61-62; 67-91 |
| Davis' Landing, Cp. at | | c. 1860 |
| Defiance, Ft. (Ft. Goliad, Ft. LaBahia, Presidio La Bahia) | Goliad | 1836 |
| Del Rio, Cp. (Cp. San Felipe, Pt. of San Felipe) | N. Del Rio | 1876-91; 1914-22 |
| Dolores, Cp. | N. of Laredo | 1854 |
| Drum, Cp. (Cp. Bugle) | Opposite Guerrero, Mexico | 1851-52; 1857 |
| Duncan, Ft. (Cp. near Eagle Pass, Cp. on the Rio Grande) | Eagle Pass | 1849-59; 60-61; 68-83 |
| Eagle Mountains, Cp. at | | 1880 |
| Eagle Pass, Cp. at | Site of Ft. Duncan | 1886-1927 |
| Eagle Springs, Cp. | S. Sierra Blanca | c. 1879-80 |

E. B. Strong, Cp.  Nueces R., Walls crossing  1855

| Name | Location | Date |
|---|---|---|
| E. B. Strong, Cp. | Nueces R., Walls crossing | 1855 |
| Edinburg, Cp. | Edinburg | 1853; 1860; 79-80 |
| El Pico, Cp. | 15 mi. NW. Laredo | 1855 |
| Elliott, Ft. | Near Mobeetie | 1874-90 |
| (Cp. on the North Fork, Red River, Ct. North Fork Red River, New Post on the Sweetwater) | | |
| Escondido, Cp. at | Near Bakersfield | c. 1878 |
| Esperanza, Ft. | Matagorda Island | 1863-64 |
| Ewell, Ft. | 40 mi. SE. Cotulla | 1852-54 |
| Faver's Ranch, Cp. at | N. of Shafter | 1879 |
| Florilla, Cp. | S. San Antonio | 1849 |
| Ford, Cp. & Prison | Near Tyler | 1862-65 |
| Francois, Ft. | | n.d. |
| Frazier's Ranch, Cp. at | Near Ft. Stockton | c. 1879 |
| Galveston, Pt. at | Galveston | 1862; 63-65; 65-70 |
| (Includes Galveston Bks., Fts. San Jacinto, Travis, Crockett) | | |
| Gardenier, Cp. | 40 mi. from Ft. Clark | 1854 |
| Gates, Ft. | Near Gatesville | 1849-52 |
| Goliad, Pt. at | Goliad | c. 1867 |
| Graham, Ft. | 18 mi. W. Hillsboro | 1849-53 |
| Grayson Sp., Cp. at | | c. 1879 |
| Green Lake, Pt. at | Green Lake | c. 1867 |
| Greenville, Garrison at | Greenville | 1869-70 |
| Grierson, Cp. (Cp. Grierson's Spring) | 65 mi. SW. Ft. Concho | c. 1878-80 |
| Griffin, Ft. (Cp. Wilson) | 20 mi. N. Albany | 1867-81 |
| Grove, Cp. | Near Hempstead | c. 1863 |
| Guadalupe Mt., Cp. | Guadalupe Moutain | 1858; 1879-80 |
| Guadalupe Peak, Cp. | Guadalupe Peak | 1855 |
| Guadalupe River, Cp. on | 1 mi. from Victoria | 1848-49 |
| Hamilton, Cp. | Near Ft. Brown | c. 1853 |
| Hancock, Ft. | Fort Hancock | 1882-95 |
| Harney, Cp. | Opposite Guerrero, Mexico | 1853 |
| Harvey, Ft. | | n.d. |
| Head of the Concho, Pickett Post at | W. Ft. Concho | 1869; 1880 |
| Hebert, Ft. | Near Houston | c. 1863 |
| Helena, Pt. of | Helena | 1868-70 |
| Hempstead, Pt. of | Hempstead | 1866-69 |
| Hidalgo, Cp. | Near Hidalgo Village | n.d. |
| Holmes, Cp. | 12 mi. above El Paso | 1856 |
| Houston, Pt. at | Houston | 1865-68 |
| Houston, Ft. | 2 mi. S. Palestine | 1836 |
| Howard, Ft. | | n.d. |
| Hudson, Cp. (Cp. on San Pedro) | San Pedro & Devil's Rivers | 1854-61; 62-63; 67-68; 1871 |
| Independence Sp., Cp. | | 1856 |
| Inge, Ft. | 2 mi. S. Uvalde | 1849-51; 51-55; 56-61; |
| Indianola, Pt. of (Cp. Leona) | Indianola | 1865-69 69 |
| Inge, Cp. near Ft. | ½ mi. SE. Ft. Inge | 1853 |
| Iverson, Cp. | Near Clear Fork of Brazos | 1858 |
| Ives, Cp. | 4 mi. from Cp. Verde | 1859-61 |
| J. E. Johnson, Cp. (Cp. Johnston) | NW. San Angelo | 1852 |
| Jacksboro, Ft. | Jacksboro | 1865-66 |
| Jackson, Ct. | Rodeo | 1854 |
| Jefferson, Pt. of | Jefferson | 1867-71 |
| Johnson's Run, Cp. on | 40 mi. E. Ft. Clark | 1858 |
| Johnson's Stn., Picket Pt. at | | 1869 |
| Kingman, Cp. at | Kingman | 1885 |

| Name | Location | Date |
|---|---|---|
| Kiowa, Cp. | | 1885 |
| Kirby, Ft. | On Charco Grande de Agua Dulce R. | 1851 |
| La Moras, Cp. | N. Ft. Leaton | 1854 |
| Lampasas, Pt. at | Lampasas | 1867-70 |
| Lancaster, Ft. | 7 mi. E. Sheffield | 1855-61; 61-65; 67 |
| Langtry, Cp. | Langtry Station | 1885 |
| La Pena, Cp. on | 43 mi. SE. Ft. Duncan | 1854 |
| Las Laxas, Stn. at | 50 mi. above Ft. Ringgold | c. 1850 |
| Lauderdale, Cp. | Above Brenham | 1861 |
| Lawson, Cp. | Midway between El Paso & Uvalde | c. 1859 |
| *Leaton, Ft. | Presidio | c. 1849 |
| Limpia River, Cp. near (Cp. Burbank) | 15 mi. N. Ft. Davis | 1853; 1855 |
| Lincoln, Ft. | N. D'Hanis | 1849-52; 1880 |
| *Lipantitlan, Ft. | Near San Patricio | c. 1835 |
| Live Oak Creek, Cp. on | 1 mi. from Ft. Lancaster | 1854; 1867 |
| Livingston, Pt. at | Livingston | 1868-70 |
| Llando, Ft. | Near Ft. McIntosh | 1859 |
| Llano Estacado, Cp. | On Pecos R. | 1859 |
| Lockhart, Pt. at | Lockhart | c. 1867 |
| Lone Tree, Picket Post at | | 1869 |
| Lopen, Cp. | 43 mi. above Rio Grande City | 1856 |
| Los Ceritos, Cp. at | Near Laredo? | 1855 |
| Los Lajos, Cp. at | | 1856 |
| Marcy, Ft. | Near Corpus Christi | 1845-46 |
| Marshall, Pt. at | Marshall | c. 1869 |
| Mason, Ft. | Mason | 1851-54; 56-59; 59-61; 66-69 |
| Martin Scott, Ft. (Cp. Houston) | 2 mi. E. Fredericksburg | 1848-53; 61-65; 66 |
| Mayer's Sp., Cp. at | | 1880 |
| McCulloch's Stn., Cp. at | | c. 1860 |
| McIntosh, Ft. (Spanish Presidio, Cp. Crawford) | Laredo | 1849-61; 65-1945 |
| McIntosh, "Ft." | 1 mi. from Ft. Brown | 1868-69 |
| McKavett, Ft. (San Saba River Post) | At Fort McKavett | 1852-59; 68-83 |
| Mercer, Ft. | | 1850-53; 55; 65 |
| Merrill, Ft. | 25 mi. NW. Corpus Christi | 1850-55 |
| Miles' Supply Camp | 13 mi. S. Canadian | c. 1874 |
| Mountain Peak, Cp. near | Near Ft. Davis | 1856 |
| Mt. Pleasant, Pt. at | Mount Pleasant | c. 1867 |
| Mud, Ft. | Near Clarksville | c. 1863 |
| Nacagdoches, Pt. of | Nacagdoches | 1831-36; 67-70 |
| Nevill's Spring, Cp. | Near Ft. Davis | 1885 |
| Newport, Ft. | | 1860 |
| Nueces, Cp. on | Nueces R. | c. 1879 |
| Ojo Caliente, Cp. at | Below Ft. Quitman | 1880 |
| Palo Altos, Cp. | 9 mi. from Matamoras | 1847 |
| Palo Blanco, Cp. | | 1855 |
| Pandes, Ft. | 2 mi. above Ft. Brown | c. 1849 |
| Pecan, Cp. | Near Brownwood | 1850-56 |
| Pecan Sp., Cp. at | Near Ft. Stockton | c. 1878-80 |
| Pecos, Cp. on the | Near Langtry | c. 1878-80 |
| Pecos River, Pt. (Cp. at Pope's Well, Cp. Pope, Capt. Pope's Wells) | SE. corner of state | 1856-60 |
| Pecos River, Cp. | | 1849; 1854 |
| Pena Colorado, Cp. (Cp. Rainbow Cliffs) | 4 mi. S. Marathon | 1879-93 |
| Pendencia, Cp. | 35 mi. ESE. Ft. Duncan | c. 1859 |
| Perdido, Cp. | 40 mi. E. Ft. Davis | n.d. |
| Permanent Camp | 2 mi. from Arden | 1867 |

| | | |
|---|---|---|
| Phantom Hill, Ft. (Pt. on the Clear Fork of the Brazos, Pt. at Brazos, Texas) | 18 mi. NE. Abilene | 1847; 51-54; 67; 72 |
| Phelps, Cp. | 20 mi. below Ft. Ringgold | 1852 |
| Pilot Grove, Pt. | Near Whitewright | 1868 |
| Pine Spring, Cp. | | 1878 |
| Pitt, Cp. | Near Victoria | 1848 |
| Polk, Ft. (Post at Point Isabel) | Point Isabel | 1846-50 |
| Port Lavacca, Stn. | Calhoun Co. | 1848-49 |
| Presidio, Cp near | Presidio | 1880-83 |
| Preston, Ft. | Near Denison | 1840 |
| Quitman, Ft. | 80 mi. S. El Paso | 1858-61; 62; 68-77; 80-81 |
| Ranche de Laxas, Pt. | | 1854 |
| Rancho Salemna, Cp. | Near Ft. Ringgold | 1854 |
| Rancho San Ignacio, Cp. | | n.d. |
| Red River, Cp. | 120 mi. from Cp. Cooper | 1859 |
| Redmand's Ranche, Cp. at | 63 m. NW. Ft. Ringgold | c. 1853 |
| Refugio, Pt. at (Spanish Presidio in 1807-36) | Refugio | c. 1867 |
| Relief, Cp. | Near Ft. Davis | 1855 |
| Rice, Cp. | 120 mi. SE. El Paso | 1884-85 |
| Richardson, Ft. | Near Jacksboro | 1867-78 |
| Ricketts, Cp. | 10 mi. N. Edinburg | 1852; 53; 65 |
| Ringgold, Ft. (Ringgold Bks.) | Rio Grande City | 1848-59; 59-61; 65-1906; 1917-44 |
| Rio Grande, Cp. on the | Near Ft. Quitman | 1880 |
| Rio Pedro, Cp. | Near Ft. Duncan | 1854-55 |
| Rio San Pedro, Cp. | On Rio Pedro | 1859 |
| Rock Creek, Cp. on | | n.d. |
| Roma, Pt. | Roma | 1852 |
| Rosario, Cp. | Rosario | 1860 |
| Ross' Stn., Det. at | | c. 1860 |
| Round Top, Pt. at | Round Top | c. 1867 |
| Sabinal, Cp. | Sabinal | 1856 |
| Sabine, Ft. | Sabine Pass | n.d. |
| Salienena, Cp. | 30 mi. above Ft. Ringgold | 1854; 1856 |
| Salmon, Cp. | SE. Abilene | c. 1864 |
| Salt Lake, Cp. | N. Ft. Brown | 1854 |
| Sam Houston, Ft. (Post of San Antonio, Cp. Almus, Cp. at the Alamo, San Antonio Infantry Bks.) | San Antonio | 1845-46; 49-53; 57-61; 65- |
| San Diego, Sub-post of | San Diego | c. 1879 |
| San Elizario, Pt. (Cp. at Presidio de Elizario) | San Elizario | 1847; 49-51; 1862 |
| Santa Maria, Sub-post at | 10 mi. SW. Harlingen | c. 1878-80 |
| Salintas, Cp. | | 1855 |
| Seco River, Cp. | | 1849 |
| Seguin, Pt. at | Seguin | c. 1867 |
| Seven Springs, Cp. at | Near Ft. Davis | c. 1878-79 |
| Sherman, Pt. at | Sherman | c. 1867 |
| Sherman, Ft. | Titus Co. | n.d. |
| Smith's Ranche, Cp. | | n.d. |
| *Spanish Bluff, Pt. at | E. Fork Trinity R. | 1804 |
| St. Joseph's Is., Depot | St. Joseph's Island | 1845 |
| Stanley, Cp. | 4 mi. N. Victoria | n.d. |
| Stockton, Ft. | Fort Stockton | 1858-61; 61-65; 67-86 |
| Stuart, Cp. | | n.d. |
| Sulphur Sp., Pt. at | At Sulphur Springs | 1868-70 |

| | | |
|---|---|---|
| Supply Camp (Mackenzie's Permanent Supply Camp) | Spur | c. 1871-75 |
| *Tenoxtitlan, Ft. | W. Bryan | 1830-31; 31-45 |
| *Teran, Ft. | 2.5 mi. from Rocklaw Dam | 1830-31 |
| Terrett, Ft. (Cp. Lugubre, Pt. on North Fork of Llano R. | 14 mi. W. Roosevelt | 1852-54 |
| Trinidad, Cp. | Lake Trinidad | n.d. |
| Turan, Ft. | Angelina Co. | n.d. |
| Turkey Creek, Cp. on | 42 mi. from Ft. Duncan | 1854 |
| Tyler, Pt. at | Tyler | 1867-70 |
| Uphazy, Cp. | Near San Antonio | 1854 |
| Van Camp, Cp. | 13 mi. NE. Ft. Stockton | 1859 |
| *Velasco, Ft. | Mouth Brazos R. | 1831 |
| Verde, Cp. | 8 mi. W. Center Point | 1856-61; 61-65; 65-67 |
| Victoria, Pt. at (Victoria Military Stn.) | Victoria | c. 1867 |
| Virginia Point, Bt. | 5 mi. from Galveston | 1861 |
| Waco, Pt. of | Waco | 1855; 1866-70 |
| Walker's Ft. | On Brazos R. at LaBahia R. | 1879? |
| Washington, Ft. | At Pass Cavallo | n.d. |
| Weatherford, Pt. at | Weatherford | c. 1867 |
| Wilcox, Cp. | East Fork, Trinity R. | 1858 |
| Willow Springs, Cp. | SW. Ft. Davis | 1885 |
| Wolf Canyon, Cp. | | 1854 |
| Wood, Cp. | Camp Wood | 1857; 1861 |
| Woodville, Pt. at | Woodville | c. 1867 |
| Worth, Ft. | Fort Worth | 1849-53 |

## UTAH

| | | |
|---|---|---|
| Battle Creek Settlement, Cp. | Near Salt Lake City | 1859 |
| Bear River, Cp. at | N. Brigham City | 1859 |
| Birch Creek, Cp. on | | 1859 |
| Cameron, Ft. (Post at Beaver) | Beaver | 1872-85 |
| Carson River, Pt. on | Near Big Bend of River | 1860 |
| Clara, Ft. | Near Santa Clara | n.d. |
| Clarke, Cp. | San Pete Valley | 1859 |
| Crittenden, Ft. (Cp. Floyd) | Fairfield | 1857-61 |
| Crossman, Ft. | 6 mi. W. Neflic | 1858 |
| *Deseret, Ft. | Near Deseret | n.d. |
| Douglas, Ft. | Salt Lake City | 1862- |
| Duchesne, Ft. | Fort Duchesne | 1886-1912 |
| Eastman, Cp. | 14 mi. S. Neflic | 1859 |
| Echo Canyon, Cp. in | Near Echo | 1859 |
| Fillmore City, Cp. near | Fillmore City | 1858 |
| *Gunnison, Ft. | Gunnison | n.d. |
| *Hamilton, Ft. | Hamilton | n.d. |
| Haven, Ft. | | 1860 |
| Herriman, Ft. | Salt Lake | n.d. |
| *Kanab, Ft. | Kanab | n.d. |
| Lolos Creek, Cp. on | Lolos Creek | 1860 |
| Murray Camp of Instruction | Murray | 1885 |
| Ogden Station | Ogden | 1878 |
| Paige, Cp. | San Pete Valley | 1859 |
| Porter, Cp. | | 1859 |
| Rawlins, Ft. | 2 mi. from Provo | 1870-71 |
| Rush Valley, Cp. | 23 mi. W. Cp. Floyd | 1859 |
| Sevier, Cp. | At Sevier | 1859 |
| Shunk, Cp. | 25 mi. SW. Cp. Floyd | 1858 |
| Thornburgh, New Ft. | On Ashley Creek | 1882-83 |
| Thornburgh, Old Ft. | Duchesne & Graeves R. | 1881-82 |
| Timpanagos, Cp. | 8 mi. from Provo | 1859 |
| Tyler, Cp. | | 1859 |
| Wingfield, Cp. | Ham's Fork 15 mi. above Green R. | c. 1857 |

190

# INDEX

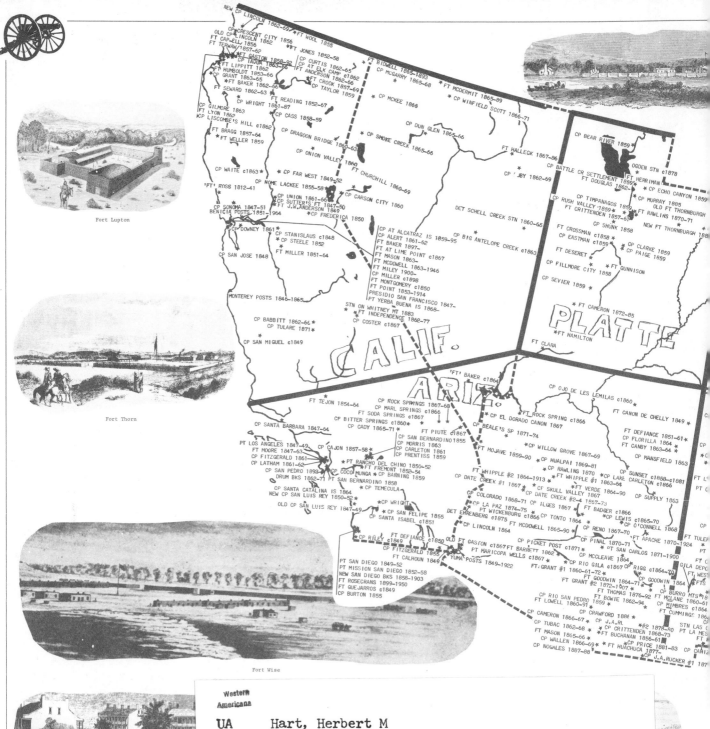

Fort Lupton

Fort Thorn

Fort Wise

Fort Smith